Chaos Shamanism

Reclaiming Your Indigenous Soul

Other Titles by Barry Goddard

The Medicine Wheel (Moon Books 2022)
978-1785359675

Surfing the Galactic Highways: Adventures in Divinatory Astrology (Moon Books 2022)
978-1803410104

The Stolen Queen (Pine Winds Press 2025)
978-1805141952

What People Are Saying About

Chaos Shamanism

Chaos Shamanism is an absolute must-read, especially if you are curious about the Medicine Wheel, transformation, wholeness and balance, and are prepared to leap into the Chaos like The Fool in the Tarot. Emphasis is always placed on respecting traditions, while being prepared to re-invent as necessary. Enter the chaos with trust, integrity, an open heart and mind, but always keep your own Soul. Barry's words of wisdom have helped me re-align myself with my own inner teacher, connecting deeper in a Shamanic sense by the balance of grounding and connection to my own Ancestral Spirits. Not just words, but feeling it in these busy and chaotic times. A great read that really kept me stimulated.
Michelle Corrigan, author of *Your Quest for a Spiritual Life* and *Something to Bear in Mind*

Barry teaches a fresh, alive, and original take on shamanism that speaks to our times, full of enlivening and liberating insights that inspire the reader both to live more fully and to make their spirituality deeply their own.
Ben Craib, co-author of *Slay Your Dragons with Compassion*

Barry Goddard challenges the structured, often sanitized approaches of Core Shamanism, inviting us instead into the raw, unpredictable currents of Chaos Shamanism. With a deep reverence for the wild intelligence of spirit, he reminds us that healing is not a transaction or a certificate but an ongoing, personal reckoning with the unseen forces that shape our lives. His reflections on embodied wisdom—whether through trees, spirits, or the mystery of lived experience—offer a potent call to those who seek true depth in their practice. *Chaos Shamanism* is a necessary, provocative read for anyone ready to move beyond formulaic spirituality and into the untamed soul of the work.

Renee Baribeau, award-winning author of *Winds of Spirit* and *A Pilgrim's Guide to Walking Wisdom*

Chaos Shamanism

Reclaiming Your Indigenous Soul

Barry Goddard

London, UK
Washington, DC, USA

CollectiveInk

First published by Mantra Books, 2026
Mantra Books is an imprint of Collective Ink Ltd.,
Unit 11, Shepperton House, 89 Shepperton Road, London, N1 3DF
office@collectiveinkbooks.com
www.collectiveinkbooks.com
www.mantra-books.net

For distributor details and how to order please visit the 'Ordering' section on our website.

ISBN: 978 1 80341 845 2
978 1 78535 988 0 (ebook)
Library of Congress Control Number: 2024926981

A CIP catalogue record for this book is available from the British Library.

Design: Lapiz Digital Services

UK: Printed and bound by CPI Group (UK) Ltd, Croydon, CR0 4YY
Printed in North America by CPI GPS partners

Contents

Preface

Shamanism is a Spirit, winging its way down from pre-history. It is rooted in our belonging to the natural world. It has no founder, no holy book, no teachings that are not dispensable. It is the original spirituality, seen as through a glass darkly by the major religions, but often clearly so by their heretics.

Shamanism is a current of energy, a high voltage cable. The teaching of Shamanism is as much about the transmission of this spirit, this energy, as it is about words. This is the real meaning of lineage — the passing down of that current through the generations.

And it is also playful. People get so serious when it comes to their 'spirituality'. There is no such thing as 'spirituality'. There is only life to be lived in a balanced way.

This book originated in unscripted short talks I made for YouTube. I generally spoke from whatever thoughts were presenting themselves that day. This is the most traditional, and I think the best, way to teach. Whoever heard of a medicine person reading from a prepared text? No, the traditional way allows for spontaneity and play, and allows room for the Spirit to speak.

Why 'Chaos' Shamanism? All traditions turn into religions, to a greater or lesser degree. It is inevitable, and a necessary launch pad for many of us. We need to know 'what's what', and who the guy with the 'answers' is. A good teacher will allow for this, and hand the projection back. But inevitably, it seems, the forms will take over. The Upper, Middle and Lower Worlds become real places, instead of ways of structuring experience. A Sweatlodge has to be built in exactly the right way. Teachers come to believe in their pedestals. And so on.

Chaos Shamanism has arisen as a necessary and ongoing protest against Shamanism-as-religion, much as Dzogchen, with its emphasis on direct experience, represented a return to the original spirit of Tibetan Buddhism. It is Chaos in the deeper, ancient Greek sense of the ground of existence. It is also Chaos in the sense that it cannot be pinned down, being open to all practices and teachings, and allied with none. As such, it is particularly suitable for the age we live in, where by necessity we pick and choose from the available traditions.

Chaos Shamanism is heretical in the best sense. 'Heretic' comes from the ancient Greek word *hairetikos*, meaning 'able to choose'. Chaos Shamanism shows us how to do that with depth and with wisdom.

Creating this book was for me an exploration of what Chaos Shamanism might mean. It seems to be a live idea that keeps unfolding. I wasn't even planning to write a book. All I had in mind was one short video about this new idea that had come to me. And then I found I needed a second video. After that it escalated. I edited the transcripts for people on Facebook who prefer to read rather than watch. And then I realised the transcripts were adding up to a book. So I just let it happen. The book has been a gift that has taken me by surprise. An overall plan for it never developed. I just let it take its own form and length. This is truly in the spirit of Chaos Shamanism. The form of the book, as well as the content, gives a taste of what Chaos is about.

I hope you can hear me talking as you read. And I hope something of the power and freedom of the idea of Chaos also comes across. I use Chaos in a number of ways, but in the last analysis it means remaining close to your heart in whatever you do.

1

Chaos Origins

I'm going to write around an idea I've had for what I call Chaos Shamanism. I've looked it up on the net, and there is only one reference to it, so I think I can feel free to unfold it in my own way.

I came up with the idea as the result of a bit of a visionary moment in some Fairy Woods in Doncaster. I had started talking about teaching Shamanism — like offline, in person — I don't know what the term is for it these days. I wasn't currently doing that, but I have plenty of experience and plenty to say, and I knew I'd be good at it. But I didn't quite know where to start. I started talking, and it just all came out. I was feeling deeply about it, and weeping as I talked.

It's like there's something bubbling up within me, something strong to say and I want to run with it. But I'm not in a hurry. I'm hungry, I have things to do. But I don't feel ambitious, I don't feel I have much to prove: I'm old enough to have had most of that knocked out of me! Besides which, I wrote some books a few years ago and I found a publisher, and so that's sort of taken care of: "OK, you've done something now!"

So I thought if I was to teach, what type of Shamanism would it be? It wouldn't be any particular kind of school or tradition. Rather, it would be an attempt to return to the original spirit of Shamanism, outside of any particular forms. You see these breakaway attempts to return to the source in all the major spiritual traditions. This is because people always turn them into religions. They turn a tradition into a set of forms which they bow down to and worship, and teachers that they bow down to and worship. They think that's the thing, that aligning themselves with all that is what will make them holy or whatever it is they are trying to become – enlightened, spiritual, maybe just better than other people!

But in the final analysis, it's not about aligning yourself with a tradition, it's about aligning yourself with your own guidance, that which comes from within you. That is what people find very difficult, but that is what a good teacher helps engender. A good teacher doesn't go, "Follow what I say, understand what I say, because I have thought it through much more deeply than you ever could." Well, he may have done, but that's not the point, which is don't identify yourself with a tradition, but benefit from it, be inspired by it, appreciate its depths.

Of course, all teachers will SAY don't follow me, follow your own wisdom. And you have to work out how much they mean that, by what the people around them are like, and by what you are like around the teacher. Do you lose something?

Traditions may be thousands of years old. They carry 'egregore' with them, the energy that builds up over time around ideas and symbols and ceremonies, and that is powerful. Egregore is a gift from the ancestors. We need to respect traditions, but not be beholden to them. At the end of the day, you have to step back: it's about you and your own soul.

If you are Shamanic, your soul is the natural world. You and the natural world are the same, you belong to her. The natural world is alive, it's inspirited, and our belonging to that is the foundation of Shamanism, because that is the foundation of how indigenous people are in the world. It's not even an idea for them. For us that has to be an idea, but for them it's like it's the air they breathe. "Well of course it's alive, of course we're part of the natural world, what crazy person are you that you could think otherwise?"

Well, we are those crazy people, we have this dead universe. Christianity fell apart and out of that came an inanimate cosmos. Why did that happen? Maybe because it had an image of torture at the centre of it: the crucifix. However profound its teachings might be in certain ways, there is also an image of torture bang at the centre of their mythology, with the threat of eternal hellfire too. And now we have a dead universe. It's almost like we're in cultural trauma from what the crucifix did to us. It created despair and killed the cosmos. And we haven't woken up yet, we are still numb. Perhaps there is truth in this. Something must have made us the first culture in history to see matter as dead, and you have to look at what came before.

Of course the universe is alive, we're alive, everything's alive, rocks are alive, you can feel their presence. I live on Dartmoor in the UK, which is covered in tors, piles of ancient volcanic slabs thrusting up from the tops of hills. They have a strong, warm physical presence, and I speak my appreciation to them when I visit.

This aliveness of everything is what Shamanism has to offer the modern world: a remedy for what I call the Great Forgetting that the world is alive and inspirited and pulsing with beauty, and takes care of us. We don't put the Spirit somewhere else up there in heaven: it is here, infusing everything.

Nature worship, in a sense that's what it's about. I don't know if you watch Jordan Peterson on YouTube, I'd recommend him. But I have an issue with him: he tries to put down how we feel about the natural world as Baal, worshipped with a Golden Calf in the Old Testament, and condemned by God. Mere nature worship, he thinks of it. You're wrong Dr Peterson, nature contains everything, and because we are nature, we contain everything, we contain the whole universe. Peterson is trying to reclaim Christianity, beginning with Bible stories, and in a way fair enough. But he doesn't ask why it went into such steep decline. What was/is wrong with historical Christianity? It's the old story of Christianity putting itself above what came before and, if it got the chance, it might well ban the pagan ways all over again. In the meantime, our task is to re-experience the natural world as the place of the Sacred.

So, Chaos Shamanism. Chaos is an interesting word, which we think of as mere disorder. Well yes, it's not order, but neither is it disorder or disarray, which is what it came to mean. It's an ancient Greek word, referring to the vast abyss of Unknowing, the Great Mystery out of which everything, the Cosmos, arose. It is what came before what we call the Big Bang.

We think that because we can't order things in human terms, then that is a negative, it's disorder. But that is just the limited rational mind. The Chaos has its own order, its own logos, but it is not one that the tiny human mind can grasp. Chaos Shamanism is Great Mystery Shamanism. It is out of the Great Mystery flowing through us, the Great Mystery that is who we are, that we have our own inner guidance. This is the essence, the original source, outside of any forms, that Chaos Shamanism stands for.

You see this attempt to return to the source in other religions. In Buddhism, they have sunyata, which is emptiness, and essentially the same as Chaos. It's the great void, the Great Mystery. And then people turned sunyata into a thing, so they had to say no no, emptiness is itself empty. So then you have to have another type of sunyata, the emptiness of emptiness, and they have to keep doing that because people keep turning it into a thing. We can't help but think in terms of things. 'Spirit' becomes a thing, and Chaos will become a thing. And then we might need to invent another level of Chaos, and say that Chaos is itself Chaos! It's a continual process of rebelling against people's tendency to turn ideas or practices into absolutes, taking them literally, writing them in stone. And then they tell other people they're not being respectful, because they didn't hold the pipe in the right way, or they didn't give thanks in the right way, and that's disrespectful to the pipe. I'm not entirely saying no to that, I do respect tradition, but actually it's the spirit that matters.

There's a good story from Tibetan Buddhism about someone who was reciting the mantra of Avalokitesvara, the Bodhisattva of Compassion. He recited it as Om Mani Padme Ox for years, and it worked, it changed him. But he'd got it wrong, it should have been Om Mani Padme Hum. However, it still worked because he was doing it with the right intention. So you see the point.

In medieval Christianity they had dancing in the churches. Eventually they banned it, because when you dance you make your own connection with the Spirit, and you can't have that if you're trying to run a religion. Maybe that is what the Sufi dancing is about, a return to a direct connection with the Spirit within the formalised religion of Islam.

With Shamanism itself, we continually need this return to what is essential, because you see it turning into religion left, right, and centre, almost everywhere, not because anything's going wrong, but because that's what people do. They think there really is a Lower World and a Middle World and an Upper World, and that power animals live in the Lower World and spirit guides live in the Upper World, and the Middle World's where you go to find your lost keys. OK, there's a certain amount of truth in that, but really it's just Spirit working through you, it has no name or form. If you just feel that working through you, it's not that you haven't got there yet because you don't know what your power animal is, and that you're backward. Actually, it may be that you're ahead of the game, you don't need those intermediaries. I love my animal helpers, don't get me wrong, I love all of that, but they are intermediaries. The warmth and love of the Great Spirit comes through them. The physical presence of power animals, of animal helpers reminds us of the physicality of Spirit.

You only have to let the soft animal of your body love what it loves, wrote the poet Mary Oliver. You don't have to be good, you don't have to repent, she said, you only need to do that, and then you have your source of guidance and joy.

Moment by moment. Chaos Shamanism is about listening to the spirit, to that inner guidance or outer guidance, it's kind of both. Listening moment by moment and living from that, putting it first. Putting your guidance before tradition, while respecting tradition. But that inner guidance needs to feel comfortable around the tradition, and there may be bits that don't feel comfortable, so don't think there's something wrong with you. Trust that inner guidance, trust the bits that feel right, and discard the bits that don't. A good teacher will always guide you towards that.

Chaos Shamanism: inspired by tradition but not beholden to it, and listening to Spirit at all times.

2

Tradition

I want to say something about tradition, because Chaos Shamanism is outside of tradition. It's about being sensitive to the Spirit at all points and prioritising that, putting that before tradition or teachings. Now that might sound like arrogance or hubris. Who are you to have a different opinion about the teachings around this Elder, maybe he's in his 80s, isn't that disrespectful? Who do you think you are? Well no, it's not disrespectful.

I went through this one myself in my late 30s. I was part of a Buddhist set-up, and there was a teacher who was by then in his 70s. He'd been my teacher for about 16 years, but something in me changed. It's like I'd imbibed what he had to say, and I'd benefitted from that, but I could increasingly also see the limitations of how he saw things, where he'd got it wrong. I started putting my own judgement in this first, and other people would try and make me doubt myself. "Oh, you just haven't understood," they would come back at me, because it's very natural for people to think well here's this guy, it's the Buddha, it's Jesus, it's the Dalai Lama, who are you to say that they're wrong and you're right?

It's often the limitations of the teacher that are in certain ways the greatest gift to you, because that's where your soul is calling out in its own voice, "I don't agree with that," and you say to your soul, "Shut up, who are you to have an opinion?" But you need to have that opinion, you need to find the things you don't agree with and cherish them, they will save you.

People regularly say that they don't always agree with me, but they never say what it is they don't agree with, they're just saying I don't always agree with you. I respond, well good, it would be dreadful if you did always agree with me, you'd be like some sort of cult member. To be fair it seems to be women who say that. The men just come out and say what it is, they are happier to risk a debate; men are known for being more disagreeable.

There always needs to be that gap between us and whatever teacher or tradition that we're inspired by, that nourishes us. Chaos Shamanism stands for that gap. It is the soul speaking from that gap.

More broadly, where is our society in relation to tradition? This is the main point I want to come at, which is that we don't have one in the modern world. There are plenty of minorities with their own traditions, but all the mainstream has are the remnants of Christianity, and that still works for some people.

What we have are TS Eliot's *"Heap of broken images"*, from his famous poem *The Waste Land*.

Christianity is no longer our unifying myth. If anything, the scientific creation theory is now our unifying myth. But it is lacking the Sacred, the Spirit, so it doesn't even qualify as myth.

We haven't got a central set of myths for the culture, and we haven't got one tradition that goes way back in history, and that's not normal. But there's a freedom in that, as well as a limitation, and this is where Chaos Shamanism comes in. There's a freedom in not having a tradition that you feel obliged to be part of. Imagine being a woman in a very traditional Muslim culture, and you wanted to go your own way and not marry who you were told to marry. That would be absolutely outrageous from the point of view of the culture. You'd go through a huge amount of self-doubt, and you'd need an awful lot of courage and self-belief to do that. And you would no longer belong to your people, you would be an exile: that can be a terrible fate.

It is the same in any traditional culture, if you want to live outside of the way it sees the Universe. Even in an indigenous culture it wouldn't be very easy. The Muslim example I used was quite extreme, but it illustrates the point, that it can be very difficult to live outside the norms of your culture.

Maybe we overvalue breaking free of the norms because of our emphasis on the autonomous individual. We downgrade them to a 'brainwashing'. The norms, albeit often restricting in some ways, can be very old and contain a lot of depth, apart from their function of holding the community together. That is what the term religion comes from — that which binds together.

You don't want to be just reinventing old traditions without deep consideration. The elders can do this, slowly; they have earned the right to, because they've mastered the tradition. If a tradition is alive, it will always be adapting in this way to changing times and circumstances.

Our situation is entirely different. It gives us the freedom to follow our own Spirit to where it calls us, and to take from whatever speaks to us, whether it's Shamanic traditions from across the world, Tibetan Buddhism, Chinese Acupuncture or, in my case, astrology.

We are surrounded by a cornucopia of traditions, and some of them will speak to you. Trust that, and follow it. My emphasis in this book is necessarily the 'pre-civilised' traditions of indigenous peoples.

The freedom to follow our callings is the spirit of what is called the New Age. Of course it has its downsides as well. It can be approached superficially, and that is what I want to address here. How do we do this with integrity? We have the freedom to follow our own Spirit and to build something that really suits us. But it's not just like going shopping and picking and choosing. It's not whimsical, it's deeper than that.

Maybe you decide to align yourself with a tradition, or at least dive into it for a while. I don't think fully aligning yourself with any tradition, in the sense of identifying yourself with it, 'converting' to it, is the right thing to do, because ultimately we are outside of any tradition. On the other hand, the overidentifying with a tradition or teacher, and eventual waking up from what you have done, is quite a common path too.

Traditions are there to help the individual soul unfold, to find its connection to everything, and its own gifts and meaning. They are there to serve us, they are not things in themselves. But if we're part of a tradition, we need to master it before we have the right to reinvent, otherwise it does get superficial.

Most importantly we need to master ourselves. I don't mean in the sense of mastery over. I mean that we need to have been with ourselves for many years. That's the real path: being with ourselves, coming close to ourselves, which in turn brings us close to everything. That, in a way, is what any tradition is about: bringing people close to themselves. People usually have got busy lives, and they tend to naturally look outwards. They don't look inwards and assess the values they're living from, and the deeper choices they have about who they're going be. But in a sense that is what life's really about: choosing moment by moment who you're going to be. Do you want to be the sort of person that kids themselves, that is dissembling, that is not courageous about who they are? Well, sometimes we are like that, but then maybe we realise we've let ourselves down.

It's the moment-by-moment choice, the ongoing living with ourselves outside of any tradition, that matters. We have a knowing that is inherent. We have a conscience that is inherent: something in us feels wrong if we don't tell the truth. That isn't just brainwashing or cultural conditioning. In a way the cultural rules should reflect that kind of innate knowledge.

Chaos Shamanism is about always living from these choices about who we want to be. And those choices have a context of a freedom to select the paths and traditions and teachers that call us. That's the great thing nowadays. In my early years, Buddhism called to me strongly. It eventually fell apart around me, and Shamanism and Astrology pulled me in, and have been with me ever since. Within Shamanism, the Medicine Wheel in particular had a deep magical pull that I couldn't explain. These traditions are enduring within me, but I feel the freedom to move around them as I please, to see what works for me. And to reinvent.

The Medicine Wheel is a good example. I wrote a book about it in 2021. I'd had no traditional training in it, and I reinvented it for myself. What gave me the right to do that was that I'd spent 40 years as an adult with myself, struggling with myself, making my mistakes, willing to be with my shadow stuff, not anaesthetising my demons too much, being honest with myself. Enough of the time, at any rate. I see that as my main qualification to write the book. There was also the fact that I'd been around the Medicine Wheel for about 25 years, and I had allowed it to become part of who I am.

Incidentally, some people would say that what I did was cultural appropriation, that I had no right to do that; the Medicine Wheel is from a foreign culture, a minority oppressed one at that, and I am stealing what little they have left. Some would say that, others would not. It's not like there is a singular indigenous authority that declares these things. Some Native Americans, or Indians, as they call themselves, would say that, and others wouldn't. Some would say go for it, you need to run with this thing, these teachings are valuable, so make them relevant to your land and share them.

This is how Chaos Shamanism works: you stay with yourself, you learn about yourself, learn how to be, probably over decades, and that then gives you the right to run ceremonies and to teach. You have something to say, and the right to reinvent as you go along. There's your empowerment. You don't get initiations or empowerments from outside of yourself. You get them from within, by staying with yourself, staying at that coalface of who you are, warts and all. There is joy in that as well as difficulty. It is more difficult than worldly achievement, and not so obvious. It's a slow path.

3
Chaos Shamanism Is a Deep Thing

This idea of Chaos is a deep thing. We think of it as a superficial thing, when things just aren't ordered, or haven't been paid attention to. But that's using the word Chaos to mean untidy, teenage bedroom, disarray.

We saw earlier that it comes from the ancient Greek, and refers to the vast Abyss that was there before the Cosmos arose out of Chaos. First arose darkness and night, the god Erebus and the goddess Nyx, the male and female dimensions of the dark, and out of them arose light. Also arose Gaia, the Earth, and Tartarus, the depths beneath the Earth. Everything arose out of Chaos, it's the source of everything. Chaos is that potent source of life, of everything, of the universe, of the dreaming, of the creation.

The ongoing creation: that's what we're tuning into when we do Chaos Shamanism. We're tuning into the ongoing dreaming of who we are, and the collective dreaming of the universe, that keeps it coming into being. We become aware that life isn't something that just randomly happens to us, which is how it can seem if you're just looking outwards. If you look inwards, you realise that life is being created all the time, mysteriously, it's not under our control, and that flow of creation is who we are.

Where do thoughts come from? They just seem to wander in. Nor do we decide on what we are feeling. Feelings are a continual flow, like a river, and they can be pleasant or painful. Our job is to come into relationship with it all, with this ongoing creation, which we experience through the continual bubbling up of thoughts and feelings and bodily sensations and dreams and hints from Spirit. And events on the outside too; we roll with them when they need rolling with, and we grapple with them when they need grappling with.

Shamanism without the Chaos is religion. In religion you get in the way of the Chaos, of that access to Spirit. You put up boundaries that say this is how it should be. This is how you Journey, this is how you call in the Spirits, and all that. I read a long response on Facebook to a question about how to do Shamanic Journeying. It was a whole description of the three worlds, and exactly what you need to do where, and what soul retrievals and so on are about. It sounded enormously complicated, and that you would need to put yourself in the hands of an expert before you went anywhere near it.

But it's not complicated, it's simple. Everything is simple. That's what Chaos reminds us of. It doesn't mean you can't have complexity – which I distinguish from complicated – but there's always simplicity behind it.

When you're doing anything – if you're in a Sweatlodge, if you're on a Journey to the Lower World, if you're doing a ceremony around the Medicine Wheel, if you're praying in a Pipe Ceremony, if you're doing an astrology reading, whatever it is you're doing, you need to be asking yourself, why am I doing it? What's the purpose of it? That is what gives the depth. There's always a very simple purpose behind everything, which is to be living from that deeper source within us, that thing that's calling us, that loves life, that has living to do. Maybe death is when you've done the living that was to be done this time, and it's time to go off on the next thing, whatever that is.

Chaos can sound like a superficial thing, and maybe you think you're the one with the real depth, because you've done 20 years training with a Siberian Shaman or a Native American teacher. Well, it probably has got a lot of depth, so I don't want to go to the opposite here. It's a delicate dance of appreciating the depth of proper training that takes many years, and the being true to the Spirit within us at all points. A proper training should lead us to the point where you can just let go of it all.

Sometimes you just need to let go of all those practices you have built up, however beautiful and profound. Take the Sweatlodge, which has got so much in it, everything is deeply symbolic and is surrounded by beauty.

And by the way, symbols are not an intellectual thing for indigenous peoples, they do not just stand for something, like let's pretend. No, they ARE that thing, the Sweatlodge IS the womb out of which you are reborn. It also IS the whole universe while you are in it. That's what ceremony does, it shifts reality, and makes it sacred.

There are, of course, lots of different ways of doing Sweatlodges, as many as there are peoples. The traditional Sweatlodges will have a lot more of that kind of symbolic content than anything we can run. We have to kind of just be true to the spirit, and keep it simple to keep it real. The complex symbolism is not ours, it is foreign, it is something we can probably never be truly part of.

Last time I led a Sweatlodge was about five years ago. It was lovely, it flowed, it was like a feminine presence came in and took over and just led it. People had a good time. Different people experienced it differently. For some it was really hot, for others it was gentle. The goddess took care of that. I didn't have much in the way of tradition behind me, just a few basics. But that's all I needed, because I'd done the 20 or 30 years being with myself, which is the real training, and which any traditional training will be moving you towards.

In a traditional training they may stick you out on Vision Quests, where it's just you and the natural world. It's a deep and demanding thing. You have nothing to distract you from the deeper questions about your life, and a vision of it may arise. It's very demanding to keep asking yourself what is the purpose of why I'm doing what I'm doing. It's much easier just to go to church on Sunday, and do what the priest tells you, or go to the Sweatlodge and do what you're told — of course we need to do that as well, because it's a collective thing, that has its own power and beauty, and which brings Community together. We do what we're told, but within it we need to be aware of why we're doing it. We're not just doing it because when we've done it, we can tick a box and feel virtuous and spiritual. No, there's no point doing it unless you're with whatever it is in you that you're here to be with. We all have something to be here with, to take care of, and to live, deep within us.

In Chaos Shamanism, we're always going back to the source. We're respecting tradition, we really honour it, we learn from it when we're around it. But there's always that gap we need to live from, that space where we find our souls, independently of whatever practice or ceremony it is that we are doing. At the same time, we are fully immersed in and wholehearted about whatever it is we are doing. But we are also human, we become identified with those practices to some extent, and we start to lose the gap. And so it can be good to just drop them all sometimes and stand alone with the Chaos, the Mystery.

In the same way that there's a gap between us and tradition, there also needs to be a gap between us and the surrounding collective values. Tradition and the collective values will overlap if we belong to a traditional culture. Though we don't have much in the way of tradition, there are certainly collective values around us now. Collective values are necessary, for they hold the community together. They are not just the brainwashing that some people think. They orient us, even though we might eventually need to move beyond them. In the same way, religion holds the community together. But these values are necessarily limited, at least in the way they are applied, if not in themselves. We sometimes need to be able to stand apart from those collective values, and that can be quite tough.

If you do this Shamanic thing, you're probably part of the counterculture that began in the 60s as a necessary protest against the materialism and the lack of spirit within society. But it has its own shadow, because it was itself a rebellion. We need to be able to stand apart from that collective shadow of the counterculture, which is authority, money, and a reflex opposition to convention. We end up thinking that we're above the world, that we know better, that capitalism is evil, and all that sort of thing. Well, we couldn't run the world any better. You encounter this very often in spiritual groups of whatever sort, this kind of putting down of the world as though we know better. "The world's in a dreadful state." Well, the world's just the world, it is what it is, it's not good or bad. And remember news isn't news unless it's bad, so we're skewed anyway by the media.

We need to be part of the world. The feeling of being above the world, that is part of the ethos of so many spiritual groups, is a prop, a dishonest one that is there to make you feel good about yourself. Chaos Shamanism doesn't have this easy get-out clause: you're part of the world, you're equal with the world. You're in the world, which in a way is all we're here to do: to incarnate, to undertake the difficult task of bringing spirit into matter.

4

Prayer and the Natural World

This chapter corresponds to the fourth video on the subject of Chaos Shamanism that I made for YouTube. I was still taking it episode by episode, not knowing if there would be another one, thinking that maybe Chaos Shamanism was an interesting idea, which would shortly be fully unfolded. Each episode was unplanned, beyond a rough idea that had presented itself to me as the thing I wanted to talk about. There was no plan at that stage. It was the opposite of a plan! But it was very much in the spirit of Chaos Shamanism, as it needed to be. I walked my talk in the way this book came about.

The word 'Chaos' can sound a bit hard or harsh. It's not a soft word. It doesn't obviously convey feeling. It can seem like it's just an idea. But it's not like that. It's about being close to your heart, which doesn't work in a rational, human-ordered kind of way. Chaos reminds us of that. I think it is a word best approached with the imagination, as the vast primal abyss out of which Gaia emerged: she provides the feeling and beauty nested in the word Chaos.

We need our human rationality. We need it in order to run our lives, but underneath it all, that's not who we are. It's about remaining close to that. I read a book many years ago now called *The Spears of Twilight* by Philippe Descola. He was a young French anthropologist who spent two years with the Achuar Indians in the Amazon jungle. He's now a sort of mandarin, a grand guy in French anthropology. But he was a young researcher then, and he lived with these people. He said that for some of them, everything they do is a prayer. I thought wow, what a way to live.

What does that mean, that everything you do is a prayer? It means you're connected with your heart to everything that you do, and that you're wishing for a good outcome. You're asking with gratitude for a good outcome. Prayer is founded in gratitude. It means a conversation with the natural world, that's one way of putting it, a sort of Navajo way. It's not about asking a deity, it's about being with the natural world, because we're part of it. It's founded in the sense that we're taken care of, we're helped, and that we can maybe get further help from that benign power. I'll leave it at that with prayer for now, and return to it more fully in Chapter 27.

It's interesting what nature is. I'm going on a slight digression here, but I'm feeling it, and this is Chaos, so I can! We have two kinds of attitudes or archetypes in the West towards nature. We have nature as pristine, as fragile, as Gaia, as the mother who takes care of us. And then there's nature red in tooth and claw. The first one is Rousseau. He also thought that man is born free, but is everywhere in chains. Piece of nonsense, if you ask me. Although we do know how to play as children, and we can forget how to play, but that's something else. Then there is the Hobbesian attitude, that life is nasty, brutish, and short. We have these two archetypes of nature running alongside each other. They are contradictory, but that's OK. We just need to hold those opposites. It's only the rational mind that has to have everything neatly tied up and reconciled.

I think the environmental movement tends to lean one-sidedly towards nature as pristine, benign, and fragile, and that she must be protected from the nasty humans. This may not be stated, but that's often the underlying feeling. And that gets mixed up with Shamanism, because of course we love the natural world, we remember we are part of it. But we also know it's tough, that nature is red in tooth and claw. The Chippewa Cree used to send their teenage boys naked out into the wilds on their own for a month, with just a knife and a blanket. They would have to learn to survive. Of course, Health and Safety would get you for child abuse nowadays if you did that. But the Chippewa Cree understood and appreciated this other side of nature. How can you not, when you are living close to the edge of survival? It is maybe a sign of our softness and decadence that we think one-sidedly of the Earth as fragile and in need of our protection. Just to add, the Chippewa Cree would have someone looking out for the boy in the wilderness, but he did not know that, so his lesson in survival was genuine.

Nature doesn't guarantee your survival. The business of rights to happiness and life and liberty is a human invention. Nature doesn't think like that. An antelope on the Serengeti doesn't think it has a right to life, it knows it had better look out sharp, or it won't have a life anymore!

Nature is both of these things, and she can take care of herself. Of course we need to take care of her as well, be respectful when we ask her for things. She has riches that she gives freely to us, she gives us of her oil, she gives to us of her rare earth elements. We humans have this technological inventive genius, and it's part of our nature. It's something unique that we bring to the table.

I don't want to over-egg that uniqueness, because if you read Frans de Waal's books — he was a great primatologist who died in 2024 — he showed that there's nothing in humans that isn't also shared by animals, whether cognitively or emotionally. He's written two books on that: *Mama's Last Hug*, about animal emotions, mainly those of chimpanzees; and then another book called *Are We Smart Enough to Know How Smart Animals Are?* The point being that animals sometimes have types of cognition that we don't have.

There is a continuity between humans and animals, but at the same time we bring, amongst other things, this huge inventiveness, and we need to value it, because it's natural to us. Our job is not to oppose that inventiveness out of fear, but to support it, and work to keep it in balance. Our Shamanic job, if you like, is to keep humanity in balance with where it's going, rather than clinging on to a pristine past, as if how we are now is somehow wrong and unnatural and killing the Earth, and all that sort of attitude. You can see this in environmentalism in its extreme form, the fundamentalists who hate humanity and all its works. Some of whom even think of humanity as a cancer, and that any changes in the Earth due to humans are automatically bad, simply because humans caused them. Well, we're Shamanic, we love humanity and we love all of nature: we love the nature of each creature and plant, and we love our own nature. So be discerning in your sympathies for the environmental movement. Not just the obvious nut-jobs who go around wearing death masks and glueing themselves to roads, but the more widespread and less obvious putting down of humanity. It is life-denying.

So back to the ongoing prayer of some of the Achuar: it would require a considerable depth and attention to be living from that place all the time, and listening to that place, and not doing something if it feels wrong. There is a whole other area there, to do with feelings, and trusting feelings and not trusting feelings. It can be another of the shadows of the counterculture, which is that we may mistrust reason and overvalue feeling: if I feel it, well then I'll do it, I'll believe what it's telling me. But it's not like that. We need to consult feeling as part of the whole complex of feeling, thought, instinct, body, imagination, inspiration, and experience. We need to consult all of these things, and through that we gradually learn which feelings to trust and which feelings not to trust.

A good example is romantic feelings. They can blow us right off course, which I'm sure is something we've all experienced. Or you know if you've woken up and you're in a mood, then you learn not to trust what it's telling you about the world, that the world's terrible and what's the point of being here. That's your mood, and what you also learn is that you can't just get rid of the feeling, you have to make friends with it or at least reach an accommodation. A therapist told me that she sees her job as helping people to tolerate themselves. We're learning to tolerate certain feelings, to live with them, make friends with them, stopping judging them, but not acting on them either: we build self-possession. On the one hand we're not putting ourselves down and judging ourselves, but on the other hand we're quite rigorous with ourselves, we need to be honest with ourselves. That's a whole other area, which we'll look at further in Chapter 14.

5
Soul and Spirits

Chaos is a protean word. (So is Shamanism, for that matter.) It has a number of closely related meanings. In this chapter, I am using it to mean the essence of Shamanism. The essence is Spirit, always coming back to Spirit, living from Spirit. That thing in you, we can't say exactly what it is, for it can never be pinned down: it's more than us, it's bigger than us, it's the place that we have to live from, without which life doesn't have meaning. That is the essence of Shamanism: living from Spirit, in the context of belonging to an inspirited — or ensouled — natural world.

'Core Shamanism' has become one of the standard ways of introducing our subject. Its name implicitly lays claim to the essence of Shamanism. It refers essentially to a series of techniques for journeying to drums within a prescribed cosmology, and doing healing work on that basis. It works, but it's a very narrow way of describing the heart of this great project that we're undertaking, which is the reclaiming of indigeneity for the modern world: the universal indigenous ways of feeling about, and relating to, the world.

We lost our indigeneity through our big institutionalised religion, Christianity, and then through Science. Science is a big religion in its own way, because most of it is based on beliefs in certain absolute truths about the universe, that we cannot verify for ourselves. If you like, Christianity told us that Spirit lay elsewhere — in heaven — and then Science finished off Spirit altogether. Job done!

Somewhere the soulfulness of the world, that is also fire, earth, air, and water — or, more concretely, sun, rain, soil, and wind — somewhere that connection has been lost. Nowadays the world is dead, and redemption lies in the scientific and technological enterprise, which will make us as gods, while explaining the deep mysteries of the universe.

We need to find a way of coming back to the simple soulfulness and connectedness of the indigenous ways. There's nowhere to go, there's nothing to do, there's just life to be lived through the Spirit in us, and the Spirits around us.

The Spirits. They are often where we are told Shamanism starts. But the 'Spirits' may not be your thing. I say Shamanism begins not with the Spirits, but with remembering the natural world, which is everyone's thing. What are these Spirits? I don't exactly know. People talk about their animal helpers and their Spirit guides. I have different animal helpers that turn up at different times. I mean when I work. But also they may just be around. One was around a couple of years ago getting me to write a fantasy saga. But that's another story.

I began with Core Shamanism in 1997. I did that course, but for me it's broadened and changed since then. Sure, I can lie down and journey to a drum, but actually the Spirits are just there anyway, like over my shoulder, and they shift into me physically. That's the thing, I don't go and meet the Spirits. Some indigenous people say no they come to you, you don't go to them. They even say there's something wrong if you have to go to find them. And that's how it works for me: they come into me, I don't go and find them. I don't journey miles and miles down to a Lower World and go looking. I'm not invalidating that, but there's this other way, and it's just like they're there, over my shoulder, so to speak, because the Spirits are always with us.

They kind of are us and not us. It depends how we define 'me'. In the narrow sense, they're not us, they're outside and they come to us. In other ways, they are us, in a bigger sense. We kind of are the universe, and there are these helpers who understand us intimately. They know how we're unfolding. You could say they're gods of the unconscious, but even the unconscious makes it too personal and narrow. This is something bigger, it's a bigger cosmology. We must never forget that we're part of a cosmology, an intimate part of a multidimensional cosmos, and we have our contribution to make, which in a way is not for us to explain or over-analyse. It's just whatever 'does it' for us, in a deeper kind of sense. It's a visionary thing.

That's one way we could see the question of how to live Shamanically. It's about belonging to an inspirited natural world, while also doing that thing that calls you, that thing that you love. Life in this sense is joyful and soulful. But it can also require courage and patience and honesty. It is easy to make excuses, to put aside the things that really matter in the interest of the things we just think matter, or that we 'ought' to do.

The 'oughts'. Often the people around you, maybe the society around you, will tell you who to be. That's just the way it works. It has its rules, it's trying to survive and prosper, and so the collective tells you who you ought to be. Often that's helpful for people. But if you've got something else going on, you need to get rid of these 'oughts'. They are someone else's idea. We need to do the things that we love. Of course, we have responsibilities to fulfil, and that's part of life as well — economics, family — they help us incarnate and connect. But outside of that, you know you have something that you're here to live. It's why you're reading this book.

Do you ever get that sense there's something in you that you haven't lived yet, that needs living? I get that all the time. Usually it's joyful. Sometimes it's difficult, particularly if I am having to move on to something very new. If I'm not living it, I can easily turn to alcohol to anaesthetise it. I gave up alcohol altogether for the first time in early 2024, and six weeks later this book came pouring out. There is a creative spark or urge, and eventually you have to go with it, or you may get ill, or very out of sorts in some way. That is what the Shamanic Illness in traditional cultures is about (see Chapter 9). An offer you cannot refuse. Spirit is essentially creative, and we are here to live creatively.

You never know what it is that people will love. I'm an astrologer, a discerner of the stories in the sky at the moment of your birth. Why I should love that, I do not know, it's a mystery. I just do, and there's an end of it. When I look at a chart, I never know what people's specific interests are going to be. I can have a good stab at it sometimes. But really it's a mystery. (Sometimes, however, I hit multiple nails on the head all in one go. That is the ancient sky gods whispering in my ear.) It might be horses, it might be astrology or painting, it might be building things, it might be trees. I don't know what it is that gives you your joy, which also gives you your challenge and stretches you.

The Spirits will help you with your callings. It is what they are for. We may or may not know what our Spirits are, but it doesn't matter. Sometimes it's quite clear there's a Bear around me, or a Wolf. At other times there's just something working through me. If you just have a sense of something and that is all, trust it. Not knowing can be good for us humans. The Spirits are there to help and to guide. They will guide us in the direction of that which we love. They support us in that, and it's a challenging place to live from. It will stretch you and also probably give you considerable self-doubt. As well as joy.

What I'm going to ask is, what would you like to be good at, if you thought you were capable? What would 'do it' for you? Often we put these things aside because we think we'd be no good at them. Self-doubt is natural and even necessary, because you're not yet good at it. You have to earn your confidence, rather than go to an analyst and attempt to build 'self-esteem'. That's one of my central maxims for life: get good at something that you love. And it will clear up a lot of your problems and demons in its wake.

You can think that it's just not practical to follow your calling, that you can't have horses or whatever it might be. But I think there's always a way to do the things we love. This is where the faith in Spirit comes in. We get help. We find mysterious openings occurring. But only when we take the initial steps. Then the Cosmos can respond, and it usually does. We can at least do a bit of whatever it is, we don't need to necessarily do an awful lot of it, just a bit to keep that connection. Over time it will grow, and opportunities that you could never have thought of will present themselves.

That is the main point I wanted to address in this chapter: finding that thing, or those things, that you love. It's a good exercise. The thing that maybe you're not doing, because you think it's just not practical, or that you'd be no good at it. All these excuses we make. It's about living creatively, it's about the Spirit being able to go beyond just following some set of rules and attaining respectability. You're bringing something new into existence, it's your own, and that's the deepest fulfilment, the deepest joy. That really is incarnation. Incarnation isn't just about earning a living and being responsible; no it's about something much deeper and bigger than that. It's about bringing in that creative Spirit and living it, doing something with it.

6

The Secret Teachings

You may have heard of Chaos Magic, which has been around since the 1970s. Someone who'd been doing it for many years explained it to me once. She said that the way it works, is that you create a ceremony for a particular reason, for an outcome, and it's unique. But the way they create those ceremonies draws as inspiration from other magical traditions. A diligent practitioner of Chaos Magic will spend a fair bit of time researching magical traditions from all around the world, and using that as a kind of databank. You can see the Chaos element, in that there's no set tradition; rather, you're allowing the form to create itself, rather than having a preset form in which you put your intentions, or what I would call prayers. Artistically, it is akin to the Romantic tradition, in which the creative impulse is primary, and the form secondary.

Chaos Shamanism can be Romantic in this sense too, in that sometimes we will create ceremonies in this way, that are tailored for the occasion or for the intention. But at other times we may be following a traditional form. Where we differ from Chaos Magic is that ceremony is just one part of what we do.

In ceremony, we pray for outcomes, we put a heartfelt intention out there, and this is another word for magic. You can't pre-determine exactly what the outcome's going to be. It'll often take you by surprise, but outcome there will be if the prayers are heartfelt. How could there not be? When something is heartfelt, you're connected to the whole universe and the universe responds, because it cares for us. In a way that's what magic is; it's an inner thing, it's the secret teaching. It's the intention behind the forms that contain the primary power, not the forms or spells themselves, whatever other impression you might have got from Harry Potter.

We do magic, but it's in the form of prayer, beginning with the expression of gratitude for all those things in our life that work, and then asking for what we need help with, or where others need help.

So that is a comparison point between Chaos Shamanism and Chaos Magic. I also want to compare Chaos Shamanism with the vision for Buddhism in the West that my old Buddhist teacher had.

What is our modern context for Shamanism? Here we are, high and dry in a society that in many ways has lost its roots in the indigenous connection to the natural world, that soulful connection to the elements, and everything that comes out of that. And we're trying to recreate it. We're in a great position, because we've got indigenous traditions from all around the world to draw on and to be inspired by. And that for me parallels the Buddhism I was involved with in my 20s and 30s – my misspent youth, as I half-jokingly call it.

The teacher's approach was to take the essence of Buddhism and re-express it in a form that is relevant to modern society. So not committed to any one school, but drawing on all of them. He was English, and his qualification to do this was that he had spent 20 years as a young man in the East, practising various traditional forms.

It's a great idea, but his trouble was that he started it far too early. He hadn't done his own inner work. He was one of these people who had a genuine insight at a very young age, but then identified with that, and kind of remained the same. His understanding of the essence of Buddhism – which is an inner thing – remained partial, and in some ways quite cold and intellectual.

He did have something, but he hadn't been through the demolition, the dark night of the soul, the underworld journey, where you come into relationship with all that is in you that isn't bright and shiny and idealistic. You start to make friends with your demons, you develop a deeper honesty about who you are. It gives you humility, because you realise you are no better or worse than anyone else. It gives you a heart. You are re-born after a long night-sea journey. It revolutionises who you are, and the way you see the world.

It is out of this long, difficult process that you truly grasp your soul for the first time. (This topic will be discussed further in Chapter 9, **The Shamanic Illness**.) It is this that any spiritual tradition is pointing to. It is an initiation that is at the heart of the Shamanic traditions, and therefore of Chaos Shamanism. It's an inner experience, an alignment with what is deepest in us, and a deeper alignment also with the Spirits around us.

Chaos Shamanism grasps the essence of Shamanism, amidst all its varying forms. It is the same kind of idea as my Buddhist teacher had. But it is me in my 60s saying it, not him in his 40s. I've had more time – and, I think, willingness – to sit at my own coalface, and in a way develop more humility and a broader self-knowledge.

When I teach, I like to begin by talking about the things I find difficult, the things that make me anxious; how I have to make sure I don't drink too much because I do like it, it is a get-out from my creativity; the things that can make me angry sometimes, the things that can make me lose self-possession; the self-doubt I go through, at least in the early stages, with just about everything I do. I like to talk about all those things, because it keeps me on the same level as you, because we are all the same. I haven't got a special experience that puts me above other people. I've just stayed with myself. Live closely to yourself, that's all we're here to do.

When I am open in that kind of way, then other people feel emboldened to do that, they feel it's OK, that their faults aren't terrible and unique. It's like no, you're the same as the rest of us.

We don't need to judge the demons and the tribulations, we just need to come into a relationship with them. It's all you have to do, it's both simple and difficult. Everything comes out of that.

This ongoing journey with the shadow side, the far-off place it takes you to, and the transformation that comes with that, is the secret teaching. It is not something that can be summed up in words, for it is an experience, usually hard-won. My old Buddhist teacher summed up the essence of Buddhism through certain teachings. There was nothing wrong with those teachings, but they were only pointers. He was an intellectual, and never properly broke his way out of that. It is the same with Michael Harner and his 'Core' Shamanism. He was an academic, and he effectively reduced the essence of Shamanism to a set of techniques. There is nothing wrong with the techniques. But it is missing the point.

In Buddhism you do get the secret teachings, the transmissions. I think something can be transmitted from person to person, from Spirit to Spirit. It's not in words, it's not in forms, it's more like being around that person and being open.

I went to an online Shamanic initiation. It was a three-part course, and the initiation was into a goddess. I lasted for just the first session. The teacher was recounting the traditional ways they work, which is great, but it didn't mean much to me. Why would it? But I felt I got it after the first session, I felt I picked up something from him, something around him was now around me, even online. (And why not? These things are outside the usual rules of time and space.) So that's the transmission, and it's also another form of the secret teaching; you just need to be open to it, and this other kind of thing can happen.

In traditional Shamanic cultures you get Spirits being passed down families, from father to son, grandmother to granddaughter, and so on, and I think it's got something of that nature. There's a special feeling. You can feel some people's connection to the Spirits, and it comes with a grounded quality when it is Shamanic, for ours is an Earth path. We are not light workers.

This connection is not the only way of being Shamanic. Not everyone works consciously with the Spirits. This can sometimes be a point of contention around the definition of Shamanism, some saying it is just the Spirit work, others saying no, it is about the broader attempt to reclaim indigeneity. Academics, who invented the term, came to use it in both senses. I prefer to use it in the broader sense.

I personally feel that inner connection with the Native American ways. They somehow seem to come my way. I'm not going to big it up, but there's a connection there, which I think comes across when I talk. I did, after all, write a whole book on the Medicine Wheel.

All the practices and ceremonies and teachings are a support to the inner knowing, the inner connection. It's quite special, it's very alive, it's got a fantastic taste to it, like ambrosia or honey. It's always a mystery, and we can't resist it. We know we're meant to be around it, it has that deeper kind of pull. I have felt that around Tibetan Buddhism as well as Shamanism. It will be around any tradition that has hung on to the inner knowing. It is easily lost in the outward forms, or in the charisma of the teacher, which can look like the inner knowing, but may largely be his personal needs projected outwards. Chaos Shamanism stands for that impulse to keep reclaiming the inner traditions from their tendency to ossify in forms and hierarchies and books, or to be compromised by teachers who haven't done enough inner work.

7

Transmission and Tradition

Chaos Shamanism sounds like the opposite of tradition. In reality it couldn't be more traditional. What is tradition? It's a means of fostering, of nourishing, of creating a spirit within the human being, in which we're aligned with ourselves, with our own nature, which is the nature of the world. There's no split between us and the world outside. The purpose of any spiritual practice anywhere is becoming aligned with that whole. When I use the term Chaos Shamanism I'm going straight to that alignment.

I mentioned transmission in the context of the Secret Teaching. It is a sort of osmosis of that deeper alignment, from one being to another. One person is open, and they receive it from the other. One tree sees the other flowering, covered in beautiful blossoms, it smells the perfume, and is also inspired to flower.

There's a book called *The Philosophers' Secret Fire: A History of the Imagination* by Patrick Harpur, which I highly recommend. He talks about a sacred tradition, or a perennial tradition, a passing down of fire from generation to generation. You see it in what is known as the Western esoteric tradition, which existed, often in secret, alongside Christianity. Magical traditions, astrology, alchemy. A good astrology teacher, for example, essentially communicates their connection with the presences of the planets, or the gods they are named after. It is there that the passion for the subject lies. You also see it in its own way in the Shamanic families out in Mongolia or Siberia, where there are Spirits associated with certain families, and that fire is passed down, shared; it's kind of transpersonal as well as personal, to use Western terminology.

That is the real transmission, that is what really keeps a tradition alive, because it IS the tradition in its deepest sense, and it is a universal. A tradition will die with just its outward forms.

In the modern West, we have no widely accepted traditions. We have no forms that go way back, that have that kind of deep resonance, embedded at the centre of who we are. You can see people's longing for it, in the way they will sometimes hang on to every word and every scrap of ritual from a Mexican Shaman, or pay good money for an online initiation into Mongolian teachings they have to keep secret. Or the attempts to create a 'Celtic Shamanism', when all we have is scraps from what was effectively a foreign culture, even if we are genetically related to them. All we have, in TS Eliot's words, are *"Fragments I have shored against my ruin."*

Be done with it all, I say. It's a poverty mentality. Don't give your power away to indigenous Shamans, we have the power just as much as they do, if we are prepared to put in the work. And don't scrabble around in Celtic fantasies, in the delusion that you are creating a tradition. Own what you have now, the modern Western person that you are. And borrow shamelessly, just like Shakespeare did.

We can borrow forms, like Chaos Magic does to create their ceremonies. We can borrow to help engender that inner alignment, to help promote it. We can pick and choose, but not in a superficial way. We choose according to where we're genuinely called. We sit with it, we see where we need to go. But it takes time, it's not just of the moment. It's not just, oh today I feel like this and tomorrow I feel like the other, like you see some people playing around with their identity.

Identity isn't such a big deal, by the way, it's a shaky, temporary thing, that is as much decided by other people as it is by us. Indigenous people, who see the self as more relational than we do, would understand this.

You can be firmly drawn towards certain practices or teachers, and it can be a deep thing that you do not understand. It may turn out to be enduring, or it may be just for a while. But there is a depth to it that you cannot resist. It is in this context that I talk about 'borrowing'. It can be more than borrowing, it can be a deep and lasting immersion, as it has been for me with the Medicine Wheel. I'm drawn towards the Far Eastern Shamanism as well, I don't know anything about it, but when I see them dancing there is a recognition in me, because they dance what we call Journeys, and it's also how I work. It's the same kind of inner thing there. Also for me there is astrology, it's like it is in my bones. And it has a connection with the Medicine Wheel through the four elements, which are used in similar ways.

What we're doing with Chaos Shamanism is we're re-encountering the real, universal tradition. We have the freedom to do so because we're not beholden to all these different ways, valuable as they are, great as it is when a whole community finds its meaning within those forms.

We're somewhere else, and the great opportunity we have is to seize hold of the essence. We can do this because there's no one stopping us. There are people who attempt to, and there always will be. There are people who say you're not allowed to do this-or-that practice without permissions, or that it's deeply disrespectful and cultural appropriation if you even go near it. There will always be these voices, and they key into our own self-doubt. Nowadays it also plays into the woke guilt, that we are the historical oppressors, and we must walk on eggshells around indigenous people and be super-respectful. I am sure a lot of them laugh at us for this. It's so weak, so life-denying.

I just say fuck all that, all those disempowering voices, and excuse my French. And my Spirit Animal says so too, so there! You just have to have the chutzpah, the hubris, the impudence to head out and run a Sweatlodge or whatever, when you've maybe only been in a Sweatlodge once, and you've hardly got a clue, but you've got a few basics, and you know it did you good. And if you are proper and respectful and go on a 20-year training instead – and I am not speaking against that – then all those people in your area will not benefit from Sweatlodges for all that time. Think about it like that. Or Pipe Ceremonies, or Journeying, or Trance Dances or whatever. But for heaven's sake don't create an identity out of it, or you'll do as much harm, without knowing it, as good. A lot of that goes on. Just stay equal to people, and let them see your vulnerabilities, specifically, and that will help keep you in a good place.

The Dalai Lama used to be known for handing out initiations to whole crowds of people. They are initiations into the inner energies. They take Buddha and Bodhisattva forms in the Tibetan tradition. There are many of them, and they become objects of meditation.

You could look at these meditative forms as frozen spirit guides, which I'm sure a Tibetan Buddhist would love me for saying! But I think there's a truth in it. The original yogi in his cave in the mountains has a vision, a powerful figure comes to him, and he passes on that living energy to those who can receive it. But then the tradition gradually gets hold of it and fixes it in words and form, and bows down and worships it as the most holy of holies. Tibetan Buddhism loves its sacred superlatives, which they dole out unsparingly on their lamas. What was originally a living energy becomes fixed, and the meditation on it can almost be like you are brainwashing yourself. But the original inspiration is still there if you can approach the figure in a fluid and open way, and allow it to take the form it wants, and move and speak as it wants.

The Dalai Lama's handing out of initiations *en masse* goes right against the tradition, where people are supposed to be properly prepared, so that they can receive it. And rightly so. He has been criticised for it, but these are exceptional circumstances. Valuable inner traditions are being lost as his culture is destroyed and dispersed, and some of the initiations may take, some people may be able to really run with them. So good on him, I say.

Not that I don't have a personal reservation, which is that these Bodhisattva figures lack ordinary humanity. They are transcendent beings of light, they are powerful, they have an incredible beauty. But they lack ordinary humanity. They are full of spirit, but lack soul. That is why I like some of the rough Chan master depictions from China, who can be shaggy, almost beast-like creatures.

Shamanism is immanent rather than transcendent, meaning that the sacred is to be found within the world rather than beyond it. It is religion that creates transcendence, which is another way of saying that people get put on pedestals. (I am usually a bit wary when someone says they are a light-worker for a similar reason. I can feel the earth element as missing.)

I think there's a political agenda behind the transcendent model. It is about religions trying to control people, by getting them to think that being an ordinary human being isn't good enough. What have we left if that is taken away, because an ordinary human is all we can ever be?

There is nevertheless a good point in what the Dalai Lama is doing, and it is similar to our position. We just have to run with these things as best we can.

I don't want at any point to give the impression that I am laissez faire about how we run with the bits of tradition we find along the way. I am probably less so than most; I am quite conservative in many ways. I have lost Facebook friends for saying that people are rarely in a position to be a spiritual teacher until they are a bit older, because otherwise they are nearly always creating an identity for themselves out of it, which is obvious to everyone except their followers. It would probably be preferable if they stepped back for ten years and dealt with whatever it is in them that needs to create an identity – which is always at other people's expense.

But you can run these things without being in the role of teacher. Do it just because people need it, and trust it if it happens, and trust it if it doesn't happen. Let it be Spirit led. It is a great training.

8

The Wider Context

'Chaos' in ancient Greek times referred to the vast Abyss out of which arose order, the Cosmos. Not that the vast Abyss doesn't have its own order; after all, it is brimming with potential, a cable of infinite voltage, on which mere humans can only gaze with awe, out of the corners of their eyes. But it is not a human order. It is more akin to those bigger patternings of our lives that we sometimes glimpse, and that are beyond our control. The sensing of Chaos keeps us close to what matters; it is another way of talking about the Great Spirit, the Great Mystery.

Chaos has come to mean disorder or disarray, and in that sense it describes well the current cultural context, in which the unifying myth of Christianity no longer has the compelling power it once did. Most of us would perhaps subscribe to its scientific replacement story, the bones of which are the Big Bang and Evolution. It may be rationally compelling, but it is not imaginatively/spiritually compelling in the way that humans need, to provide a meaningful context for life; for where is consciousness, and where is value?

In 1919, in the wake of WWI, Yeats wrote his prophetic poem *The Second Coming*. It begins:

Turning and turning in the widening gyre,
The falcon cannot hear the falconer.
Things fall apart, the centre cannot hold,
Mere anarchy is loosed upon the world.

These lines describe the collapse of the Christian story in the modern world. And the outcome? These lines at the end of Yeats' poem, which many of us know from Joni Mitchell:

And what Rough Beast,
Its hour come round at last,
Slouches towards Bethlehem to be born?

The authoritarian horrors of Communism, a quasi-religion, were one manifestation of Yeats' Rough Beast. There have been others: Nazism and extreme Woke, for example. Arguably also net zero carbon, a defining belief for many, but which keeps the developing world in poverty, unable to use the oil riches that we continue to consume so freely.

Collectively, the collapse of a unifying myth puts us in jeopardy, whatever the limitations of the Christian myth were. All certainties gradually disintegrate: we have now reached the point where we can no longer even define what a man or a woman is, one of those fundamental categories we use to orient ourselves, to understand our existence.

It is cause for concern, because the religious impulse is central to humans, and if we do not have an adequate vehicle for it, we will create inadequate vehicles for it. We enter an age where, as Yeats put it,

The best lack all conviction,
While the worst are full of passionate intensity.

To risk being political for a moment, I would argue that 'cancel culture' is an example of Yeats' 'passionate intensity', in which the laudable aim of protecting the rights of minorities is subverted by an intolerant mob, who will forcefully silence, and reputationally destroy, anyone who disagrees, even mildly, with the way they see the world. It has religious elements, which can also be seen in extreme environmentalism.

I am saying this not so much to make a political point, as to provide a context for modern Shamanism: the decline of institutional religion, and the 'rough beasts' that have become its substitute.

Philosophically, we live in an age of no absolute truths. This is called Postmodernism. While this is always true on a metaphysical level, words never being more than pointers to deeper truths, it is not helpful for the average person. Their concerns lie elsewhere in busy lives. A more straightforward metaphysical explanation of the universe is required, that they probably interpret with more certainty than is warranted. But that is regular humanity for you, it has always been that way. Astute propounders of religious truths allow for this.

Postmodernism is a sympathetic philosophy for healers and mystics, for our power and wisdom come from living close to the mystery of things. It is uncomfortable for most people: for them, it is a case of "mere anarchy is loosed upon the world."

I have no solutions to offer for this lack of unifying myth(s). Maybe the problem was that we only had one of them, a recipe for fundamentalism, which we eventually, and rightly, threw off. Indigenous peoples may have a plethora of creation myths, which they do not need to reconcile. Science has inherited from Christianity the notion that there can only be one truth. Postmodernism is perhaps the first step in addressing this problem. Allowing space for contradictory ideas to live, without having to reconcile them, is a good practice, which opens us to deeper truths. Try believing, for example, both the Biblical and scientific creation stories. If not the Bible, then another one that has imaginative appeal for you: it is that which makes it a genuine belief.

This is the religious context in which Chaos Shamanism is giving birth to itself. Any new mythologies will need to gather organically around it. It is a favourable context for those with the psychological strength to live in uncertainty. It gives the freedom to be eclectic, to pick and choose from existing indigenous traditions, and to adapt them as necessary. We don't necessarily appreciate our freedom to do this, and to speak as we wish in public. This is historically rare, and we cannot assume it will last.

The main opposition to this Chaos approach would be from within the modern Shamanic world, from people who regard tradition as the only right way; or from those claiming to speak on behalf of indigenous peoples in judging this approach to be 'cultural appropriation'.

Fortunately, we can quietly go our own way, for there is no overarching authority to whom we are answerable. Chaos Shamanism entails being true to the spirit within, and opposition to that from the voices claiming to represent tradition can be just the kind of 'worthy opponent' we need to become confident in what we stand for. This was my own experience some years ago on Facebook, in the face of someone who claimed to know what Shamanism is and isn't, and wanted others to regard him as the authority in the matter. That opposition eventually left me much clearer of my own position.

Shamanism, by my definition, is the attempt to reclaim, and live from, the indigenous soul, in the context of a humanity that tends to forget its intimate connection with an inspirited natural world. It is a spiritual starting over, bringing us back to how humans were for perhaps 95% of our existence.

I think we need to learn from, and trust in, Christianity's demise. I observe the influential podcaster Jordan Peterson devoting much effort in attempting to resuscitate Christianity, starting with the Old Testament stories. Yes, there are profound truths to be found there, as in any religious text. And he does a good job. But it seems to me like a desperate attempt to bring back the past, if only because he never asks why Christianity declined so catastrophically in the first place, and the limitations of a God who would, for example, like to see gay men stoned to death. Peterson also likes to put down indigeneity as mere 'nature worship'.

I say trust the fact that Christianity failed, and learn from it. Metaphysically, we live in a volatile age, dangerous for the 'rough beasts' it continues to spawn. But we also live in an age of unique potential, where humanity's technological brilliance – a part of our nature that needs to be trusted and embraced – needs to be re-allied with our belonging to the natural world. Christianity, in its assigning of the world to the devil, cannot do this. Science, the new religion, needs to be open to consciousness – or maybe 'soul' is a better word – being an inherent part of matter, its subjective pole. The subject of what I call the Great Forgetting is discussed further in Chapter 15, **Soil**.

Chaos Shamanism reclaims what we have forgotten about ourselves, while having a complete openness to the forms which this new alliance between techno-human and indigenous human may take. It can be part of the way forward.

9

The Shamanic Illness

A Shift in Authority

I want to say something about the Shamanic Illness, that phenomenon amongst the Shamans from the remote cultures of the Far East, and how that relates to us, what it's really about. This is in the spirit of Chaos Shamanism, where we are always asking that kind of question, instead of being confounded by the exotic and foreign nature of these things, and maybe bowing down before that. They are humans just like us, and we can always find a reference point in our own experience.

The way it's put, is that the young person who's supposed to become a Shaman gets ill. This is because he's trying to be like an ordinary guy. And the Spirits come knocking, like the dark stranger in the middle of the night come to tell you your Fate. And they go, "You've got to be a Healer", as well as everything else you do. In those cultures, it's not like you become the holy man and you get paid to do it. No, you still have your ordinary life to fulfil, and then you have these duties on top, and people don't necessarily want that.

I think it's also more than that. Allowing the Spirits in can be deeply scary, and they're more comfortable with who they are and who they've been brought up to be. And here they are, being taken outside the collective norms, the collective way of seeing things, which is a difficult thing.

As the poet TS Eliot said,

Humankind cannot bear very much reality.

That's how humanity works. It's important to recognise that we all think we're independent individuals with free minds and the freedom to choose, but that is only true on a superficial level. We go along with the collective norms and the collective way of seeing things. We think we have thought it all through, but in reality we hold all our beliefs for emotional reasons, and they are given to us with the authority that the collective holds for us. We use reason just to support what it is we want to believe anyway. That is why it is so easy to find yourself in an argument about certain ideas: they are beliefs that tell you who you are.

The authority that the collective holds for us is fundamental. The Covid lockdowns were an interesting case in point. Most people buckled down to the new rules immediately. They believed implicitly that there was a very dangerous disease at large, purely because they'd been told that. Fear had taken hold. I was more sceptical about it; I thought it was a bit overblown. You also saw a minority of people going to the opposite extreme, reacting against it, rebelling against it, and coming up with wild theories about secret agendas. That was no less a collective phenomenon, and was quite characteristic of the counterculture, with its frequent paranoia about authority.

I was a bit rebellious about masks myself, even at my advanced age. I recognised that, and I just had to get over myself, though it still took about six months. I thought the masks were ridiculous, and I still do. But sometimes you just have to conform, and it wasn't going to harm me. So there was a bit of self-knowledge for me.

You can learn a lot about collective humanity at such times.

We see it also with the net zero carbon idea. Without going into the rights and wrongs of that, you see how the collective has been persuaded into a sense of emergency, based on apocalyptic thinking. People tend to bow down before politicians claiming the authority of science, and it is not hard for politicians to herd scientists along the lines they need them to go, for they are not always a very courageous bunch, and their jobs would be at stake if they didn't conform. I don't think it is so much a conscious desire to control on anyone's part; it is more that the collective gets swept into these currents, and everyone goes along with it, politicians, scientists, and the man in the street, each in their own way.

It's not very difficult to whip the collective into a sense of crisis. Back in the day, it was the nuclear weapons crisis, then it became the environmental crisis. After that, Covid was the crisis for a bit, and now we're back to the environment. But now there's the potential AI crisis that might end the world, or so we are told.

I suppose it gives a point of certainty, and a sense of right against wrong, and a comforting feeling of an authority that is claiming to be in charge. These crises are a bit like mind-viruses that go around, they are epidemics.

So that's the perennial collective mindset. When you get onto the Shamanic path, or any spiritual path, you are stepping outside of it: the Spirits become your authority, your guidance, instead of the collective beliefs and the sense of belonging that comes with that. It's a big deal.

It's usually a process, and quite often what we do at the beginning is to step outside of one collective mindset and into another one. It's kind of inevitable. We loosen up a bit, there's something new in ourselves that we're listening to, but we don't fully trust that guidance from within yet. So we look to teachers and traditions, and we accept their authority. That is natural and usually necessary, but it is limited.

What the Spirits want is for you to trust them fully and implicitly, because they ARE you in a broader sense. But that takes time. It is a lifetime's work, probably. It is a huge and deep shift. They want you to leave the group mindset behind, not by being anti-it, which often is also a temporary part of the path, a phase, but by living quietly alongside it; probably putting your head in your hands at the nonsense that goes on, but in a sympathetic way, and spreading a bit of the Spirit perspective where you can.

It was certainly gradual for me. And there were crises too, that only resolved by throwing off more of the collective mindset. These personal crises are common, and they bring us back to the Shamanic Illness, because a crisis is what it is.

We don't necessarily want to go there. We may prefer the security and certainty of the previous way of being. We might be miserable, but at least it's a familiar misery, we know what's what. You could say that the Shamanic Illness occurs for reasons of 'better the devil you know'.

So the young Shaman-to-be gets ill. It may be an illness that is very hard to diagnose, a strange illness. We see a lot of these strange illnesses nowadays, but I'll come back to that.

It's not until he accepts the Spirits into his life, that he becomes well again. I'm sure it doesn't happen for all of them like that, or necessarily even for most of them. Some of us are only too happy to accept the Spirits into our lives, because we can find the collective values stifling, we can't breathe. It can be like, "Oh I can breathe at last, yeah I bloody will do this thing, I'll accept this vocation." It gives life, it gives meaning, it gives it depth, it gives all of those things.

Your point of authority is shifting, you no longer look to the rules and norms of the society around you. You look to what Spirit is telling you. They're not necessarily contradictory, and in a reasonably healthy society they're not going to be too contradictory, we can do both.

In our counterculture it can be almost a point of honour to be in an oppositional mode, to be anti-establishment, and certainly anti-Tory or anti-Republican. But if you look at a traditional Shamanic culture, you don't read stories of the Shaman being in opposition to the political leaders, like he knows better. Well maybe he does know better in some ways, but he'd be diplomatic about it. The Spirits will tell him things, and there's a good chance the political leaders will listen to that, coming from him. They'd be working together, they wouldn't be in opposition like we so often put ourselves. It is so wrong-headed to be taking political sides, as we often do, and effectively setting ourselves against half the population. Our calling is to go beyond that polarised way of being in the world. And be the poets that the political leaders listen to.

The Shamans have their own otherworldly authority, Spirit speaking through them, and yet they're integrated with normal life. That's what we need to do. As long as we feel ourselves to be in opposition to society and the way it works in that fundamental kind of way, I think we're in a kind of spiritual bypass. I think it says something about ourselves, I don't think it says something about our insight. I think it says that we're not bringing Spirit into matter, we are floating above the fray and looking down on it.

Of course society will always need tweaking, but you need to ally yourself with it and tweak, not just sit there in opposition, condemning the leaders and glueing yourself to pavements or whatever: that doesn't achieve anything. You need to work with the culture you are part of, create something, build something. That's because Spirit isn't just about us, Spirit wants to be expressed and do good within society, so we need to be part of that society.

OK, so I haven't got that far into the Shamanic Illness itself. I wanted firstly to make the important point about the locus of authority in one's life changing, and the implications of that, because it has a lot of bearing on why the Shaman gets ill in the first place. So let's head directly in again.

We do get the equivalent in our society of this kind of calling, when people get ill with syndromes like ME, irritable bowel syndrome, multiple allergies, fibromyalgia, all these sorts of gradual diseases that can be debilitating, that are quite hard to diagnose, and quite hard to prove they're even there, medically.

This can be very distressing, because they get called psychological. And we go no, no, no, it's not 'just' psychological, it's real. Well actually, it's both.

'It's psychological' suggests you are malingering. But 'psyche' means the soul, and 'logos' means the word, so psychology is the word of the soul. It's your soul speaking, saying I'm ill, I am out of balance. All diseases are also psychological, for how could your soul not be involved? But we have this idea that if there is an element of the soul in it, then it is to that extent not real, and you're malingering. This is because we see the mind and body as separate, in the same way that Christianity saw Spirit and the body as separate, and its offspring science translated that into mind and body being separate. So no, these illnesses are real, but like all illnesses, they're also the soul. There is something unlived that needs to be owned, and that can take time.

The Heart of Initiation

This is from Mary Oliver's poem *The Journey*. I've abridged it.

One day you finally knew what you had to do, and began,
though the voices around you kept shouting their bad advice—
though the whole house began to tremble
and you felt the old tug at your ankles.
"Mend my life!" each voice cried.
But you didn't stop. You knew what you had to do....
Little by little, as you left their voices behind,
there was a new voice which you slowly
recognized as your own, that kept you company
as you strode deeper and deeper into the world,
determined to do the only thing you could do—
determined to save the only life you could save.

The above lines describe a central theme of the Shamanic Illness. It's about claiming your life, not just being part of something, a role, a well-defined identity that you can trot out at social occasions, which is how normal society works. It's how relationships also work, in that psychologically we adopt roles. There's nothing wrong with this, it's 'normal'. But we are nevertheless in a role.

In the initiation that is the Shamanic Illness, we are stepping outside of any such societal roles. There's something very powerful that wants to claim us. And it can force the issue, so to speak, by making us ill. In my mid-30s I had a fatigue for a few years. I call it fatigue rather than tiredness, because I wasn't tired in a normal sense. I just couldn't carry on in the way I had been. The fatigue was as though the plug had been pulled; there was no energy there. I realised that I'd taken my life force as my own to use, and that's not how it is. You are used by it, we are in the service of life. Life has a blueprint, a destiny, a something that is writ for us in a living sort of way, where we have choice all along. Life is about saying yes to that. It's not about getting fixated on an idea of who we should be or what we should achieve, and forcing ourselves along those lines.

I'd been very wilful, overseeing a Buddhist set-up in London – several communities, businesses, and a public centre, all according to certain ideas. Ideas which I'd stopped believing in, but still I pushed myself to do this thing, that maybe it would come right somehow. I was doing it partly to prove something to myself, which isn't necessarily all bad, and to the people around me. The organisation had been in something of a crisis, and eventually we pulled it all together and it reached stability. As that point approached, I started going into a meltdown, in which I could apply myself to nothing, unless it was this mysterious thing called Shamanism which was buzzing around in my head. Astrology also spoke to me in this way.

When I listened to that kind of inner ambrosia, for that's how it felt, instead of listening to these ideas from outside myself, the Buddhist tradition and the teacher, I had all the energy I wanted, I was full of fire. I'm not saying the Buddhist ideas were wrong, but they weren't mine, and I'd been using them in the wrong way, trying to change myself from the top down, so to speak, instead of allowing the depths to speak on their own terms. (That said, some of the ideas were the teacher's interpretation of Buddhism, and they were definitely wrong.)

I think this is central to the recovery from the Shamanic Illness: learning to listen to something deep within yourself – to the Spirits. And having the courage to act on that. It may not make sense from an ordinary point of view. It may be very threatening to your usual life and to what other people think of you. I had to leave the whole life I was in, and the friends I had, and oppose a lot of people in positions of authority who were prepared to say that I'd got it wrong. *"Though the voices around you kept shouting their bad advice."* I had to leave all of that. This process, this turning about, took me right through most of my 30s.

It was a turning about in the sense that my point of reference underwent a major shift from 'out there' to 'in here', so to speak. It had always been considerably 'in here' – I'd been attempting to practise Buddhism, after all – but it shifted decisively in that direction. My point of authority, my guidance, was now more firmly within, even though it took me some years to fully trust that. I would slip in and out of it. But it was enough to catapult me out of the life I had, my whole world, and to start afresh.

There was a voice within, in the deeper place that is beyond the narrow self, that had its own agenda for me. It was, in a way, who I'd always been, without knowing it. That is what these crises do. They remind us of who we are in a deeper way, that we have, so to speak, forgotten. We need initiating into it, because it is so outside who we have been up until now.

Initiation is something we don't have in a formal sense in our culture. In some traditional cultures, the teenage boys may be put out into the wilderness, where they have to learn to survive.

In some rituals they may have physical scars put on them. They're taken away from the women and brought into the world of the men. Girls have their own initiation when they become capable of having children. Giving birth is an initiation, and men don't have that, which is why initiations need to be created for them. For one thing, men need to learn to bear suffering, which happens to women naturally through childbirth.

We don't have ritual initiations, and sometimes people bemoan that. "We haven't got initiation so we can never discover this profound thing, we can never move on to these next stages properly, we never become proper adults, because it is initiations that move us on in this way."

I think that's the wrong way of looking at it. It's not the Chaos Shamanic way of looking at it. The ordinary way of looking at it, the religious way, is that you have certain rituals, and you have to go through them to come out the other side initiated. Chaos Shamanism always says form is secondary. What matters is finding the meaning of the ritual, and living it. So what is at the heart of initiation? At the heart of initiation is something new being born in you that isn't just a rearrangement of the old, and you need to be opened up in order for that to happen.

This is why in the rituals you may be put through some difficult trials. They demolish you, so that you don't know who you are anymore. Maybe you're naked in the darkness, and you no longer have a name. You're waiting for a new name to come. A ceremonial space is created, in which the old has to die — or is at least suspended. That's what happens when you go into a Sweatlodge: it's a death and a rebirth. You go naked into the darkness, and you come out reborn, a new person. These forms just point to that, and they can help with it.

But — and here's the Chaos point — initiation is something that happens anyway. Life initiates us if we're open to it, if we're lucky, painful as that often is. Many people, maybe most people, are content just being normal, they don't want anything outside of normal, and that's fine, that's who they are. They have their own particular path to follow, and life will still take them on to the next stage in the usual kind of way, though it is unlikely to be the kind of radical change that Chaos Shamanism points towards.

But if you're reading this, then there's something else going on that needs to be listened to: the ongoing initiation into the new, that life becomes once you're on this path. The initiation may begin from the outside, as it were. You can lose all sorts of things, particularly if you're not being open in the way that is needed. The Spirits have chosen you, you could say, and they're not going anywhere. They will be ruthless if necessary, such is the imperative for life to keep moving on. You may lose people close to you, your job, your physical and mental health, your money. All these things that are really painful can happen. The Spirits are willing to demolish us. Such painful events can of course occur anyway. They don't necessarily point to a deeper meaning, they are just life doing its thing. But sometimes they happen for the purpose of taking us apart, so this new thing can be born. Or rather, so that we can decide at long last, after many trials, to claim it, as in the Mary Oliver poem.

It can be a long slow process, and brings us back to the Shamanic Illness. People can lose their health. I think when the illness is hard to diagnose, that is often particularly key; it is probably showing us that there's something we need to start listening to, taking seriously. Then you may gradually, over the years, get well, as you learn to listen and live from that listening.

Even now, 30 years on, I will get twinges of the fatigue if I start pushing myself, if I have too much of a plan about what I'm going to do, and I act accordingly. Maybe I'll do ten minutes gardening, and then I just can't do anymore, not because I haven't got the capability, but because of the way I've decided, "Right I'm going to get all of that done." The Spirit goes, "No, no, no, we'll decide what you're going to get done, not you. Just go at it in a gentle reasonable sort of way, and we'll tell you when to stop and start. When you're functioning from Spirit you can keep going forever, you'll have all the energy you need."

I've emphasised the hard-to-diagnose illnesses as particularly suggestive of Spirit being at work. But it can easily be more straightforward than that. You regularly hear about how, say, cancer has changed someone. The Spirits really mean business. They may be prepared to bring you to the point of death if you don't yield to them. They have a different perspective on death to us, and they are not fluffy! They demand everything of us.

This Shamanic path is a serious thing. Your physical as well as your psychological survival may depend on being true to it. It is not an add-on for Sundays. It is the most important thing in your life, it is the *sine qua non* of everything else. And it is deep. Its roots go as deep as existence itself, into the vast unknowable Chaos.

For He on Honey-dew Hath Fed

The Shamanic Illness is an archetypal event, which has come to us from the Shamanic cultures of the Far East. The young Shaman or Shamanka – a traditional term for a female shaman – gets ill and doesn't recover, unless they accept their vocation as a healer, or more broadly as a person whose life is fundamentally guided by the Spirits.

A Daimon (see Chapter 13) has seized you, and your life is no longer your own in a narrow sense. The Daimon – or the Spirits, they are interchangeable, poetic terms – gives you your power to live. Your life becomes a matter of continually doing that which you have to do, what the Spirits want you to do. It's a deeply meaningful and joyful way to live.

It is a powerful thing, and quite different to how most people live. If you have that in you, don't expect to find community, don't expect people to understand you. If you're lucky, you'll have one or two friends that you can talk to about this stuff, so just cherish them. And even they may come and go over the years.

If you've been through this kind of dismemberment, it could well have been a very difficult time. In our society it is not necessarily straightforward to find someone who can help to guide us through, to tell us what's happening. You might even find people wanting to medicate you, to help you become 'normal' again. Bringing perspective to these times is a regular part of my job as an astrologer. The outer planets – Uranus, Neptune, and Pluto – represent Spirit under three different aspects: creativity, ensoulment, and death and rebirth.

When they are active, we have to yield to them, and therein lies the difficulty. Life no longer makes sense as it did. It's a classic midlife crisis, except in the Shamanic cultures they seem to have it when they're teenagers.

In a way I had it aged 20, when I went through this kind of revolution. It was happening anyway, but three months of magic mushrooms and my metaphysical quest, as I call it, became central. I became much more serious about it. I'd also had an initiation into the shadow, into the demons in me, and that was really difficult. That's what a 'bad trip' is: it's an initiation into the shadow side, and that's a good thing. It's not like something's gone wrong. We need that initiation, we need to be able to live with it, be friends with it. (See Chapter 30 on **Teacher Plants**.)

The proto-Shaman may die. That's how serious the Spirits are about us accepting our vocation, accepting what is deeply within. The mysterious thing around which we cannot always plan our life very much, for we don't know where it's going to take us. Month by month sometimes, we just have to be open to where the Spirit is pulling us, how it needs us to live. It doesn't work 9 to 5. We may not do an awful lot with it, and we may therefore feel we're failing, that we're not properly living it. But no, Spirit has certain things for us to do, and they are deep things. Spirit will send the right people our way, if we don't go chasing and advertising too much for people that we can help. And then maybe we just fiddle around and do other things much of the rest of the time.

We don't have those kinds of worldly judgements of ourselves anymore around being 'busy' — the Protestant Work Ethic — because fundamentally it's about the calling. It can happen in less dramatic ways, where you maybe just quietly get on with something that has always been calling you, and it doesn't disrupt your life. Or it happens in bigger life-changing ways, that can be initially very disruptive and difficult, where you no longer live from the values of the people around you, but from something else that you've had to find for yourself.

You see artists living in this kind of way. Ask them what their next painting is going to be, they probably won't know. They don't usually work to order. Nick Cave, the rock musician, works 9 to 5 at his art, but he's an exception. And you get the impression that even then he is only formally in his office 'working'. He probably spends much of the time staring out the window, as you have to if you are creative.

You may do nothing for ages while something brews below the surface, and then you may do nothing but work for weeks. That is Spirit for you. Less successful artists — and only a very small minority have major success — will often get judged for not being regular people and regular workers.

Here are a couple of lines at the end of *The Holy Longing*, a poem by Goethe:

So long as you have not experienced this, to die and so to grow,
you remain but a troubled guest on this dark earth.

You will remain troubled, your life will never be quite working, as long as you wriggle and rationalise to avoid what you know you must do. It might not bring you to the point of death, but you will feel something is wrong, that there is something in you unlived. You remain a troubled guest in your own life, because there is this other thing. You need to taste the dark earth, bring Spirit into matter.

There is also *The Rime of the Ancient Mariner* by Coleridge, a long poem that opens with:

It is an Ancient Mariner and he stoppeth one of three
'By thy long grey beard and glittering eye
Now wherefore stops thou me.

The Ancient Mariner had a tale to tell, he had a look in his eye, he'd been to another world. The Illness takes you to this other world, you've seen it, you've seen how things really are behind the usual parameters within which we live and think and value.

The Ancient Mariner had shot an albatross, he knew he shouldn't, but still he did it, bringing terrible misfortune. Everyone died on board the ship, except him. He was surrounded by ghosts and skeletons, the wind died, and he was in a dead sea. He'd been on a terrible journey, and it changed him forever. When he came back, if he saw someone who he sensed could listen, he'd grab them and tell them his story. He saw the wedding guest, a regular guy on his way to a wedding, and he stopped him. The guest was gradually getting later and later for the wedding, but he knew he couldn't but listen to this Ancient Mariner: the look in his eyes, and the compelling tale he had to tell. Eventually he missed the whole wedding, because he had no choice but to hear it. The wedding guest was being initiated into another world by the Ancient Mariner.

Maybe that's something we do as well. We've been to that place and we've taken back something of it. We have a tale about what matters in life, a tale that is profoundly moral, because it concerns how to live and how not to live: cherish the albatross, do not harm it. The albatross is your Daimon, your guide, and will bring you good fortune. Or maybe you need to first betray the Daimon in order to find him.

Here are a few more lines, from the end of *Kubla Khan*, again by Coleridge:

And all should cry, Beware! Beware!
His flashing eyes, his floating hair!
Weave a circle round him thrice,
And close your eyes with holy dread
For he on honey-dew hath fed,
And drunk the milk of Paradise.

We have that, and if people come close to us, they will experience that taste, that will help awaken the calling, the pull to the faraway place, in them. In a way, we never know that we're having that effect. We're just being normal when speaking of this thing that is real to us, but to them it's something else. It's like you've got this quality, this something about you, and it speaks to something in them. They may just say you are authentic, and you are, but it can be a deceptively deep and magical and otherworldly thing too. So don't underestimate the effect you may have on other people just by being what for you is ordinary and honest.

Back to the Illness. It's not just that we want to stay in our comfort zone. We also want to be like everyone else, we want their acceptance, we want that belonging. These are deep human drives, and we're being taken out of that in a fundamental way. Of course, we still feel ourselves to be part of humanity, in fact more than ever, but we are also like God's Fifth Column, we are agents of a foreign power. That gap in ordinary belonging can be difficult. But it also forges us, forces to stand on our own two feet existentially, with roots as deep as the universe.

With these callings, there's something to do, there's a gift that comes with them. It may, archetypally, mean being a healer of some kind, and the Spirits through you help people heal, become whole, for that is the meaning of heal. But the calling can take many forms: storyteller, astrologer, artist, animal whisperer... What it is for an individual, you never know, it's a mystery — that which draws us irresistibly, that which the Spirit tells us we must do. We don't have a choice, we're drawn towards these things, it's what we have to do. As Jung put it,

Freedom of will is the ability to do gladly that which I must do.

It is a nice way of tying up fate and free will, because life is both fated and free; they are not contradictory.

We are often held back from accepting the Spirit calling by self-doubt. We don't think we can do it. Who am I to write books? I still get this in little ways regularly. In 2022 I was writing a fantasy novel that a Wolf had suggested I write. I hadn't written fiction before, and sometimes I'd stop for a month at a time, and I would start crashing. I'd stop because I didn't think it was any good. If I'm honest, I do think the novel is quite good. The style's maybe a bit undeveloped, a bit rough, but there's a rawness to the tale, there's a nugget in there, and I can write in a way that keeps the reader interested. But I didn't believe in it — I still don't in some ways — and so I would crash. I would drink too much, and I'd feel depressed. Nothing was working anymore, I'd try this, try that, everything except the one thing I had to do. As Mary Oliver says, *"One day you finally knew what you had to do you, and began."* As soon as I'd sit down and start writing again, I'd feel OK.

Self-doubt is part of the initiatory fire. We all go through it. We have to earn our confidence. (You can't 'affirm' your way out of 'low self-esteem': you just have to get good at something. That is the purpose the discomfort serves.) In the end you just have to do it anyway. Singing is a good example. Very few people are prepared to sing, because they think they're no good at it, and they're worried about what other people will think. But maybe they'd secretly love to sing, to freely give expression to the joy in their souls. (Everyone seems to love singing in the Sweatlodge, where our voices are relatively anonymous.) The calling can be just like this. You need to do it, and it often requires grit and courage. But there's also joy in there, and you feel that you've got your life when you do it. Claim that calling when it comes knocking at your door. Or rather, let it claim you. It might come knocking very hard!

10
The Not-Knowing of Chaos Shamanism

Chaos Shamanism is not something that you can build a body of knowledge about. It's the opposite. You build an edifice, a deep foundation, of not-knowing. It's paradoxical, but it's when we know, or we think we know, that we limit ourselves.

Gnosis – knowing. It's really about not knowing, the wisdom that wanders into us when we're not fixed about what we think we know. I've sometimes seen the opposite in the Shamanic world: people quoting all this stuff from Native American or Siberian cultures, and identifying with their ability to do that. You can see it makes them think they know something, and it's giving them a 'spiritual' identity. It's not enough to be ordinary and English. No, they want a flavour of Toltec or Navajo adhering to them, and they think that intellectual knowledge will give them that.

But the real path, the Inner Path, is about the opposite of this. It's the same with practices that we may spend many years doing. We think they're going to take us somewhere. "I've done 20 years meditation so I'm actually quite advanced." And then you realise, oh there was never anywhere to go. All I ever had to do was just be with how I am now, and be comfortable with that. Whatever it is, just be with it, just be close to yourself and don't judge it, don't try and make it better. But it can take 20 years of trying to climb the mountain to realise there was never any mountain to climb. It's why they say the good is the enemy of the best. Because when you're good, you're always trying to become better. Whereas with the best, you've dropped all of that, you're just comfortable with being you, which the good person never is. You're like the Lion, King of the Jungle, you just sit at ease with who you are.

Lewis Mehl-Madrona, who is Cherokee-Lakota and a conventional doctor, says that in a traditional indigenous society, most people will have a fairly simple set of beliefs about how the world is. It's only the medicine people who realise that actually we know nothing, that it's all the Great Mystery. That's where their power comes from, because they're not standing in the way with their beliefs about how things are. Lewis talks about this in the context of postmodernism, the modern philosophy that says there are no absolute truths. He says this is uncomfortable for most people, but sympatico for medicine people.

I think postmodernism has a lot going for it, because it is accurate in its contention that there are no absolute truths. This is because words can only ever be pointers, approximations, they are not the things themselves. They point to the Chaos. Words are the finger pointing at the Moon, as the Zen saying goes.

But there is such a thing as objective truth, which is necessary for ordinary life. Such truth is relative from an absolute point of view, but it can be slippery and even insidious to deny it. That animal over there is a cat. Yes, it's an agreed-upon term, it is only a word, but it is nevertheless true within this limited framework of time and space within which we find ourselves. It would be a lie to say it is not a cat.

It is the same with men and women. Animals know very well the difference between the genders. It is only confused humans who are losing this very basic knowledge. It is because we apply the metaphysical truth of postmodernism to objective truth, where it does not apply. This breakdown is ultimately a result of the loss of the arbiter of truth, which is a unifying set of mythologies, stories that we agree upon.

As always with Shamanism, the answer lies in the natural world. Be as the animals are, and listen to what your body tells you. You will know the difference between the genders again, and be able to speak it with confidence. It is the Chaos that tells you. Animals live in the Chaos, that continual flow of feelings and perceptions and impulses that is outside our control, and whose source is forever a mystery. It tells us how to be, if we align ourselves with it, and don't allow the human double-edged sword of abstraction to predominate.

Even so, it's all ultimately contingent. Space and time themselves, which are instinctual more than verbal categories, are not attributes of the universe. Our minds create them in order to make sense of experience. All is unknown and unknowable. This is relatively easy to understand intellectually. But emotionally it is a shocking, terrifying truth. Postmodernism is shocking, properly understood. If you are not shocked and terrified, you have not understood.

Postmodernism fits very well with being a medicine person or some kind of healer, because you are dancing in the flow of uncertainty, which enables Spirit to speak freely through you. You're not standing there with your advanced ideas about how things are, or what power animal you want to turn up, or trying to subtly bolster your identity as a healer because you want to be taken seriously, all that sort of thing. You're just not going there. Or maybe you are, and you may still do a reasonable job, but it won't be as good as it could have been if you weren't so much in the way.

What I took from Lewis' statement about indigenous people's beliefs is that human nature tends to be somewhat fixed and limited, and that is a universal. It's not like indigenous people are somehow magical and spiritual, and we're the ones who've lost it because we've been brainwashed, which is how some people think. Sure, indigenous peoples tend to have a sense of belonging to the natural world and a respect for it as a living presence that we have lost. But indigenous people are also ordinary humans just like us. Most people do have a fairly simple set of beliefs about how the world came to be.

For modern people, our simple beliefs about the universe are that firstly there was the Big Bang, then there was the evolution of the star systems, and then life appeared by chance, that had its own evolution, and here we are. In this way we've also got a simple story that makes us think we know.

But it's not like that if you look closely. It's full of holes of unknowingness, that aren't just gaps in scientific knowledge. They are bigger and more profound than that. Any theory is just a modelling. It exists within a profound unknowingness that we prefer to sidestep. What came before the Big Bang? We don't know, it's an absolute mystery. People don't really look very hard at that. If you ask a scientist, they might say it's before time, so you can't say anything, as if that is an answer. Well that's true, but it means actually you can't know, it's the Great Mystery. Scientific theorising has brought you to the brink of the Great Mystery. How wonderful. Just sit with that, be awed by it.

But that's not the usual response, which is more like science has explained thus far, and eventually it will explain everything. It is no different to letting the church take care of the big questions, while we get on with day-to-day life. Being awed by the Great Mystery is not everyone's cup of tea, and never will be. It requires attention and effort and honesty; it requires living in uncertainty. Science doesn't have the big answers, and nor does the church. Nobody has the answers, and nobody ever will.

It is much easier to fantasise that we know how things are, while never examining that belief very closely. Just as the origin of the universe is the Great Mystery, so is the origin of life. The more we understand the complexity of even the simplest life, the more does the possibility of it having arisen by chance chemical interactions look vanishingly unlikely. Evolution likewise: its plodding, purposeless mechanism of natural selection and random mutation has been shown mathematically to require far longer timescales than the lifetime of the earth allows for. Besides, our inner knowing tells us that life has beauty and meaning and intention behind its arising. It is the great dreaming of the soul, as it ushers forth ever new forms of life.

Socrates was said to be the wisest man in Athens because he was the only person who knew he knew nothing. That is the actual situation. We know nothing. Chaos Shamanism acknowledges the not-knowing, while building the psychological and existential wherewithal to live within that. Some of the time, at least. We are only human. Chaos Shamanism in the full sense is always for the minority. Most of us need some sort of set of beliefs to hang on to. We all need at least some provisional beliefs to live in this world. Those beliefs are stories, including the scientific theories. Provisional they may be, but they can delight and enrich the imagination, and entice us towards what is ultimately true. Just as Science does, when it brings us to the edge of the Great Mystery.

There is, for example, a Californian Indian creation story. In the beginning was just water, and earth was needed so people could be made, so a turtle dives down to the bottom of the water and brings back some earth. And it goes from there. That kind of story nourishes me, and in a way it goes deeper in me because I'm not trying to set it in stone as what 'actually' happened. It's a story and therefore it's true. It's a truth of the imagination. To be paradoxical, it is also how the world actually began, because the world began as an imaginative act.

Chaos comes from an ancient Greek creation myth. It was there before anything, just this vast abyss of nothing, of unknowability. There wasn't even the water, there wasn't even God at the beginning, there was just the vast Abyss about which nothing can be said. There's a deep truth in that. It is the Great Mystery behind the Big Bang. Out of that abyss came the world.

We're not given any reason why the world came forth. And that's because there isn't one. Reasons are a human thing. Why does the soul body forth dreams at night? It is the same thing. The cosmic soul dreamed a universe into being. The universe is not real in the way we think it is. Visions are said to be more real than this reality. In the same way, the universe is not literal in the way we think it is; it is more akin to visionary reality, and is the more real for that.

The poet William Blake comes to mind. When asked about the sun, and whether he sees a disc of light, famously responded:

> *Oh no, no! I see an innumerable company of the heavenly host crying "Holy, holy, holy is the Lord God Almighty!"*

A good creation myth keeps us close to the universe as visionary reality, and the imagination as the ground of being. (In that respect, the scientific story is lacking.) Leaving room as it does for other creation myths to be believed alongside, it also points towards the ultimate unknowability of things.

That includes your own unknowability, being a mystery to yourself. On one level, we need to know who we are in terms of what calls us, what pulls us, what we've learned from experience, what kind of temperament we have. But an identity? If asked about ourselves at a drinks party, most of us have things to say about the job and family and home and interests that we have, and that tells the other person who we are. It also tells us who we are. That is why it can be so discombobulating when one of those pillars, such as career or marriage, founders, because we no longer know who we are anymore. But that is a good place to be, from a Spirit point of view, if you can handle it. Because it's closer to how things are, closer to the unknowability of who we are. What is real are the currents of feeling and thought and sensation that pass through us. What is not real is the identity that we create around it. It is, however, normal and necessary for psychological stability. In the Chaos path, that identity is gradually dismantled.

Identity has become a big deal in current times. People are encouraged to identify along lines of race and gender and sexual orientation, and to celebrate it if in a minority, and to feel guilty if part of the majority. It is healthier to do the opposite, to ignore these considerations as being important to who you are, because then you are closer to how the universe actually is. The self is a fragile thing, fragile because ephemeral and mind-created.

Some form of identity being necessary for functioning in this world, it is probably best to let others decide who we are.

When people stress their identity and how important it is to them and how you have to respect it, or someone else's identity (it's usually someone else's!), I think they are being delusional, to put it bluntly. These eggshells we are meant to walk around about people's racial, sexual, and gender identities. It shouldn't be such a big deal. Of course we need to be respectful to each other, but this is something different. Identity is neither here nor there, it is nothing in the grander scheme of things. It is a group label, and we are so much more than that. It is our connection to the whole universe that is real and lasting. Of course we belong to certain cultures, and it's important to recognise where we belong. But beyond that we actually have this profound unknowable connection to everything, and that's where we need to live from, and our identity just gets in the way of that, so get over it!

11

The Medicine Wheel: Balance

In this chapter I'm going to start coming down to a particular form, in a way that I haven't so far. That's going to be interesting. It would be easy to get the idea, particularly if you're a bit rebellious, that Chaos Shamanism is about being above the restrictive forms, and that we're beyond all that. But it's not like that at all, it's the opposite. It's about being able to go into the forms more deeply, because we're approaching them on a level of experience and questioning rather than on a level of ideas and blind faith.

For an example of that, I'll go over to astrology. The Sun and the Moon have particular meanings, and they're written down in the books according to the stars behind them, and various other factors. My approach is to say that if you're doing the astrology reading, just let the Sun be with you. You can feel the Sun, because you know it, you experience it. Then it's as if it'll speak through you, and yes you have all your intellectual understandings, and they contribute, but primarily there's this other thing that speaks through you. It's divinatory or intuitive. It is, if you like, the Sky Spirits speaking. (As an astrologer, some of my Spirits are in the sky.) We may say things we have no reason for knowing, we just know that we need to say them, we know that there's some kind of truth in them that we would probably never insist on. In this way the intellectual understandings of the Sun and Moon that we have been taught act as a launch pad for the real thing, which is our own direct connection to those sky gods. They may bring in meanings that aren't in the books, and what do you do, when the venerable tradition and your venerable teacher say one thing, and your inner knowing bounces in with something else? It is an instructive place to be.

We're inspired by tradition but we're not beholden to it. That's how I began this exploration of Chaos Shamanism. We're maybe deeply in some tradition, we understand the Medicine Wheel, the Pipe Ceremony, the Sweatlodge, we appreciate them, we love them, we love to be part of the community that happens when we do them. Or the Trance Dance, the Despacho Ceremony, whatever it might be. But while being fully in it, we also have that gap which enables us to be with the real meaning of it, rather than worrying too much about whether or not you're doing it in the right way, or maybe what other people are thinking of you.

I was once around a traditionally trained guy from South America. We had built a Sweatlodge, and we needed a few leaders of them, because we were going to have several sweats. I asked him if he'd lead one, and he thought about it and replied that he was sorry, but he couldn't, his tradition wouldn't allow him to, because it wasn't built in quite the right way.

I'm not going to disrespect him. There is something in really holding to a tradition and doing it exactly as you're meant to. It has all sorts of layers of beauty and meaning in it, of honouring what's come before, and the ancestors who created it. It has all of that, and that's beautiful, and you want to be able to be in ceremony in that kind of context. But you also need to be able to step outside and just go whatever, I know the essence of what this is about, and we're going to run with this according to the circumstances we are in. When in Europe, a South American Sweatlodge belongs to the past. It needs to be used as inspiration. That is what the Spirits want. What does it mean to a European that the Sweatlodge is not built in exactly the right way? It is absurd, when you think about it.

When needs must, you drop all of that, you don't just not run a Sweatlodge when you know you could do something that would help people. Because that is what we are here to do:

help people. Are you here to help people, or to do things in the correct manner?

There's a Native American guy called Jim Tree, who wrote a book called *The Way of the Sacred Pipe.* He emphasises that the Pipe Ceremony needs to be done with a lot of respect for the Pipe and for the Ceremony itself. He wants people on the one hand to get to know the tradition, but on the other hand to be able to adapt it as necessary. He wants people to feel they can run them. It is the Chaos Shamanic position: inspired by tradition, respectful of it, but not beholden to it. Jim Tree has a saying:

If it works it's real, and if it's real it works.

I think that's a really good principle.

The South American guy could have run a really good Sweatlodge. It just wouldn't have been the way he was taught. He was a relatively young guy. It could be that his path will lie in finding the courage to listen to the side of him that knows perfectly well that you just need to get people into the lodge, however it is built, in a sacred kind of way, and get them praying, getting connected to the stones, all of that, just do it. If he is not listening to that voice, he is disempowered by the tradition. And, in my view, getting his sense of power through the indigenous pedestal that the Europeans put him on. He may spend the rest of his life in that kind of way. Plenty of teachers do. Or he may shift. You never know with people.

Chaos Medicine Wheel. That's what I'm slowly circling around and approaching. How do we use the Medicine Wheel, coming at it from a Chaos point of view?

We need to start by asking what the Wheel is getting at. In its simplest form, it is just four stones, that we use to help become a balanced human being: balanced within ourselves, and balanced in relation to the world around us. Each stone embodies a different power, and becomes a point of reflection. The powers of Fire, Earth, Air, and Water. Very immediate and concrete.

Balance is the purpose, and needs to be remembered at all points when engaging with the Wheel. Remembered not so much as an idea, but as a feeling, as an awareness, in a relaxed kind of way.

In the modern West, we think more in terms of wholeness than of balance, though they are not incompatible ideas. That is because we emphasise and value the autonomy, the primacy of the individual. We maybe overemphasise it. It arguably came out of Protestant Christianity, which itself arose as a rebellion against Catholicism, where only the priests could have a hotline to God, so to speak. That's a way of keeping people disempowered and under control. Protestantism said no, everyone has their individual relationship to God. I'm not a great believer in the Christian God. I'm more a Great Spirit sort of guy. But there is nevertheless value in this position. We do need our individual connection. But it can go too far, and one way in which it's gone too far is that we forget to value community sufficiently and the natural world around us. We don't value and respect that as we need to, we easily get out of balance with that.

Traditionally, if someone is ill in a community, then that affects the whole community. That person needs to get well for the sake of the community, as well as for their own sake. You may get the whole community, or much of it, present at a healing ceremony, praying for the recovery of the ill person. The ill person may not even be there if he's too ill. This kind of thing works. Indigenous people have an experience of the individual as relational as much as they do autonomous. Just the fact that you can pray for someone, and it helps them get well, shows you on your pulses just how connected we all are.

So that's worth thinking about, because we get so het up about our individual rights and identity.

There's a book called *Drawing Out Law* by Professor John Borrows, who is a Native Canadian. In the book he is looking at the different ways the white people and the Indians look at law. He says let's take abortion as an example. We frame it in terms of a woman's rights over her body, and it's like OK, that works, he respects that and he's not trying to argue the rights and wrongs of it. But he says the Indians don't think like that. Let's shift it to their framework, where you have a community, and the father is held to account, he is made to be responsible, while the mother gets a lot of support from women, because people are much more networked and connected and part of each other's lives. What happens as a result is that you get a lot less abortion. That's what can happen when you shift from the individual as autonomous, to the individual as relational. Things happen in quite a different way, and it doesn't make one approach right and one wrong. Let's take the ideology and polarisation out of it, and be pragmatic: if it works it's real, and if it's real it works.

The Medicine Wheel describes the world around us, as well as being a point of reflection for the individual. We come into balance in the context of belonging to the natural world. To use the Medicine Wheel most effectively, we will probably need to make a shift in the way we think of ourselves, away from the individual and its emphasis on rights and identity, and towards being relational and belonging. It can be a relief to let go of much of what pertains to being an autonomous individual, to take it less seriously, and to get on with simply being part of something bigger than ourselves.

12

The Elements

The Medicine Wheel at its simplest is four stones, one for each direction: North, South, East and West. They also correspond to the elements of Fire, Water, Earth, and Air.

There are many other correspondences to these four stones. They make a cycle. We have, going from East round to North: birth, childhood, adulthood, old age; spring, summer, autumn, winter; the timeless, past, present, and future; morning, afternoon, evening, and night. There are also yellow, red, black, and white; Eagle, Coyote, Bear, and Bison. These are all in the Wheel I use. You get quite different set-ups in different Wheels. There are Wheels all over the Americas, no one quite knows where they came from, which I think is great, though central America seems to be the main contender as a possible origin.

In a way, and I reckon most importantly, the Wheel becomes a symbol that sinks into your unconscious, it becomes part of who you are. That was what happened to me almost immediately when I saw my first Medicine Wheel, after many years immersed in Buddhist symbolism. This was in the 90s. I saw a Medicine Wheel and it just had me, it intrigued me. I knew nothing about it, but it was like wow here's this thing that is a teaching, and it describes everything. What I particularly loved about it was that it was earthy, it was here, it wasn't a teaching about up there, or about what's ultimate in a faraway sense. It is a teaching about what's ultimate here right now, because everything's here around you and within you, we contain all within us.

Above all, perhaps, it was the intimate involvement of the earth that grabbed me. The earth as alive and sacred. I had been in a Buddhist tradition for 17 years where that had been put down. It was otherworldly presences that one was meant to aspire to. They were not ordinary and human. And when the elements were brought in, they were arranged hierarchically, in progressive levels of refinement. The earth element was at the bottom as the crudest, and that was definitely something you wanted to transcend! All it did was to eventually make me ill and unbalanced.

It isn't that Buddhism per se is necessarily like that, though I think it often tends in that transcendent direction. It was more that the Buddhism I was around was Westernised, and so contained the imbalances around the relationship between the body and the spirit that have vitiated Western culture for over a millennium. I was ill, if you like, because Western culture is ill – even though it has a lot of good things going for it – and the Shamanic outlook, the indigenous outlook, was the cure for me, and therefore can be for the culture. That maybe sounds a bit pretentious or evangelical. It's not really, it's more of an observation or an insight.

My encounter with the Medicine Wheel was deeply healing, on a metaphysical and other levels. I've written a whole book on the Medicine Wheel. There are so many things that can be said, that's the beauty of it. The book I wrote was an opportunity to say everything I thought about everything! The Medicine Wheel contains the whole universe – it describes the Cosmos that arises from the Chaos at the Centre of the Wheel – and it's also you, and that's because we are the universe.

Let's pull back to the word Chaos. We are gradually uncovering its meaning as we go along. It is both simple and multifaceted. I can imagine it could get confusing, because I've been unpacking it in lots of different ways, with many connotations. You just need to remember that Chaos brings us to the heart of things, brings us to what we're really about it, brings us to the centre of the Medicine Wheel. Chaos is that vast Abyss that is at the heart of things, that beautiful soft beating heart at the centre of the universe and at the centre of you.

Perhaps the best way of envisioning Chaos is to feel that mystery at your centre, that force of life that is always in you, heartfelt and joyful. That is Chaos, in the sense that we don't know where it comes from or where it's going, it is just something very deep and fundamental. Chaos in this sense is also at the Centre of the Medicine Wheel. The purpose of the Wheel is to help us to keep coming back to that centre in ourselves, which is easily lost amidst the busyness of everyday life, and the collective currents and beliefs and ideas that sweep us along.

I want to talk about the Medicine Wheel in as simple a way as possible, because that's what we have to do in the modern West. We have no traditions, but we can borrow them and we can dance between them, and we can do the same with the Medicine Wheel. You can have 20 stones in the Wheel if you like, but I don't think that is a good starting point. Firstly, because it's hard for that not to be just the imposition of a foreign culture on yourself, at least if it is done all in one go. And secondly, because when you get that complex, it moves up to the brain, to the intellect, which in one way is fair enough, because there's all sorts of nuances of meaning there, but you tend to lose that connection with the symbolism once it gets intellectually complex.

As long as it's simple, the unconscious can hold it, you can hold a symbol that is white in the north, red in the south, yellow over here and black over there, you just hold it, it can become the centre of your dreaming, the centre of your life, the centre of your universe. That's how I've used it, mainly along with the four elements of Fire, Water, Earth, and Air. If you like, those Elements are Inspiration, Healing, Incarnation, and Perspective, just to make it a bit more concrete. It's a way of describing all those different aspects of who we are in a symbol.

The Wheel is round. It affirms the Greek philosopher Plotinus' dictum that 'the native motion of the soul is circular'. You find these circles, or mandalas, throughout the world. We tend to think in a linear way, that we're going from A to B. We need to think like that for daily life. But the bigger picture, the motion of our souls, is not linear. It circles in an ever-deepening way around its own centre, which is the centre of the Wheel. We are not 'evolving': that is a modern, linear, scientific notion, alien to the indigenous way of seeing the world. Rather, we are continually finding balance within the four elements, paying attention to one then the other as needed, while letting the bigger theme of who we are, and maybe our place in the scheme of things, take care of itself. It is not for us to know, with our tiny individual consciousness. It is good to feel that mystery of who we are and what it's all about: just sit with it, be awed by it. That in itself brings us into balance, for we are living from the centre, the trunk and roots of the tree.

This Chaos exposition of the Medicine Wheel will be about how to find balance, through an exploration of the elements of Fire, Water, Earth, and Air. Even that categorisation, however, is to a degree an abstraction. This is Chaos Shamanism, which always remains close to experience.

For Fire, what we usually experience is the Sun and its warmth. The idea of Fire is a generalisation behind that experience. The same with Water. Unless you live by the sea, your main experience of water is probably going to be rain. I'm talking natural world here, because that is where the Medicine Wheel is based, rather than indoors, where you could say radiators and taps for Fire and Water. It's not quite the same! The Earth element is the soil, which we can put our hands into, get them dirty. The Air element is the wind, for we experience Air most tangibly when it moves.

Sun, Rain, Soil, and Wind. It is very immediate and tangible. It keeps us close to experience when we think this way, even if we are indoors, because they are very present to our imaginations in a sensory kind of way. That simple, raw experience has its own delight and beauty, and it draws us right in to the deeper considerations of life that are at the heart of the Medicine Wheel.

You may hear or read all sorts of great teachings about the Medicine Wheel, but at the end of the day, you need to drop it all and come back to your senses. That's an interesting expression, isn't it, coming back to your senses? There's a lot in it. It says that is where reality is, rather than the abstractions we are in, as humans, much of the time.

It is easier to learn the theory than to sit closely with experience. It is easier to learn the dozens of correlations you find within the directions and intermediate directions of the Wheel than it is to still the mind and sit honestly with yourself. It is, of course, a good thing to learn all the correlations, and how the directions interact with each other. But thinking you then know something as a result is religion.

We drop all of that and we come back into experience, into the heart and the senses. We feel the warmth of the sun, the rain and the wind on our faces, we dig our fingers into the soil. Nature is very good at bringing us back to ourselves, she reminds us of who we are, which is her. In a way, that's all the Medicine Wheel is doing, that's all that this great project called modern Shamanism is doing, it is bringing us back to that experience of the Elements, and in-so-doing bringing us back to who we are. What else is there to do, what else is life about, but continually coming back to who we are, remembering who we are?

That's why amongst the Chippewa Cree, and probably other peoples as well, humans are known as the newborn ones, recently arrived, because we're the only species that doesn't know who it is. You look at the other animals, they know how to live, they know who they are. We're the ones who scratch our heads and get out of balance all the time. So that's why we need things like the Medicine Wheel, to show us how to come back into balance, how to orient ourselves – that's why you have the directions there as well. Maybe I'll bring them in also, but I want to keep it simple, because you can get lost in this maze of meanings, you can become a Shamanic theologian! And then you've missed the whole point.

13
Sun

Keywords: Initiation; the Sees-far Place.

I'm going to launch into the Wheel proper, so to speak. In other words, the four directions around it. We've been looking at the centre of the Wheel, its chaotic heart. Chaos in the sense of that mystery out of which experience is always unfolding: thoughts and feelings, where do they come from? We don't know. Why are we here, what's the universe about, how did it begin, how will it end, where did life come from? All these are unknowable and unanswerable. We live from that mystery, and the purpose of the Wheel is to keep bringing us back to that, because that's when we're in the centre: it's when we know who we are, when we know we know nothing, and that we can know nothing. We have something, but it can't be put into words. It's like we kind of know that we're part of this whole shebang, this whole universe, that we're connected to it all, we feel it. But that's about as far as we can go in knowing anything. I reckon that after we die, we return to a full sense of being connected to everything, of being everything and everywhere at once, and we go, oh yes of course, why did I think I was separate?

We will now unfold the Wheel into its elemental aspects of Fire, Water, Earth and Air respectively. Google "Medicine Wheel stones" and you'll get the idea of what it looks like. I suggest you have a Wheel while you are reading this, it will make it more experiential. You just need four stones, one in each direction. The altar of your local church points East, while North is to your left as you face it, and South to your right. West is behind you.

You can paint them if you want — yellow, red, black, and white, in that order. It is what I have done, but you don't need to. In fact, I think you gain something in having raw stone, so to speak. You can put your Wheel anywhere – this is Chaos, after all. Maybe in your garden or maybe on your table, maybe you take it down sometimes. But it's good to have it as a sort of reference point. More than that, it becomes a symbol, it gets in you, it even carries your dream. It certainly carries your sense of the Sacred, that which is of highest value in life.

When I was living in a caravan for a while, between lives, I had a Medicine Wheel on the grass outside. The sheep would tread on the stones and chip the paint! The Wheel was carrying my life forward. I didn't know exactly how, and I didn't need to. I still have it in my current garden, all these years later, and it is still taking care of me, along with a fairy tree I have planted next to it. Fairies are a universal, and I am sure they have learnt all about the Wheel from their American cousins.

But without further ado, let's go on to specifics. What I want to do is to discuss each element in turn: what they're about, and how to bring them into balance, beginning with the East, with Fire, with the rising Sun, because that's where things begin.

As I say, I want this to be experiential. So have your Wheel somewhere, but also experience the Sun. The Sun's just come out just now as I'm writing – it also did that when I made the video and got to this point. Go outside and experience it when it's next out, let it just hit your face, just enjoy the sense pleasure in that. OK, nothing might go through your mind, and you might not have any great insights, but nevertheless you are connecting to an ancient symbol, an ancient reality. A symbol doesn't just stand for something, it IS the thing, it IS in this case the new life of the East. That's what Fire is, it's the new life that's always bubbling up. The Sun literally brings new life and growth in the natural world, and it is the same with the Spirit.

So there's that to be connected with in the Sun. It's always there, and it's in the nature of life to be always moving on. It doesn't stand still, it's always unfolding into the next stage. Who knows, the next stage might even be death? But that doesn't mean less life, it's just life in a way that we don't understand from where we are now. But even within life, we never know the next stage.

We can sometimes have a sense of a design for our lives, a larger pattern that peeps through at moments of great change, or when we look back on our lives. Maybe even our death has that sort of sense — like Socrates, who needn't have died when he did, but his Daimon suggested otherwise. The Sun is also that level of things. The East is known as the 'Sees-far place', because of that perspective it gives, *sub specie aeternitatis*. That is why the Eagle is also in the East — it flies high in the deep blue vault of the sky, and looks down from infinity. The East is also the place of initiation.

Begin by going out and experiencing the Sun. There's an ancient power to it that can speak through you, it will feed you, and you'll be paying attention to that new life in you. It's so important to pay attention to that level, because we get caught up in the everyday, keeping life going. Life can just be about survival, and it can seem like a luxury to think in terms of creating and bringing in the new. It's like, I'm just trying to put bread on the table, I'm just trying to make sure I can pay the next gas bill, I'm trying to get the kids off to school. Fair enough. But however much there is of that, there's always the new life, there's always at least a trickle of that, and you need to remain with that feeling. You may not be able to do an awful lot with it. It may even be your ordinary life that has that trickle of the new. You may have young kids, you're watching them grow and you're keeping them growing, that is the new life. Or it might be a new job that interests you in some way. So Fire may be coming out through the ordinary, or it may not be. If the ordinary is only 'needs must', then you need to find it one way or another.

Start inwardly: what is it in you that wants to live, but that isn't being lived, that you would love to be doing, or that you feel you HAVE to do? Often we're on this kind of path because there's something we have to do. It's the Daimon. Or you could say the Spirit Guide. The Daimon comes in like an archangel from the Sun, from the East. So think about that in your life, what do I HAVE to do?

It can be good to look back as well, at what's 'done it' for you during the course of your life. What did it for you when you were a kid, that gave you a sense of magic and wonder and openness and imagination, of adventure and excitement? It's all those kinds of qualities that are in the Fire of the Sun. And what did it for you as a teenager, and what did it for you in your early 20s and so on? Maybe write it all down and look at the connecting golden thread. You'll see there's a bigger design that's been unfolding all the time.

When I was a kid, there was a picture book with a wizard in it that drew me strongly, and which has always stayed with me. In my teens, it was the occult, through reading about it, that fascinated me. When I was 20, I liked to wear a dressing gown that stood for the magic. And eventually as an adult, after some wrong turns, it became Shamanism and Astrology: both grab me from deep within, and have done for years. You can see the thread connecting all those things.

Trace your life back in those sorts of terms, come to know yourself in that way, and take that side seriously. Society at large doesn't necessarily take it seriously, and why would it? It's not the job of society at large to take it seriously. Its job is to make sure that we're safe and that there is prosperity. That's what it's there to do. We can feel a bit railroaded by that, and maybe also by our parents' ideas for us. But their job is just to get us to the point of being a functioning member of society. So there's a good chance your aspirations and your imagination weren't affirmed, and that's because most people are just normal, they are muggles, to use JK Rowling's term for it. You need to let your Daimon claim you, and take it seriously, and don't rely on anyone else taking it seriously.

If you look back on your life, you'll see that when you were most fulfilled, when life had most meaning, was when you were doing whatever that thing was that carried the magic for you at the time. I had a big thing at the beginning of 2024, writing was no longer enough, whether it was books or regular posts for Twitter and Facebook. Something in me was going a bit mad, and I realised I had to speak. So I started making short videos, and everything came right, I flourished again. There's something in me that comes out when I speak, that isn't there when I write. And it's not just about me: others seem to benefit too. There's always some bigger picture at work with the Daimon.

Those things that drive you mad when you don't do them: that's the Daimon, and it can be ruthless. It may demand sacrifices. The philosopher Kierkegaard arguably sacrificed his engagement, because his Daimon required him to be unmarried. The same was required of the Jungian analyst Robert Johnson, via a dream interpretation from Jung himself. The Daimon is not necessarily interested in our happiness. What matters to it is that we do the thing we're meant to be doing. It may not give us conventional happiness, but it will give us joy, and that is something worth sacrificing a lot for. I saw a manic-depressive talking on a documentary, and he said the extended misery he went through was worth it for those moments with the angels that also came. You can find a good exploration of this theme of the Daimon in Patrick Harpur's *The Philosophers' Secret Fire*.

I'm perhaps making it sound more dramatic and painful than it will be for most of us. The point is that there is always new life in us to be lived, and the Sun, the first point of the Wheel, if we spend time with it, will remind us of that, ask that of us, show us what that new life is.

The Daimon gives a perspective on life as caused by the future rather than the past. It frees us of the 'parental fallacy', that we are essentially a product of the influence of our parents. No, when we look back, we may discern mysterious ways in which events prefigured what was to come. Elon Musk was named by his father after a fictional commander on the planet Mars. I find it much more plausible to think of this as Fate reaching out from the future and pulling Musk towards it, rather than his central life purpose of bringing humanity to Mars being merely the incidental product of the shaping hands of his father. In the same way, the British Labour Prime Minister Sir Keir Starmer carries the same Christian name as Keir Hardie, the first Parliamentary leader of the Labour Party. As a schoolboy, Winston Churchill told a friend that one day he would save the country from invasion. He had extraordinary escapes from death on the battlefield, as though Fate was reaching out a hand and preserving him for what was to come: it was something he felt himself.

Nor is the Daimon just for what we think of as the 'good guys'. In *The Soul's Code*, James Hillman elaborates on this principle, and includes Hitler as an example.

The irruption of the Sun in a big way into our lives can cause a crisis. We may have one big crisis during our lives, a turning point, or maybe we have more than one. The Shamanic Illness is such a crisis. It's a crisis of something new trying to come in. We can go through the whole thing while not knowing where it is going for much of the time. Sometimes we do know, it's like this side of us, this gift to be claimed, though we may not be ready for it yet, for the old has to be demolished first. We might think we're ready, and we want to be able to get on with our lives again, but we're not, and the Spirit knows. It will hold us back. A bit of help from someone who's been through this kind of thing — who maybe has a sense of the Spirits knocking at your door — can make a big difference. They can help you start to anchor to the new reality that is coming upon you.

Sometimes these times of change, of crisis, of illness even, of unknowing, can go on and on for years. I spent about three years from the early 90s where anything I tried to do outwardly just seemed to go wrong: it just didn't work, it always went to pot. But if I listened to the inner voice that was emerging, that was drawn to Shamanism, then I felt fine. But even that was a slow and gradual thing. It took its time; it had its own course. We're not in charge: that's what it showed me. This is one of the great learnings that we get from the Sun, because it is where Spirit comes in, and feeds into the rest of the Wheel.

Or you could say it goes straight from the East across to the West. You could look at it like that as well, because opposite the East is Earth, Soil, which is body, or Incarnation. It's Spirit coming into matter, into the Earth element, and that is also outside of our control. Take the body: we have two arms, two legs, we're human, and we didn't choose that. We didn't choose to be born and we won't choose our moment of death, probably. We don't choose when we get ill. It is Spirit that decides these things. Or the Moirai, or the Norns, the spinners of Fate, take your pick.

The Sun is inspiration, and it is well-known that we don't choose that; inspiration comes calling at a time of its choosing. This insight is a great antidote to the Western myth of the lone hero carving out his place against a hostile nature. That heroic myth is vital — it gives courage and creativity and a sense of adventure – but it needs to be in the service of nature, or the feminine, if you like. It tends to think it is top dog, and that is where it gets out of balance.

The axis across the middle of the Wheel is called the Blue Road. It's the axis of Fate, you could say. Running from North to South is the Red Road, the Good Red Road as it gets called. You could call it the axis of Free Will. We have choice here, because it is Water and Air, Emotion, and Mind, and that's where we can manoeuvre, that's where we have choice about the thoughts and feelings we're going to give free rein to, and what we are going to keep at bay and not act on, or not let take over our minds. And that then provides fertile soil for when the Blue Road activates, when Spirit comes in. It has more of a place to land.

I want to say a bit more about the nature of these crises. You get them delineated in Psychosynthesis, which is a sort of slightly Jungian Psychotherapy School. An Italian called Assagioli started it, he was around at the time of Jung. He had a concept called the Self (a bit like Jung). It's essentially transpersonal, it is outside the ego and conscious intention. At certain points in life, it's time for a new element of Self to be born. And the old has to adjust itself, because when a new element of Self is born, it's not an add-on. It's a new centre, like when I wrote at the start of the Shamanic Illness chapter about a shift in authority. There's a new centre to us, and everything has to be rearranged around that. The need to rearrange, and our reluctance to do so, is the crisis. Eventually, if we are willing, we know what it is we have to do, what it is we have to accept, what it is we have to live from. It can be like, "I can't carry on living like this," we can get driven to that point. This is how Pluto, Lord of the Underworld, sometimes works for an astrologer. Once you've given in, so to speak, something new can happen. This can be a tremendous relief, like letting go of what has become a great burden.

You can see these periods of change starting sometimes, when the energy starts to go out of something that you've been strongly engaged in. It's time for it to die, so that a bigger self can begin to emerge. It's like you fall out of love, but you don't notice it at first. The enthusiasm, the passion you had: you suddenly notice, oh it's been leeching out, it's not there anymore. It's dying, and you maybe find that hard to recognise or accept, so you struggle to get it back again.

But that's not the way to go. The way to go is to trust it. We'll get to trust when we do the South. There is something new to be found, and you have to trust in that, even though you may not know what it is. But the human tendency is often to scrabble for a handhold in what has the become the loose and sliding shingle of the old life.

The East, the Sun, is the Timeless. The South is the Past, the West is the Present, and the North is the Future. You can get the sense of a design, a pattern to your life at these times, when you're strongly in the East. It's like suddenly there's illumination, and it's outside of time. I was watching a Siberian woman called Snow Raven, who can be found on YouTube. She gives a long interview, in which she says that her people, whose culture is strongly Shamanic, believe that everything is always happening at once, there is no past, present, and future. And they're quite right. She puts it in terms of belief, but really it needs to be an experience. It's hard for us to experience that as human beings for much of the time; it's not really a place to live from. We need ordinary reality most of the time, or we'll get out of balance. But it's good as a belief that you have just a sense of on a day-to-day basis, but which opens out into mystical experience at special times. When the Shaman is doing his journeying, for example, and is with the Spirits.

Beliefs are OK, they are very useful pointers, providing you have some kind of feeling for their veracity, and not just something you want to be true, which is the norm for human beings. Everything at all times happening at once: it's not something we can put into words or understand in any kind of normal way. But that is the light of the Sun for you. Take a light particle: Einstein told us they don't experience time, they arrive as soon as they leave. So there's a connection with our own culture. Time and space only arise when energy condenses into matter.

I want to say something about teachers, who are also to be found in the East. They are the bringers of light, of inspiration, they show it to us, they remind us of it in ourselves. Teachers perform such a great service, and they've also got a bit of a bad name! They've always been up to their tricks, one way or another, because they are human, but they also bring gifts. The word 'guru' means bringer of light, but so badly have many of them behaved that it has become a term of contempt and ridicule.

A good teacher needs to be personally ready to teach, in other words in good relationship with his own shadow. He will have a shadow, he will have all those usual things that we have — self-doubt, anxiety, insecurity, anger, cruelty, a pretty bunch. We'll come to the shadow later, but we do have all those potentials within us as part of being human. We don't like to admit it. We like to think we're a good person who doesn't have things like that, and that is what makes us 'spiritual', or so we think.

Sometimes you can learn as much from the teacher's faults as you can from what he has to offer. A teacher usually does have some gifts to offer, they have something to say, and you can learn from that. But usually, well invariably in my experience, there's something out of balance also going on around them, and it becomes a matter of, can you live with that? Can you even see it? That's the first thing you learn, to be able to even see their Shadow. Can you see the way that they need everyone to love them? Or how they need everyone to believe what they believe? Or the way they demonise and cast out anyone who doesn't fit in, anyone who criticises them, reduces it to their problem? Or the way, maybe, they are fuelled by ambition and the desire to make a name for themselves — which is legit and even necessary in a worldly context, but not OK in this context, at least not too much of it. All these sorts of currents tend to swirl around them, to a greater or lesser degree, and you can learn a lot from that. That can also be what eventually saves you.

Sometimes we get involved with a teacher, and it initially helps. Our own metaphysical connection, our faith in the Spirit, strengthens. We learn to take it more seriously. But we also lose something if we get drawn into the teacher's orbit in the wrong kind of way. We get drawn into that energy field around them, which has its own kind of rules and hierarchy, that people will create, with the best will in the world on the part of the teacher. Unless the teacher is really sure of himself, it is hard for him not to feed off that adulation to some degree and so become complicit. But of course, he may well have catalysed it in the first place.

One of my litmus tests with a teacher in this regard is, can I hang out with them in an ordinary kind of way? Can I feel them, or do they have a shell around them? Can they listen to what I say, or do they always have to have the upper hand, to be in the teacher role?

So we give our power away, if only because everyone else is doing so. It is very hard to resist these collective dynamics. A good teacher will know how and when to hand it back. He won't provide you with answers, he won't tell you how to live, he'll always be nudging you in the direction of trusting your own inner guidance. That is the only job of a teacher! Not to teach you stuff, not to tell you how things are, but to get you to trust your own nascent wisdom. 'Educate' comes from the Latin 'educare', to lead out what is already there.

Realistically, we are rarely ready to fully trust our own inner guidance, though not many people will admit to that. The teacher accepts that people need a person and a teaching to look to, to rely upon, to some degree, and that may go on for years. People can easily spend their whole lives making just a small shift in this respect. And that is fine. They are doing what they need to do.

There are plenty of teachers who won't throw you back on yourself, because they need you as a disciple. Of course, they will claim to be promoting your spiritual autonomy, and that they don't want followers. And you need to be able to stand back – with the gap of Chaos Shamanism, that ability to stay close to your own experience and not be thrown off it – and see the actual situation.

It won't win you any friends if you talk too readily about what you see, because people need to be in that vortex around the teacher, and who knows what it is they have to learn? But it will save you, if you act on it, if you trust it. Because it means you are trusting your own voice, your own inner guidance, in the face of a collective that does not want you to, that will do its best to make you doubt what you see if you speak it. Speak it if you can – there is a test of courage! I have been in that situation, and it is painful, but it can really forge you. It is also, however, a matter of temperament. Some people will just slip away quietly, and good on them. Criticising in that situation doesn't usually achieve anything anyway, the teacher and the group around him are what they are.

In this paradoxical sense, we can be grateful to the teacher, maybe through gritted teeth, for his or her egotism. When we see it and go our own way, maybe after some struggle – because the teacher has, after all, helped us, and that can make it hard also to doubt him – then we trust our own inner guidance as never before, we can really start to own ourselves in a deep way. We come to the centre of who we are.

14

Rain

Keywords: Emotional Awakening; the Close-to Place.

We come on to Water in this exploration of the Medicine Wheel, with Chaos as the foundation. We are also exploring as we go along the meaning of Chaos. It is a new word in this Shamanic context. It is there because we're in a unique position. We don't have tradition, and that is a loss, but it's also a gain. It means we're free to delve into the essence of all these different Shamanic ways you find around the world. There's something universal about them. What is it that is universal? What is at the heart of them, what are they all getting at? Chaos Shamanism is about remaining close to the heart of Shamanism, and asking these kinds of questions.

It's the connection to the natural world that is fundamental. The softness and the care the natural world gives us, which brings us straight into Water, the South of the Wheel, or rather Rain. Water is in a way an abstraction, though it's not really, it's alive to our imaginations, but it kind of is abstract because it's a generality, whereas Rain is more specific. You can see it running down the windowpane like tears: tears of sorrow, tears of joy. That's the place we've arrived at: we're in something very personal now.

We began with this bigger thing, the Sun, the element of Fire: heat, initiation, inspiration, new life bubbling up. So where does it go to? It can go straight across the Wheel into the body as a sort of fated event. A new phase of life, arising naturally and inevitably. Somebody dies. You have a child. You are struck down by illness. You inherit some money. But Fire also goes clockwise around the Wheel, which means firstly into the emotions, and that's where we learn how to live with it. It's Fire that keeps our emotions bubbling up. We don't have control over what we feel, our feelings are a mystery. In fact we don't even know what we're feeling half the time, let alone where the feelings come from. Particularly, and perhaps schematically, if you're a bloke, and especially if you haven't got much water in your chart astrologically. We still have strong feelings, it just takes longer to know they are there.

So that's the first task of this place of Rain: to pay attention to what you're feeling, all the time. The South, Water, is where we're close to ourselves. This awareness is physical — in the trunk of your body, in your heart, in your stomach, right through you. In your vitals. This is the big learning of the Water place. Paying attention to feeling, and living from that. We always know what we're feeling, even if it is numbness: that is what we are feeling, and we go from there. It's what we forget to do. Maybe we are even deluded enough to think we are rational creatures who operate from reason! Research has shown, as if it is needed, that we make decisions emotionally, and we espouse beliefs emotionally. Reason is applied *post hoc* as justification, that is all it is. We live from emotions anyway, so we may as well be aware of them, be honest about them. Otherwise we are just unconscious human beings, and who wants to be that?

Why is Water the element of feeling? Because it moves a bit, and yet is contained. It's not like Air or Wind, that moves all over the place unrestrictedly, which is more like the Mind. It's not like Earth, which is fixed like the body. And it's not like Fire either, which moves pretty fast also, it roars upwards, soaring inspiration. But feeling nevertheless moves — we talk about being moved by something. And yet it's also contained. Water describes well these currents that go through us. Water IS that. These indigenous correspondences aren't just symbols standing for something, they ARE that thing, because they partake of its nature.

So we pay attention to what we feel, and we try and live from that place.

The emotion of trust belongs here in the South. I've learned to come from trust in the way that I do the videos on which these written pieces are based. In the way I teach, I haven't even got a notepad with headings written on it. I start with a few ideas to talk from and I just let it unfold, and that means I often surprise myself, there is room for the Spirit to come in with its halfpenny worth; that wouldn't be possible if I had it all planned out. Such an approach would kill it for me. I wouldn't have the same joy in it.

There is something very traditional about my approach, which with a live audience could be called responsive. You are trusting in the process, that is where we begin. You do of course need to know what you are talking about, you need a proper background and training. But then you throw that up in the air and let Spirit have its way, according to who you are talking to. Spontaneity.

Trust in life is the foundation when we are newly born. We trust in our mother. Our existence is founded on implicitly trusting that we will be taken care of. That's where our psychological security comes from. It's a very basic emotion or attitude. And we're not just cared for by our physical mother. When we get older our physical mother has done her job, and we can release her from that, thank her for that, and we discover the Earth is our real mother. The Earth takes care of us. The Earth is also red in tooth and claw, she is challenging, and we cannot ignore that. But for now, we're just concentrating on this benign caring aspect, which we learn to trust in as adults, ideally as a natural development from the trust we had in our parents.

The Native Canadian guy who used to come and stay with me was a traditionally-trained storyteller. You know how nowadays, if someone's telling a story, they have it all prepared beforehand, and then they tell it, and that's great. I love going to storytellings, and telling them myself sometimes. They belong to the North, to Air and Wind, so we'll come to that. It is stories, scientific or otherwise, that tell us our place in the cosmos and show us how to orient.

This Native friend didn't work in our way. First of all, he didn't need to prepare his stories, because he'd been trained in dozens and dozens of them. He'd been recognised as a youth as someone with the gifts to be a teacher, healer, storyteller etc. It was an oral tradition. He knew the meanings and how to expound them. At a storytelling he would suggest that people ask him questions about something that was relevant to their life at the moment. One person would ask a question, then another, and then another, and at a certain point a story would present itself to him, to tell in response to people's questions. And he would tell it. He wouldn't necessarily give a neat explanation for why that particular story, but that's what he would do, and that's a certain kind of trust. You just trust in what's happening, and that enables you to be responsive.

You can easily tell the difference between someone who is reading from a script, and someone who is talking off the cuff. Watch my short videos on YouTube at Chaos_Shamanism to see what I mean. This piece is an edited transcript of a spontaneous talk. If I had been reading out a pre-prepared script, it would no doubt be better English and tighter, and the thought probably more precise, but it would also lose some flow. Sometimes it's necessary to read out a prepared paper, but it's not half as alive, because it hasn't got the spontaneity and play, and with it the opportunity for the speaker to be fully and easily herself.

This brings out another aspect of the Rain element, which is the child as a stage of life: namely, spontaneity and play. That is how the child lives, and it is what we often need to relearn as adults, instead of thinking we need to be dutiful and serious all the time. Children know what they want in a straightforward way. We adults don't always know what we want. We can end up confused. But kids know what they want. We need to go back to that. Better than that, we need to hang on to it in the first place, so that we don't have to go back to it. We need always to keep that playful element. I like to sometimes read children's books — *Winnie the Pooh, Alice in Wonderland,* stuff like that. It brings you back into that. And it is vital for creativity. This Water place is also a place of creativity, because if your creativity isn't play, it's not really the full shebang, it's got a big bit missing. This is a point Jung made, just to quote an authority! So the videos behind this book were play for me. I've got to enjoy them or I won't really communicate my being, because it's communicating my being as much as the words I use that matters. And hopefully in reading this you will be able to hear me talking and partying!

Play becomes joy, the tears of joy running down the windowpane. Joy is different to ordinary happiness and contentment, which occurs when there's something you wanted and you've got it. It's dependent on the external: you've got a happy family, you've got a good job, you've got all those things, and you're content and happy. That's great and that's good when that happens. But then there's something else: there's an inner joy when the Spirit soars, when we're answering a call deep within us and living from that. If we are expressing and creating from that place, then there's joy, and it can happen amidst a life that might be otherwise miserable. It has the spontaneity that the child has in his or her play. The child experiences joy too, and as adults we can experience joy when we remember to go back to that child place and trust, whatever our circumstances.

The child has a naïve trust. We have a different type of trust to find. It's not just a naïve trust, although it contains that childlike attribute. It is a trust that has to be built on the fact that the world cannot be trusted in the childlike way that we trust our parents. Terrible things happen. But still we trust. Actually,

I think faith is a better word than trust here. I've been using trust because that is what came down to me in the way I was taught the Medicine Wheel, but it's too psychological. It does not sufficiently imply the overarching metaphysical dimension.

Faith in its turn has a bad name, because it has connotations of blindness. But that isn't what I mean. Faith connects us more explicitly to the Great Spirit, the Great Mystery that we cannot know, but which we trust implicitly and which is the foundation of our life. How irrational is that? Out of that foundation comes the confidence we have in life in a general way. Confidence itself comes from 'fides' or faith, and 'con' or with. This kind of confidence is irrational, because it assumes a positive outcome without the evidence for it.

Let us say non-rational instead of irrational. By non-rational I mean that which cannot be known by reason alone. By irrational I mean holding on to beliefs in the face of clear evidence to the contrary.

It is faith that gives the emotional strength that is the potential of the South. Without faith, we cannot be both resilient and sensitive. Some people are very tough because they have thick skins, and that is all. (They are often also hypersensitive to criticism.) Be like Armadillo, I say: develop a tough skin, put yourself in the fray; but keep a soft heart. I like to associate this animal with the South of the Wheel.

The story of Job in the Old Testament is illustrative of the type of faith that I mean. Job was a righteous and prosperous man, and Satan said to God that Job had faith in God only because he protected him. So God set out to prove Satan wrong, and utterly destroyed Job's life. God had an angel take away his wealth, his children, and his physical health. Job considered the destruction to be God's will, but nevertheless maintained his faith in God. So Satan was proved wrong.

In his book *Answer to Job*, Jung portrays God as an imperfect being who, through mankind, evolves. I think this is wrong.

The Great Spirit does not 'evolve'. It just is, and has infinite compassion and knowledge of how things are. It is not for us to apply modern human concepts such as 'evolution' to the Great Spirit. 'Evolution' is alien to the indigenous worldview, which tends to think in terms of balance within natural cycles: life is not 'going somewhere'.

I think the story of Job is best viewed as a myth about the darker side of life, nature 'red in tooth and claw', which is also the Great Spirit, in which that darker side is piled up in an extreme way to make a profound point about the nature of faith. Job embodies the type of faith that I am getting at. That however bad things get, we do not shake our fist at the Great Spirit, we do not go into blame mode. We find ourselves able to keep faith in life. This is a very deep and rare thing. The testing we have as adults, the suffering and disappointments we inevitably experience, give us the opportunity to look deeper, beyond outward circumstance. Life in this sense forges us.

As Christianity puts it, "The eyes of faith are moved only by God's Spirit and His Word, not by what we see through our human eyes."

It is also the lesson to be learnt from the Cross. Jesus was put through the worst torture, and his faith was tested. "My God, why hast thou forsaken me?"

It is important to be able to sift through Christianity and reclaim what is of value, while discarding that which is not, that contributed to its decline. People often either reject or accept Christianity wholesale. It is an emotionally loaded aspect of our ancestral inheritance that needs to be unpicked. The main idea I reject from Christianity – which is central to its faith – is that Jesus was a historically unique figure, the one and only incarnation of God. This is simply untrue, for if you look around the world you will find dozens of parallel figures. It is wilfully blind to look on Jesus in this way, and it gives faith a bad name. The case against is overwhelming. As for the Resurrection,

I think it is best viewed as visionary reality, which can be a collective phenomenon. It was not literal reality. It was more real than that!

In some of the Native American traditions you find the Sundance, in which participants have their flesh pierced with strips of wood, that are tied to a pole, and they dance until the wood has torn its way out and they are free. This is the same principle as we find in both Job and the Cross. The suffering, as it strips away all that is extraneous, all that we hold dear, can bring us close to the Spirit in a very deep way. The difference with the Sundance is that it is voluntary, unlike Job and the Cross. It is a sacrifice of the flesh. Sacrifice means to make sacred. We surrender on one level, to bring us closer to the Spirit on another level.

We try always to be listening to Spirit, and that gives us our strength. The world around us is ever-changing, and viewed as a theatre of desire, cannot be relied on as a foundation. But the world of the Spirit – which is also the natural world – can be relied on, it is not subject to the vicissitudes of life. It is timeless, and has our best interests at heart.

Chaos Shamanism is not a fluffy path. It looks at the darker, painful side of life full in the face. It demands fortitude – what we call trauma can sometimes become this kind of character-forming vicissitude. And within that, we find faith and joy. A deep light shines from our eyes.

Tears of sorrow and tears of joy, drops of rain running down the windowpane. We are in the Water element: feeling, emotion. When we're connected to that which is creative, that which Spirit calls us to do, then we experience joy, even if outward circumstances are miserable. But there is also sorrow, and there are the tormenting demons. We suffer in this vale of tears, as it sometimes (rather one-sidedly) gets called.

What should we do with all this? This is the Water element, this is feeling, and often we're troubled. How do we come into relationship with that? That's what I'm going to be looking at. It's a huge area, with all sorts of ways it can be looked at. It is a gateway to the soul. It's "the crack where the light gets in", as Leonard Cohen put it. The obverse of this is that often we suffer because we're not addressing that which is deepest in us, we're not living from that.

We have a choice: are we going to come into honest relationship with the demons, which we all have – the self-doubt, the anxiety, the anger, the paranoia, the jealousy, all that pretty bunch? Sometimes we just need to call a spade a spade, and not give it a psychological diagnosis. Instead of saying someone suffers from narcissism and it's probably the wiring in their brain, so it's not really their fault, say instead that they can be self-centred, they're selfish, they're vain. And that it might be a good thing if they could see it, be honest about that, recognise it in themselves.

Let's use these old-fashioned terms; in a way they are more honest and don't let us off the hook so easily. Here's another term you might have heard of: spiritual bypass. It's used to refer to people who, for a spiritual identity, go for the angelic, for something transcendental. They become 'spiritual' people as a way of avoiding their own stuff, their own weaknesses, their own troubled sides. Spiritual bypass is a kind of neutral psychological description. I'd rather use a moral description: it's more telling, it's more biting, gives more urgency to it.

So instead of spiritual bypass, first of all I would say pride: you're giving yourself a spiritual identity that makes you better than other people, because you are spiritual and they are not. Pride is a sin, and the word sin means to miss the mark. In other words, you are not being true to who you are, and you will suffer because of that, just because that is the way things work, rather than any kind of punishment handed down by God. Spiritual bypass is also dishonest, as I just implied, because you're lying to yourself about who you are. You know there are these troublesome bits in you that don't fit with who you claim to be, and you're steering clear of them, using this false identity as a shield.

So there's pride and there's dishonesty in it. This kind of moral assessment suggests you actually need to do something. It is not something just to be talked about to a therapist so that you can blame your parents (a bit of a crude judgement on my part, but there is some truth in it). It is indeed a moral judgement on oneself, but it is not censorious, it is not making us a 'bad' person. It is, however, saying that we are falling short of who we could be, and who do we want to be? Is that how you want to live? Morality used in this way becomes a powerful transformative agent. We have a conscience that is innate, that knows when we are falling short, and we feel shame in response to that.

Words like morality, sin, conscience, and shame are very unfashionable. We know better, don't we, now that we have got rid of religion and discovered psychotherapeutic childhood explanations and become non-judgemental about ourselves? I think there is a lot of wisdom in the more traditional perspective.

It's a dance with ourselves, maybe delicate at first, because maybe we are used to thinking of ourselves as a bad and inadequate person. That seems quite common. And maybe whatever it is that bothers us seems insuperable, maybe it feels fundamental to who we are.

There is a kind of self-possession, even self-mastery (but not in the sense of mastery 'over') that is the aim within the Water element. We need to get a hold of ourselves. We will suffer if we don't. We will indeed go to hell, not for all eternity, but just as a natural consequence of our unwillingness to be honest with ourselves, to choose what and what not to act upon, and what feelings we allow to dominate our minds. It can sometimes, unfortunately, be a case of better the devil you know, because we may be miserable, but at least it's a familiar misery.

It's really about making friends with these troublesome sides, but not letting them hold sway, not acting on them, at least not too much of the time — we're never going to be perfect. But at least some of the time, we hold ourselves, we stand tall. That's what we're trying to do: stand tall, instead of being bowed down and thinking we're useless and hopeless and that our demons are worse than everyone else's. I used to feel that my demons were insuperable and worse than anyone else's. But nearly every everyone seems to think like that, not necessarily because we think we're special, it just seems to be what we do. But then you get in a group, and everyone talks about their stuff and you realise that actually we're all in this together, it's the human condition.

Sometimes I'll talk about my own anxiety. That's one thing that gets me: in very practical situations, when there's a problem, I'll get quite anxious. Rationally I can see the solution, and I do what is necessary. I don't let the anxiety stand in the way of action, although sometimes I get a bit overheated. But there's fear biting at my vitals, and I approach it by standing tall enough so that it can't reach up and really grab me. I hold it at bay. In fact at some level I'm nearly always holding it at bay. It's a lot better than it used to be, but these things are incremental, year by year.

From this place of disidentification, I try to merge energetically with my dementors, and in-so-doing enable a gradual transformation over the decades. This is important inner work. It is the coalface of the South. I'd go so far as to say that if you can get a handle on yourself in this kind of way, at least some of the time, then everything else in your life will work.

However, you could also say that there's only one thing worse than having demons and tribulations, and that is not having any, because they keep us grounded, they keep us the same as everyone else. This is particularly the case if you're on some kind of spiritual thing, you're some kind of teacher, where you start thinking you're more advanced than other people. There are indeed things you probably do know, gifts that you have, and it's important to own that, if only because you can't properly give of them unless you own them. But we're still all in the gutter, as Oscar Wilde said, it's just that some of us are looking up at the stars. We still have those tribulations, those demons, and they keep us on a level with everyone else.

This is what I sometimes do when I teach. I say, OK, here's what I find difficult, and I'll be specific, because it's easy to say, oh yes of course I have faults and of course in a general sort of way I'm the same as everyone, I've got lots of humility. So be specific, and then when you do that, particularly if you're in the teacher position, other people feel at the same level as you; they're not feeling disempowered, they haven't got you so much on a pedestal. They maybe want to put you on a pedestal, but you're not letting them, you're giving it back. Furthermore, they also feel they can own up about their own demons, that actually it's perfectly OK, it's not anything to be ashamed of, and that's so important.

Honesty: that's maybe the crucial factor here. Being honest with ourselves and about ourselves. If we have someone we can tell, so much the better. Obviously, we don't want to go around telling everyone, they might rightly think you're weird. Besides which, a lot of people don't want to know about their own demons, and if you come too close by being honest about yours, that's threatening to them.

They've got these nice walls up, and a nice safe identity, and they're maybe not ready for that yet. They keep psychological stability by projecting the bad stuff onto guys out there. That's usually a sign that someone doesn't have into a good relationship with what is known as the shadow side. They've got a whole cast of demons out there, they're often politicians or CEOs, wealthy people, anyone with power or success, and certainly Republicans/Tories – that goes without saying if you are 'spiritual'. We make all sorts of judgements about their characters, when in reality we don't know them from Adam.

Success is an interesting one, because I think we often take people down out of envy. Envy is the first sin after Eden in the Bible, when Cain killed his brother Abel, because God had praised Abel and not him. That suggests how basic and common it is. Our happiness is competitive, we compare ourselves to others all the time. The antidote to envy is living your own gifts fully, which Cain had not done. Then you will feel happy with yourself, and able to forgive others their successes. More than that, you will be happy for them and admire them.

You can usually tell it is people's own shadow stuff when there is an edge to their criticisms of others, it's like they need them to be the bad guys.

Anger is another one. It does indeed drive people away, but it is not a cardinal sin. It is necessary for survival, but it can also desire the destruction of the other person. So just be upfront and honest about that red mist, if you get it. Apologise without hesitating if you need to. But like anything, you'll make it unconscious if you condemn it. Why will that demon want to be friends with you if you're treating it like that? We're back to that delicate dance again.

I want to look at our demons, the things that trouble us, in terms of how we frame them. Where do they come from? We have a very definite psychological model in the West that traces much of it back to childhood, and that doesn't seem to be the indigenous view.

I trust the indigenous view about lots of things, because it's worldwide. You find the same kind of outlook, even though their traditions of course are very different – different languages, ceremonies, different everything. But fundamentally there's the same kind of outlook on what it is to be human in this world, which says to me there is something deeply natural and sane about it, or it wouldn't be so universal and long-lasting. Their outlook is sophisticated too, it's not just 'primitive', in the sense that we moderns can think we've gone beyond that and we've made these 'discoveries' about the psyche. No, it's not like that. "There is nothing new under the sun."

I used to talk metaphysics round the breakfast table with my Canadian Indian friend who used to stay with me. We'd talk subtle definitions of words, all that sort of stuff. His philosophy, his way of seeing the world, which is traditional to his people, is very sophisticated and subtle. Probably more subtle than anything we have, and it incorporates Spirit; it's not a philosophy of justifying a dead universe, it's not cynical at all. And it's very realistic. So I look to these indigenous wisdoms, and how they view the demons.

There's a guy called Eduardo Duran, who has written a book called *Healing the Soul Wound*. He's part Native American, and also a Jungian analyst. He does a lot of work with the people on the reservation. Often the problem with them is alcoholism. The first thing he does when they come to see him, is to wave around a bit of smudge and do a bit of ceremony. It engages ancient traditions that they've forgotten, but they're still somewhere in them. If you like, it engages the unconscious. Something in them wakes up, they are now in sacred space, where all sorts can happen, and where people naturally focus on that which has the deepest value for them.

And then he goes OK, this alcoholism, it's a spirit that's come to visit you. Get to know it. What does it look like, what's its name, and so on. Introduce yourself to it in the traditional manner, say who your parents are, and your grandparents are. You need to come into relationship with it. For indigenous people, with their relational view of humans, who you are is also who your relatives are, in a way that it isn't so much for us. That's the first session he'll do with them, and he says immediately their relationship with the bottle changes.

Incidentally, Duran also says that the Indians won't accept anything less than a full human relationship with him. This is interesting in view of the conventional insistence on psychotherapeutic 'boundaries'. Obviously, they have their place in this very sensitive work. But it usually also means that the therapist doesn't reveal themselves as a full human being: you don't get to know them in an ordinary kind of way. The relationship remains 'professional'. But you can't do this to the soul. I was once seeing a therapist, and she told me that she realised that at the start that it wasn't going to work with me unless she was ordinary and chatty with me about her life. I think the Indians' instincts are right. It's as though they have hung on to something essential, despite everything they have been through, that will not accept this professionalisation of the soul. Think about it: therapy works in the same way that transmission works, that was discussed in Chapter 7. There is an energetic intermingling, and a transformation of both people, as two souls meet. But if one of them is partly hidden, however worthy the reasons, then this transformational synergy is compromised. I would go further and say that the 'boundaries' frequently serve the therapist as much as they do the 'client' (dreadful word!). It enables the therapist to function through a persona and therefore not address much in themselves that may need addressing. They are in a position of authority, and if the client feels uncomfortable with this lobotomization (as he should), then it is liable to be seen as his problem, not the therapist's. It leads to the same kinds of problems as are found with leaders of religious cults (a cult simply being a religion that has not found wide acceptance). It infantilises the client, from whom the personal life of the 'adult' therapist is concealed, much as one does with children. And it easily lends itself to an enjoyment of power on the part of the therapist.

If we were to invent Chaos Therapy, then as ever we would stand back from the forms and trust in what the Spirit is saying. Just as Duran says to the client to ask the Spirits that torment him to introduce themselves and be known, so does the therapist need to be known. Instead of boundaries, one relies on sensitivity and appropriateness, the assumption being that the therapist fully reveals themselves as an ordinary human being, unless there are clear reasons not to. In this way therapy becomes very similar to what might be called Chaos Shamanic Counselling, the main difference perhaps being the calling in of spirit helpers, as and when appropriate.

The indigenous view of the demons, and I get this from Lewis Mehl-Madrona as well, is that they are not essentially part of us: they belong to the universe, and they're coming to visit us. It's a story – everything's a story, it's not the absolute truth. Nothing's the absolute truth. But I think it's a great story, and that's how I try and deal with this stuff personally.

So I try to view the anxiety – let's call it fear – that I sometimes suffer from, as something that has come to visit me, and is trying to get its claws in and take over. And I'm going no! I'm treating it like I would a pet that wants to misbehave. No, you're not doing that, but I'm still going to be around you and share a cup of tea together. Because if you push them out, it'll just get worse. It's a dance that we need to do. It's a very different way of viewing our tribulations and where they come from. Really, we don't know where they come from. They have swirled in from the Chaos.

William Wordsworth, the poet, wrote that:

Our birth is but a sleep and a forgetting;
The Soul that rises with us, our life's Star,
Hath had elsewhere its setting
And cometh from afar;

Not in entire forgetfulness,
And not in utter nakedness,
But trailing clouds of glory do we come
From God, who is our home.

We come in with stuff, we come in trailing clouds of glory, and maybe a string of demons as well, who knows? Maybe you did some sort of deal with the universe before you were born: OK, I'll have this demon and that demon this time, because I'll learn this, that and the other. Again, it's a story, but maybe it's a helpful story.

It is a counter-story to what James Hillman calls the parental fallacy. Hillman was a well-known archetypal psychologist, who had analysis with Jung as a young man. He stopped after a while, saying he'd have been burnt up by Jung's light, it was too strong for him. I don't know that he was right about that, but at any rate he was a highly original thinker, and he was prepared to challenge deep-seated assumptions. It's fundamental to psychotherapy, and to our psychological understanding, that we are who we are to a considerable degree because of parental influence. Hillman disagreed with this. He said why should we assume that the earlier something happened to us, the more formative it is? He also saw life as a kind of fate, a blueprint unfolding, with necessary challenges along the way, so that we seize our destiny.

It's the nature-nurture argument, and there are a couple of well-researched books that give considerably more weight to nature, and less to nurture, than we are used to assuming. It is, if you like, the opposite of the 'blank slate' idea, which I think is a foolish notion. One of the books is *Blueprint* by Robert Plomin, who did many years of personal research, as well as meta-research, particularly into identical twins brought up separately. The other book is called *The Nurture Assumption* by Judith Rich Harris, and again she does meta-research amongst twin studies, and reaches the same kind of conclusion. She is limited by her scientific assumption that who we are is either nature (as in DNA) or nurture, which causes her considerable difficulty trying to explain differences between identical twins who were brought up together.

The Chaos Shamanic view would be that we don't know. There are some things we can explain, and some that are unknowable, human nature being one of them.

I am circling round to another criticism of psychotherapy, which does its best to find explanations in childhood. It's easy to create stories, and spend a lot of time with your psychotherapist exploring those stories about why what happened in your childhood explains how you are now. I could take my anxiety, and I could explain it at length with a psychotherapist in terms of my relationship with either my father or my mother, or the boarding school I went to. I could use all those avenues and come up with very convincing stories.

Now that doesn't mean psychotherapy doesn't work. The very fact that we're paying attention to these things brings them to consciousness, brings them into closer relationship with us, and that's the main thing: coming into close relationship with our demons. It's not about transforming them, and this is another key point. Who knows what part they have to play? It's like the awful Gollum in *The Lord of the Rings*, where Frodo wants to get rid of him, and Gandalf says he has a sense that Gollum has a part still to play, and of course the ring would never have got thrown into Mount Doom without Gollum. So be open to the demons bringing something useful to the table that is not obvious to us.

What we call demons often serve a purpose. Our job isn't to explain them or transform them, it's to come into relationship with them. Childhood explanations are just one more story, and there is no proper research, as far as I can see, showing that childhood events actually are causative rather than just correlational. The idea that our demons are a result of our childhood and what our parents did wrong is so deeply embedded, it's such a deep idea, that we take it as an absolute reality. It can take quite a lot to shift this axiom. But it needs shifting, we need to loosen up this whole picture and step more into the not-knowing, which always leaves greater room for the Spirit. The parental explanation of who we are is not traditional, it's not indigenous, and that's where we're coming from with Chaos Shamanism: we're trying to go back to the heart of indigeneity, and find what is universal in that.

They did not have a childhood explanation for the demons. Of course, there will be some things about us that can be traced back to childhood, though even then it needs to be held lightly as explanation, as not the whole story. But it's a matter of emphasis, as Plomin's and Harris' books indicate. It's like an overlay, and maybe it has left us with some things to struggle with that may forge us, the grit in the oyster. But who we essentially are is not a product of our childhood. Anyone who has had children will know that they come in with their own unique natures already strongly present. In an indigenous society, you might have visionary shamans who can tell you the nature of the child and its future before it is even born. As an astrologer, I can sometimes do that with newborns.

And it's the same with our demons. Who knows where they came from? Who cares, in a way? The main thing is to discern them, get to know them, and keep making the choice, to the degree we feel able, not to act from them, and not to let them dominate our minds. That in itself will gradually effect a transformation. The nature of the transformation is not for us to know, or to cause: our part is to create the conditions whereby it can happen. The Red Road of North-South creates the conditions, the Blue Road of East-West effects the transformations, at a time and in a manner of its choosing.

In being in this Water element, in being at this coalface of ourselves, we need to pay attention to the mystery of who we are, rather than seeking too many explanations; we need honesty; and we need to keep making choices about who we are going to be, and not let ourselves down. Over the years, this forges us, we become substantial, we develop a strong foundation, and we have wisdom in the workings of human nature.

I will conclude with a (perhaps one-sided) quote from the great Sir Winston Churchill:

> *It is said that famous men are usually the product of unhappy childhood. The stern compression of circumstances, the twinges of adversity, the spur of slights and taunts in early years, are needed to evoke that ruthless fixity of purpose and tenacious mother-wit without which great actions are seldom accomplished.*

15

Soil

Keywords: Incarnation; the Looks-Within Place.

We come on to the Earth element, or Soil, in this exploration of the Medicine Wheel from the point of view of Chaos Shamanism. With Chaos Shamanism, we're bringing it back to essentials, getting rid of any kind of overlay. The Medicine Wheel has got all sorts of correspondences and subtle meanings. But at the heart of it are these four ancient elements: Fire, Water, Earth, and Air. They are to be found in both in Europe and the Americas. They're an ancient way of describing both the world and the individual person.

The immediate corollary is that we therefore ARE the world around us, we're no different, we're of the same stuff. This is what Shamanism does: it connects us, or rather reconnects us, because that's what we've lost. We've lost that sense of belonging to the natural world, of belonging to the earth.

Christianity relegated the earth. Even before it was Christianity, when it was just the Old Testament, we humans were given dominion over the earth, over the animals and plants. You can interpret that as a responsibility, but also as a dominance, and I'm sure people weren't reluctant to look at it in that way also. And then the world came to be seen as the province of the Devil, as created by him, and Heaven was where you wanted to be. So that was another put-down of Nature.

And then Science arose, which sees a split between mind and body. It doesn't know what to make of mind, or rather consciousness. (Let's go one step further and call it Soul, a less respectable but more accurate term for what we are talking about.) That's because it is a subject rather than an object, and so cannot be inquired into by the scientific method, which treats everything as an object. Science puts Soul in a separate cupboard over in the corner, labelled 'for later', on the assumption that it will eventually be answered, such is the faith in the scientific method. It sits in the same cupboard as what came before the Big Bang and the origin of life. After decades of speculation, Science can still absolutely say nothing about Soul. The more they try to investigate, the more it becomes an absolute mystery.

And then we have the scientific idea of evolution, which puts humans effectively at the top of the tree, above nature. Any respectable scientist will go no, no, we're not really at the top of the tree, it's just a description of a pattern. But that's not how humans feel. We are a competitive and hierarchical species, we like to feel better than other people, and by the same token, we like to feel superior to nature.

In medieval times, you had the Great Chain of Being. God was at the top, and then angels, then men, and below them came women, and then animals, plants, and stones. It started with God and went downwards. It was fairly flattering to humans, especially to men. Evolution is the Great Chain of Being inverted, with God and the angels ditched. It starts at the bottom with stones, and you have humans unrivalled at the pinnacle. So it is even more flattering to us! Again, we're above nature. We're also split off from nature because of the Soul-Matter divide that Science inherited from Christianity as the Nature-Spirit split.

Science arose in the context of the Renaissance, which saw the rediscovery of the ancient Greek and Roman cultures. The Greeks themselves had, through their emphasis on rationality, begun the separation from nature. This was another line of inheritance of the divide we are discussing.

You can see the tangle we're in, and why we need Shamanism. It's the great project of our age, that's how I see it: reclaiming the indigenous soul, through remembering that we are an integral part of the natural world, that there is nothing in us that is outside of that. Healing the Great Forgetting in the West, that began several thousand years ago.

The reason I'm talking about all of this is because we are in the Earth element now, which is also the body. Shamanically, it is an inspirited body, because all of the elements are inspirited. Or rather, ensouled! There's a book called *Dancing in the Streets: A History of Collective Joy* by Barbara Ehrenreich. She says that in medieval times there was dancing in the churches. People would dance alongside the priest. And what happens when you dance? Your spirit comes alive, you make a bodily connection to Spirit, you become inspired. Now you can't have that if you're trying to run a religion, because you've got to have people under control. You need to have the priest as the only one with a hotline to God. He's the person you go to for answers. So they banned dancing in the churches. They allowed that kind of spirit at festivals a few times a year, just to keep the mob happy. But apart from that, it was out.

Fast-forward a few hundred years, and you have the early European explorers voyaging around the world. And what do they find, wherever they go? People dancing to drums around fires. Their response was one of disgust. That kind of freedom, that kind of connection to the body – well, that was animal, that was the Devil. So that's our cultural baggage. Christianity may be on the back foot, but the inhibition continues, perpetuated through intellectual belief rather than moral disgust, via the Mind-Body divide in Science.

The liberated animal spirit will always try to come back. You get it in rock and roll music, which was why Elvis Presley was banned from performing in some states. You get it in rave music, and you get it in Pentecostal churches, where people clap and sway to the music, and roll on the floor, possessed by spirits and speaking in tongues.

The Spirit can take us over physically. It's not going to be for everyone, but it needs to be allowable, it needs to be felt to be OK. We're not under control in a normal kind of sense when the Spirit gets hold of the body. I'll say more about that when we look at Journeying, in **Meeting the Spirits** (Chapter 21). There is a way in which the body can be deeply liberated, the animal spirit can be fully present, as something we yield to, while being fully present to ourselves. You can see how that could be threatening for some people, even if they're not part of a controlling religion, for it is taking place outside the normal 'civilised' rules of being human. But paradoxically, that 'wild' energy is very self-possessed: look at wild animals, they do everything deliberately. If you have wildness in that sense, it makes you very civilised, because you are self-possessed: there is a bigger, more natural self present, than most people allow themselves to be. (See section on Wild Shamans, Chapter 31.) In a way, I have just defined the spirit of Chaos Shamanism. It can be a bit of a gift, necessary for doing healing work.

It's time for something practical in this discussion of the Earth element. Go and lie face down, spread-eagled on the ground outside. It doesn't have to be a nice day, just dress up warm if you need to. Lie quietly on the earth, and let your body and your heart be filled with her solid presence. You will be able feel the heart of Mother Earth with your heart. Our hearts can connect, and you can feel how she takes care of you, and that she can take all your pain, and heal whatever needs healing. It's a wonderful thing to connect in that sort of way. It brings us back to who we are. We are the offspring of the earth, we're nothing but her.

So that's a very good way of connecting with the earth and therefore with who you are. Get your fingers in the soil. Almost taste it, well maybe not literally taste, it's not good for you, but you know what I mean. Smell it, rub it over your skin. Gardening, it can be as simple as that. You don't have to do advanced Shamanic practices!

You can connect with the earth just as well in a city, for there are always parks, if you haven't got a garden or window boxes. It is the attention and intention that matter. Obviously it helps to get out into the wilds sometimes. It's something I do. I live on Dartmoor, a wilderness area in the UK. I go for walks there, I'm exercising my body, which it loves, and I'm just in the natural world, solitary, with the big sky above me. It sort of shakes everything down, it sorts things out, it brings me back into balance, it connects me. It does all those things and it's very simple. I just need to be there and pay attention in a relaxed kind of way. Some of the time, maybe most of the time, I'm off thinking about something else. But some of the time I look and I appreciate.

As a bloke it can be that I've got my route on Dartmoor planned and I want to get it done, that can come to be the main thing. So I find it can be quite useful walking with a woman, because they'll get me to stop and look at something. I've got better at it over time, through walking with women, and nowadays it'll often be me who's going, look at that! Paying attention, that is so important, paying attention with our whole being. Then nature can speak to us. Rocks can speak to us.

The Earth element, in the West of the Wheel, is also the adult. As an adult we have to meet the demands of practical reality, which is the Earth element. We can't just play and do what we want, which is what we do, schematically, as children, even though we get sent to school and sometimes are made to do chores. Children are Fire (play) and Water (feeling). As an adult, we have to make life work, and that's practical, and life resists. We have to learn to do things, maybe we don't want to be doing them, nor do they necessarily go how we want them to.

What we're doing as an adult is bringing Spirit into matter. That, in a way, is all we're here to do: to incarnate. In that sense the Earth is the most important element. Of course it's not really, but it makes the point. Incarnating is a central and difficult thing to do, but it's also a joyful thing.

Christians talk about having your cross to bear, and I think they talk too much about that, they make it a bit one-sided, because life is also about joy. But it is indeed also about bearing a cross. This is not a very New Age approach to spirituality! We talked in the South, in Water, about the demons and tribulations we have within us. Objectively, life may also be hard. Life is in certain respects difficult, and we need to learn to bear suffering. That is part of life. Women have that naturally through childbirth. Young men in a traditional culture may be put in the Sweatlodge, where they learn how to bear the heat and bear thirst. Or they get put out on a Vision Quest on the hillside with nothing but a blanket. In this you learn that suffering is part of life, and you learn to bear it. It is a strength.

Moreover, would we learn anything if we did not suffer? Sometimes suffering is just suffering. Not everything has a deeper meaning. But sometimes it is because we are out of balance in some way, and it is showing us that. Suffering can really push us in this way, force us to look. In this way, suffering becomes much more than a cross we have to bear. It is the point where we learn and transform. It is what pushes the proto-Shaman in his illness to yield to the Spirits.

Bearing your cross: that can almost make it sound like that is the be-all and end-all of existence; that the most important thing is that life is difficult, and you just keep going and you'll get your reward in Heaven after you've died. But no, life is also sweet, as the Bear, who lives in the West for some Native Americans, shows us. The Bear knows about honey. The Bear is a good antidote to the 'vale of tears' of Christianity. It was what was so initially appealing to me about Shamanism, and that feeling remains: life is something to be savoured. The Buddhism I had been around previously had a downer on ordinary existence.

Life is also joyful. That's the Shamanic perspective, the indigenous perspective. Heaven is here, now. We're not born, as *The Tibetan Book of the Dead* would have us believe, because we can't handle the white light of reality after we've died, and we flee in terror and get a body, and then eventually, once we've gained enough wisdom, gained enough Enlightenment, we won't need to be born anymore. Again, the Earth just becomes this place where you don't really want to be. It's the same for a traditional Christian, living in a world created by the Devil.

I don't want to be too one-sided about this, because there is also TS Eliot's line that *"Humankind cannot bear very much reality."* It is not that *The Tibetan Book of the Dead* is untrue: it's a matter of emphasis. If the dark and difficult is one-sidedly emphasised, you have to ask, why? It's the old story of religions keeping the people under control through fear. Truth is being spoken, and that gives it credibility, but in such a way that it becomes manipulative. It is simplistic to say that there is some dark force that, if you are a good person, you will not be subject to. But it is also what many people want to hear. It is a co-creation.

I nearly always get a pushback if I critique Tibetan Buddhism. Many people have it on a lofty pedestal. There are a lot of good things in that tradition, and in *The Tibetan Book of the Dead*. But it is also a religion, like any other, and we need to be able to see the limitations. For example, I read Heinrich Harrer's account of Tibet in the 1940s, *Seven Years in Tibet*, where he was tutor to the young Dalai Lama. The religion he was surrounded by was at least as rigid and rule-bound as anything we have known in the West. Maybe even worse than in Mervyn Peake's *Gormenghast*. It is just what humans do, and why we need the Chaos principle. Indigenous people can be just as stuck in their ways too.

The Chaos Shamanic perspective has got none of this religiosity. When you make earthly life something undesirable, you're controlling people, you've got them where it matters. You promise them happiness somewhere else if they're good, if they follow your rules, and you terrify them about what will happen if they are 'bad'. The Tibetan descriptions of hell are every bit as gory and detailed and terrible as we encounter in Catholicism. Whoever created them was motivated by sadistic and Machiavellian impulses. It's what can happen when you create an identity out of being 'spiritual', as a monk or priest might do: the normal human impulses come out uncontrolled, in shadow form, and wreak destruction. Religion in this sense has nothing to do with Shamanism as a life of finding balance. The former is about group control, the latter about becoming a full human being.

There's joy when Spirit meets matter in the adult of the West, when Spirit enters the body. That's why creativity is joyful, because when you're creating, you're doing so from the whole of yourself, it's coming out of your vitals, it's not just a head thing. It's a deep thing, it tastes like ambrosia, like nectar. You know you're living in the right way when you have that joy.

It almost seems to be part of the human condition to have a big downer on the world, to see it as being in one crisis or another, and to think humanity is going to hell. I think Shamanism as a reclamation of the indigenous soul is an antidote to that. When you look, there is indeed a lot of good that's going on in the world. Take the unprecedented numbers of people that have come out of poverty, for example, in recent decades. But we don't want to know about that, we get too invested in things being awful in a fundamental kind of way. We are too invested, in this case, in Capitalism being an evil, to be able to acknowledge that it is the only economic model that actually brings people out of poverty.

It is easy to align our Shamanism with the environmental movement, and think we're all on the same side against the bad guys, whoever they may be. You've got to be really careful before you do that, because the environmental movement has no shortage of people who hate humanity; some of them go so far as to refer to humanity as a cancer. This is sick. And they think that any changes happening on the earth because of humans are by definition bad, and we've got to reverse them and come back to pristine nature.

Well, humans are part of nature too. We are, for example, releasing lots of carbon dioxide into the atmosphere. It's still very low by long-term historical standards. And what is happening? The earth is greening. The trees are getting taller, the crops are giving bigger yields, and huge semi-arid areas have greened over, because they can get their carbon dioxide without having to lose so much water by opening their pores for so long. There's good stuff happening. It personally gives me joy too, this greening of the Earth. And another one: polar bear numbers are increasing. Hunting by man was the problem not, as we were led to believe, global warming.

I'm not denying there's plenty of bad stuff happening, but there are good things happening also. You can't really see what you need to address without a proper perspective, without balance in the way you see things.

As we saw in the chapter on the Shamanic Illness, Chaos Shamanism stands outside those huge collective currents that sweep humanity along. It stands outside the ongoing crisis mentality. And it certainly stands outside the humanity-hating aspect of the environmental movement. We love humanity, and we love the re-greening of the natural world, at least some of which we have inadvertently brought about. We have faith and optimism in the future of humanity. Collectively, we have always been beset by problems, and always will. Maybe the problems are necessary for our unfoldment, the grit in the sweet oyster of existence.

Remember there's the joy, and remember the good things that are happening. Look up a guy called Bjorn Lomborg, who makes a career out of pointing out, with well-resourced evidence, the good things that are also happening in the world.

He is, in my opinion, performing a great service to crisis-addicted humanity. There is also a free app called Inconvenient Facts that gives this other side of the picture. I'm shifting over onto the North here which is Air: the Elder, the mind. Elders have that sort of perspective, where they don't get caught up in these blind, manufactured crises that we get caught up in, one after another.

So incarnation usually begins with the ordinary responsibilities of life, and then, schematically, it can move on to its deeper creative aspect.

That also brings us onto Ceremony, which is there to remind us of the Sacred. (See Chapters 26–29 for a fuller exposition of this important theme of the West.)

Children don't need ceremony, because they're in the Sacred. As Wordsworth says in his *Intimations of Immortality,*

Heaven lies about us in our infancy!

Children wouldn't call it the Sacred, but the play state is that, they are in that delight. Even then, the poet continues,

Shades of the prison-house begin to close upon the growing boy,
But he beholds the light, and whence it flows. He sees it in his joy.

Older people have the space, they have the wisdom and perspective on life, to see its deepest values, which is another word for the Sacred. We don't necessarily know what we value until things happen, and we make decisions, and you find out who you are, and what really matters, what gives most meaning to your life. It might be that without something creative, life just doesn't work properly, there's something important missing, and then you do that creative thing, which might be running Sweatlodges or painting pictures, or whatever it is that you do, and then life has got its full meaning. So there's a deep value for you there, the Sacred.

I don't think life can have full meaning without the presence of the Sacred, without a connection to the highest or deepest possible purpose. I don't like the word 'high' very much, for it has too much of a connotation of striving to become something other than we are. Rather, we are allowing ourselves to be at our deepest and most whole. That's what we do when we create, and that's what we do in ceremony.

Frank Fools Crow says that a more accurate term for what we call Great Spirit, which is a translation of the Lakota term 'Wakan Tanka', is "Holiest of Everything." In other words, the Sacred.

It can be harder for the adult to have a sense of the Sacred, because we are necessarily caught up in day-to-day responsibilities, and we lose sight of what really matters.

As Wordsworth continues, referring to the heavenly light:

At length the Man perceives it die away,
And fade into the light of common day.

A distinction can be made between the Sacred and the ordinary, even though everything, truly seen, is Sacred. Or Holy, coming from 'whole'. Things become ordinary, or appear as such, when we do them a lot. You might have a Sweatlodge, sited out in the remote wilderness. When you go there, it is unusual for you. Whatever is unusual is the Sacred, because it shifts you out of your usual state. And then you'd be doing that Sweatlodge in the same place for five years, and it gradually becomes ordinary. So you move it somewhere else in order that it becomes Sacred again. It's how humans work.

Anything unusual or dangerous can be treated as the Sacred; it puts us in that other place. Tigers, poisonous snakes, thunderstorms, lightning, night-time. All these things put us into the Sacred. Into the Chaos, where the usual order of things is suspended. In his book *The Circle of Life,* James Audlin describes at length the difference between the Sacred and the ordinary from a Native American perspective. I took the Sweatlodge example from him, but I don't entirely agree, because a particular place also becomes more sacred over time through being treated as such. However, it is a book I recommend as a thoroughgoing exposition of the Native American attitude to life.

I have used the keyword 'Incarnation' for the West. Another keyword is the 'Looks-within' place. This ties in with its association with evening, as the sun sets, dips below the horizon, and shines light on the inner world. The inner work begins in the West, that leads to the knowing of the North. It comes about by reaching back to the child of the South and its demons, and being the material vehicle for coming into relationship with, and transforming, those tribulations. It often takes until we are well into adulthood, a good way through the West, before we are ready for the encounter with the shadow side.

16

Wind

Keywords: Perspective; the Knowing Place.

Wind is the term I am using for the Air element of the North, the last of the four elements: Sun, Rain, Soil, and Wind — the more tangible version of Fire, Water, Earth, and Air. So just go outside for a minute and feel the breeze, make that connection with the Wind. I'm trying to make this experiential, because these spiritual traditions so often wander off into ideas. Even by talking about Air we're in an idea, which is fair enough, but we then easily start to lose connection to the body, to the heart, to experience. And this is what Chaos Shamanism is always pulling us back to.

It's a pulling back that we need to do almost constantly, because as human beings we so easily head off into abstraction. It's our gift and it's our weakness. This brings us to the heart of Air, because that's what this element is about: ideas and their power, but also the way they can take us away from ourselves.

Maybe it's the Air element more than anything that makes us "the animal that doesn't know who it is", because we're always being pulled off into our ideas about things, and away from immediate experience. With Fire, Water, and Earth you're always in them: Fire keeps you wanting to live, Water gives you your feelings, Earth your Body and the world around you. They are givens. Animals and plants are just in them, subsumed by them. They know who and what they are, they just get on with it. That doesn't make them better or worse. That judgement is another human thing. But we wander away from knowing who we are.

Yet Air can also do the opposite. It can also help us know who we are more deeply. It is paradoxical and tricksy.

I wrote a book called *The Medicine Wheel* in 2021, which has 84 pages on the Air element. I'm not going to inflict 84 pages on you here. I'm just going to inflict on you what comes to me now to say, and hopefully that will be some kind of essence, and in the spirit of this new idea of Chaos. I'm not referring back to what I wrote then. I see this as congruent with the traditional way of teaching, because in the traditional way you don't have a script, you respond to the audience. On the one hand, that's more appropriate for them, and it also gives Spirit more freedom to speak. Something bigger, something outside yourself can come through.

I'm starting to wander a bit now, but that's Air for you. I'm going to wander and see what themes present themselves. I was thinking about Spirit coming through, and I was thinking about the theme of being authentic. I noticed when I started teaching a few years ago, or rather came back to it after a 15-year gap, I got the appreciative comment that I was authentic. I thought, well what's that about? I didn't at the time think too much about it. But on one level I thought, well I do try and just be open about who I am, what I find difficult, which I've probably bored you to death with already; the things that make me anxious, the things that make me cross, where I doubt myself, where I can get depressed if I'm not writing, or if I'm not doing the next creative thing. My own tribulations. They're not a big deal. I'm not whining, I'm not complaining. But I'm with them, I'm not denying them either. And I thought that authentic is just about being that, in a way just being true to myself, not making the mistake of thinking that because I'm teaching, I have to display some kind of superpower, or claim to know something. And if I'm open about who I am, on the one hand the people I'm talking to feel on a level with me, and also they feel they can be open about their stuff too, that they're not worse than everyone else! So that's one level of what it means to be authentic, and its implications.

But then I realised there is another level, when I draw from somewhere else. This came out of a conversation with a friend who has watched many of my Shamanism and Astrology videos. She commented that it was fascinating to her to watch my movements and expressions. As she put it in writing to me:

> *When you look down, it feels as if you are seeking within yourself, dipping into your cauldron of reflections and knowing … and yes, with a gravity of consideration.*
>
> *When you look up, it's like a looking out beyond yourself, seeking inspiration from somewhere and something far out and far beyond…*
>
> *They feel like very different touchstones, which you are reaching for and connecting with.*

This latter level is also real, if anything it is more real than the ordinary level, and I think this is also what people are picking up on when they say I am authentic. They may not be aware of it. The ordinary level acts as a sort of disguise!

It brings us back to the chapter on Transmission, which is a big deal in the Tibetan tradition. And maybe to the idea of Spirits passing down the generations in Shamanic families. Like anything, it can easily be reduced to forms, and the spirit gets lost in a miasm of rectitude. But if you've spent years with yourself, being honest with yourself – some of the time, at least, because we are only human – then you stop trying to control who you are, you stop being so attached to your ideas of who you are. This yielding to yourself is also a yielding to Spirit, to something vaster, because we were never truly separate from that. Then something inspired and intangible can blow through you, and if people are listening in an open way, it will catalyse that in them also. But nothing need be said. You just keep on being ordinary and real and on a level, that is the key. Chaos wafts through the room, or even through the Zoom.

So if you have only encountered what I am saying here on the page, go and look up Chaos_Shamanism on YouTube and you may get a sense of what I'm getting at. And then you'll probably hear me talking as you read, which people have commented about my book *The Medicine Wheel.*

It can be difficult to write or talk about this area, because it can be like making claims for yourself. And if I start to do that, I always get a feeling that stops me. And I haven't had that feeling so far. I think it's because I am saying that anyone can do this, most of us probably do it at times. All I've been doing is adding a bit to the explanation of it, and saying how it happens. It doesn't make you 'special', rather it is part of being a full human being.

People are going to put you on a bit of a pedestal anyway as a teacher — it's their own as-yet-unlived potential that they are projecting onto you. It's often a necessary phase. I've been there myself, for years, though I might have found it hard to admit to at the time. A limited teacher will enjoy that projection, will feed off it, rather than kindly hand it back. And that takes the pupils in the wrong direction, they lose their power. So that is why I am careful not to make any claims about myself.

The Air element is also the teacher, so my Spirit-wander has kept me on message. I wrote about the Fire element as teacher, in the sense of bringing inspiration and meaning. But Air is associated with age, it brings the human wisdom, perspective. It is therefore also the teacher. Having both is necessary to be a good teacher. There are plenty of teachers who have the Fire, and they do have something to offer. But they haven't been round the Wheel enough, and they end up with messy cults around them.

To paraphrase what my friend said when she watched me on video, when I look down I am being Air, searching for my own knowing; when I look up, I am being Fire, listening to the Spirits.

Traditional cultures understand age better than we do. We mainly see age as a time of decline, it is when you 'retire'. An indigenous guy in his sixties once told me that back home, he was not an elder. The elders were the guys in their eighties, they had some real wisdom. I started to understand this in my early sixties, when I returned to teaching after a 15-year gap, and realised that I knew what I was talking about in a way I hadn't previously. Or at least, I had BEGUN to know what I was talking about! It's like I can feel what I am saying in my body, in my bones even. I got to this point because I was prepared to listen to the Spirit in my mid-40s and stop teaching. Many people cannot do that, because they are busy using teaching to build an identity for themselves, and they get stuck in that.

Ageing can be the opposite of the gentle decline that the culture often suggests. Forty years of adult life ideally opens us up and makes us a more adequate vehicle for the Spirit. Life becomes more abundant, and the transformations become deeper. That has been my personal experience. In this way the North, the Elder, is the fullness of life.

We are on the Perspective that Air gives. Air has the ability to move, you find it right up high, and you find it right down low by the ground, in the nitty-gritty of things, where it can analyse and discern, because it stands back. It's got that detailed vision which in a way is more a Water quality, the opposite and balancing direction: Water is the feeling of the South, the 'close-to' place, and pulls us back to the here and now, it brings us close to ourselves. But not necessarily with objectivity — we may mistake how we feel about something for reality. It's the combination of Air and Water that gives the detailed, objective awareness.

The North/Air is known as the 'Knowing Place'. In calling it 'Perspective', I am drawing out the particular ability that leads to the North type of knowing, which is standing back and disidentifying. But as I say, it can't do that without the Water.

The North needs the South, it is an axis. Air gives us the ability to stand back and look, but Water gives the grounding in human reality, so that we're not just spouting off big ideas.

The reason Air is in the North is because it takes until old age to master it. In a way it's the most difficult element of all. On one level it's simple, it's something we learn in childhood. We go to school, we learn our numbers, we learn to read, we learn to use the mind; we might become very mentally quick at a young age. The mind might be really well-developed. But perspective, that's something else, that's the deeper quality of the mind, and that takes people all their lives, if they're lucky. It can be a curse to be smart in our culture, because it gets you places, and you can build an identity based around being smarter than other people, that lasts the whole of your life. And then maybe in old age you realise what you've been doing, and how shallow that is.

There is also the complex work around beliefs that we come to with Air. It is well-known that we believe things not because they are true, but because we want to believe them. This work is also part of the Emotional Awakening of the South.

There's an old saying that *"a man convinced against his will is of the same opinion still."* It's an established research finding, that people make their decisions on an emotional basis, and that their views and beliefs also come from an emotional basis, which is the South, or Water. (See *The Righteous Mind* by Jonathan Haidt.)

The Air element, the Wind element. Perspective. That difficulty we have in seeing straight, so long as we continue to believe simply what we want to believe. Arguments and debates usually consist mainly of finding reasons to support what it is that you want to believe anyway. The first step towards wisdom is seeing that you're doing this, allowing inconvenient facts into your life. Are you able to do that?

Jonathan Haidt has given a TED talk called "The moral roots of liberals and conservatives". He points out what it is that people on the Left and Right each value politically. They each have things that need to be valued. Put simply, the Left prioritises fairness and compassion. And of course we need to value that. The Right has more of an emphasis on order and stability, the idea being that it's hard-won and easily lost. And of course we need to value that as well. We all value both of these things, but in different proportions.

However, are we able to see the viewpoint of the people who don't prioritise these values the same way as we do? By and large no, we just write them off, we even demonise them. So that's one maybe inconvenient fact. People don't realise when they're writing off people who vote differently to them, that they're actually writing off half the country. What kind of Elder does that to his people, writes off half of them because they have a different view on things? The whole point of an Elder, which is Air, the North, old age, is that you can unite, you can bring different sides together. You see what they each value. That is the place of wisdom. It's very easy to state, but very difficult to do. We tend automatically to vote just with one side and not the other. And that suggests that you have an emotional bias within you. Now you might always vote one particular way without thinking that the opposition are just morons, and that's fair enough. We each genuinely have different views and values. There is no right way here.

In a way it's natural to humanity to do that, I'm not railing against it. Jonathan Haidt makes an original comment on this: he says that the increased polarisation we've seen in recent decades is actually a return to normality. We had a long postwar consensus in the West, in which the left and right were able to work together a bit more than usual. This was because we had an enemy in the Soviet Bloc, and we'd had the Second World War, and bloody hell we'd better work together, we don't want that again. And then Communism collapsed in Russia, WWII was receding into the past, and you got this increased polarisation from the 1990s onwards. It's just what humans are like, we polarise, and we believe that what we think is reality. In America, the divide is even more extreme than in the UK.

The task of Air lies in seeing that it's not reality. It takes integrity and it takes humility to allow in the inconvenient facts. In this case, that people who vote differently to you invariably have a genuine value in how they see things.

We think simplistically, we don't like complexity and nuance, because then we don't know who we are, and it doesn't give us a side to join in the collective, that will support our view and therefore that sense of who we are. We are half-people, not whole people, and we side with others who are half-people in the way that we are. The Elder is a whole person — the balanced person that the lifetime journey around the Wheel can engender.

My observation is that all views that are collectively held are at best simplified to the point of falsehood. Life is always complex, and any view we have about anything needs to take that complexity into account. But we don't do this. Take Covid. We were being told by governments to "follow the science". But science is complex, it is always a multitude of views. It is the same with climate and CO2: there are many scientific opinions. (For the record, I am doubtful that CO2 plays a major part in global warming. At 1 part in 2500 of the atmosphere, I find it hard to believe, based on what seems to me to be common sense.) But government grabs the single view that suits them, and throws the authority of science behind it, and we just accept it. Or we go in the opposite direction and say it's all some kind of conspiracy to control us. That is a simplistic view too, that similarly does not require proper facts.

I'm NOT saying those collective views about Covid and climate are wrong. But they are definitely more complex, and less certain, than we are led to believe. Few of us know the science, we just trust in the authority. We don't care what it is we are being asked to believe, as long as it is simple and certain and most people around us believe the same. It really is like that.

The Air element at best understands the complexity. And that is because the Elder doesn't just believe what suits him or her emotionally to believe. That emotional preference will still be there, because Elders are not on some sort of higher plane where they don't have ordinary human feelings. But they have the integrity to be aware of it and not just go along with it, not just take the easy, unconscious option, which is what collective humanity does all the time without knowing it.

This brings us into the South, into Water, into Feeling. Air plays a central role in the Emotional Awakening which is a keyword of the South. Of knowing what it is you are feeling, and having a choice whether or not to act or speak from it. It is precisely the Air keyword of Perspective that allows us to do this.

There's an axis on the Wheel between Air and Water, mind and feeling. They need to work together along that axis. It's called the Good Red Road. It's the place we can actually work. The other axis, the Blue Road, is about being receptive to the fire of Spirit in the East, as it flows into the Body in the West. It is the axis of Fate, just as the other axis is that of Free Will. We're born, we die, we are part of a family, we have interests and inspirations: they are all beyond our control, they are Fate, they are what our life is. The North-South is then what we do with it, the choices we can make about who we're going to be and what we are going to do. We're always making these choices: are we going to stand tall, or are we going to let the dementors, those creatures from the Harry Potter novels, have the better of us?

Just one more bottle of wine and that will soothe me. Whatever it is that our addiction is. People can get addicted to all sorts of things — computer games, sex, drugs, food, relationships. They anaesthetise us, they keep us away from being close to ourselves. Addictions apart, are we going to languish, take the easy route of staying the same, because then we won't have to experience the anxieties and self-doubts and discomfort of doing something new? Is it easier just to pretend we are what others around us want us to be?

Air gives us the ability to see that we have choices, within the closeness to ourselves that the South brings. We come close to ourselves by bringing awareness into the body, and so into what we're feeling. We can always know what we're feeling; it might just be numbness, but if you stay there it will gradually open up into something more complex and more descriptive of how it is you want to be and behave, because our behaviour is feeling driven.

The central ability of Air, its disinterestedness and perspective, begins not so much 'out there' in how we think about the world, but within, with the willingness to see our own self-interest, our own emotional biases, and act, or not, on that awareness. And also what it is that gives us joy, and have the courage to act on that too.

It's a crucial awakening when you realise you don't have to act on a feeling or be dominated by it. It gives you self-mastery, it gives you self-possession, ownership of yourself, instead of being a bit of flotsam tossed around by the various currents within yourself and in the collective around you.

I had an experience of this a while ago when I was walking along the top of a beautiful valley. A feeling of loneliness took me over, and the reflex response was, oh I need a relationship, I need someone to be with, so I'm not lonely, I have to have that. And then I realised this feeling of loneliness that had taken me over was just a temporary feeling, it's not who I am. It is part of me that needs owning, acknowledging, but I also need to stand back. This is detachment or disidentification, which isn't about not owning our feelings, though it can sound like that. It's more that there's a part of us, which we maybe don't use very often, that is able to look in on them without being determined by them. And when I realised that this is just a feeling, I started to realise that actually I'm connected to everything. Once I stood back in that way, something bigger was able to come in; it wasn't just an intellectual understanding, it was far more than that, and my detachment had given it the space to arise.

It made me realise that loneliness is a medicine that pushes us towards an experience of connectedness to everything, that the universe loves us, and what a beautiful place it is. Relationships can be just a sticking plaster, a false comfort, another anaesthetic, though not necessarily so: they are the opposite if both people are really honest.

So whatever you're feeling, you don't have to be determined by it, you have that choice. There is your freedom, claim it. That is the gift of Air, of the Breeze.

I want to say a bit about symbolism, because there is so much symbolism in the Medicine Wheel, and you can get lost in it. You can get lost in lists, you can get muddled about what belongs where. And there are different Wheels with different systems. With Chaos we're standing a bit to one side of that, while drawing on them and being inspired by them.

The essential thing about symbolism is to remain close to it, to see why it's there, not just list it off and go, "Here's the North, it's air, it's old age, it's winter, it's the bison, it's all these things." It becomes a list, and then we move away from experience into the mind. The mind of course has its own positive function in being able to do that. But we need to stay close to the experience, because that's where we transform, that's where we're living, that's where we're truly alive.

We are using a particular Medicine Wheel for the sake of simplicity, but this is Chaos Shamanism, so we can draw from any of them, if we feel called that way. I hope the approach I am taking to the symbolism of this Wheel shows how to approach the symbolism in any of the Wheels. The beauty of Chaos Shamanism is that we can do this with anything, taking advantage of the times we are in, when for the first time in history we have access to all the world's traditions.

With the symbolism, you need to have not just an understanding, but a feeling for why it's there. So I'm just going to go briefly around the Wheel, looking at a few of the basic correlations.

Fire. That is the sun, it's obviously our main experience of Fire. So stay close to your experience of the sun. It rises in the East and begins the day. That is why the East is Fire, and why it's also birth – because the East is about beginnings. You can see how all these things tie together. The East is also Spring, because that's the beginning of the year, when new life bursts up. The East is also yellow, the colour of the Sun. There is all this in human life, around the experience of the Sun rising in that particular place every day. And let's chuck in an animal for good measure. I'm going to do culture specific ones, but obviously these can be changed. The Eagle lives in the East. He flies high, far higher than the mountains of the North. The Eagle has Spirit Vision, outside of time and space. He may give you dreams that map out your future. He may give you glimpses of what's coming: but remember it is outside time, it may be many years off. He will show you who you are at your deepest, who it is that Spirit wants you to become. The sun is too intense in its fire to be looked at directly, and it is often the same with the spirit vision.

Then we move to the South. If you live in the Northern Hemisphere, the Sun at midday is in that direction. That's why you want a south-facing garden in summer. It's when you get the fullness of life, which is also the child, because the child just plays. The child is full of life in a way that we often forget as adults. So childhood and summer. Water is in the South, because Water is feeling: the child is full of feeling, children just do what they want. They're very quick to feel, and then it all goes and they move on to the next feeling. They don't hang on like adults do. They live from feeling, and that is very much the way of Water; it's kind of contained but it moves and it has currents and it changes. You could say children are like a fast-flowing stream of water, ever-changing and jumping and sparkling. So hang out by a stream for that experience of effervescent childhood.

Here is a quote from AA Milne, *The House at Pooh Corner,* likening this childlike quality to little streams in the forest:

> *By the time it came to the edge of the Forest, the stream had grown up, so that it was almost a river, and, being grown-up, it did not run and jump and sparkle along as it used to do when it was younger, but moved more slowly. For it knew now where it was going, and it said to itself, "There is no hurry. We shall get there some day." But all the little streams higher up in the Forest went this way and that, quickly, eagerly, having so much to find out before it was too late.*

Also, stand in the rain sometimes, savour it, don't just write it off as bad weather! In summer, you can dance in it.

The South is red, because it is feeling, the heart. The Mouse lives in the South. He is the opposite of the Eagle: he sees things from very close-up. He helps us pay attention to the minutiae and subtlety of our feelings, that warm pulsing of life as it flows through us. The Coyote also lives in the South, the trickster. That is a big theme. But let us say it is sometimes necessary for things not to go to plan, to jolt us out of our comfort zone, our emotional habits, our limited ways of being in the world.

And the West. Soil as our experience of the Earth. This is the adult, because we have to engage with solid material reality, we can't just dance above it and do what we want. We meet the limitations of that physical reality, and have to make life work. The earth will take care of us, but we have to play our part in that. There is also the journey of the sun across the sky to the West, where it sinks below the horizon, and goes deep within the earth. That is the incarnating of the West, as Spirit intermingles with matter. West is for the same reason autumn in the larger cycle of the seasons, when life starts to die back and go inward. It is also therefore known as the 'Looks-within' place. It is what busy adults find difficult!

The West is also the shadow, all those things we don't want to know about ourselves that are often projected onto others. The South is also where we encounter the shadow, but in the West we incarnate it, we learn to use that energy instead of having it buried away. The West is black, because of its sunset, looks-within quality. The Bear lives in the West. Just as the Sun goes below the Earth in the West, so does the Bear hibernate and dream. He is the dream, the vision of the East as it flows through the body in sleep. The Bear gives the chance to regroup after the often headlong rush of adulthood. And to go within and redream our life. Because he eats honey, he is also the sweetness of life. Humans are often very problem focussed – the news certainly is! – and the Bear reminds us that life is also to be savoured and relished while we have it.

And then we come to the North which is also Air, the Wind, the Breeze. If you live in the northern hemisphere, that's where it's cold, that's where it's winter. That's where life has receded and apparently died. Life is a cycle, and cycles within cycles, as the Medicine Wheel understands so deeply. When you get old, life begins to recede. You start to withdraw from the compulsion to be in the thick of ordinary life. But that doesn't mean your life isn't still abundant within, maybe more so than ever. You can see how that withdrawing leads to the Perspective of the North. And how it comes out of Air as well, because of that ability to move and see from multiple viewpoints. The North is white, for the snows of winter. You get the Bison in the North in some of the Native American Wheels. The Bison endures the freezing winter and the blizzards. In the same way, humans learn to bear the difficulties of life, we become more equanimous as we age, we stop whining! And we make our peace with death. The Bison gives everything of himself, there is no part of him that is not used after being hunted. In the same way, the elder is at the service of the community, he is done with his own personal ambitions.

With the animals, other ones may come to you for particular directions. Trust that, and don't worry too much about finding reasons. Let them come in time. This is a Spirit process, not a rational one.

So there is some of the symbolism. Always ask why, and feel that closeness between e.g. north and the winter and old age and air and white, and how all these things connect. Just take them one at a time, because once it's complex, you're in your head and you lose that felt connection, and then you don't transform, you don't come into the centre of yourself, which is the purpose of the Wheel. It becomes just information. Information is the necessary starting point for something we can carry into our hearts and into experience. We generally need to keep it one bit at a time and feel it.

In some ways even the basic Medicine Wheel is pushing it, it's got four bits to it! But the unconscious can deal with that once you have been living it; it becomes a powerful symbol that can carry the dream of our life. I have eight points on my Wheel, and I still have to think about the intermediate directions. But I have had the Wheel for many years, it is in my garden, and my unconscious feels more than happy with all those points. But I have reached the level of complexity that I feel comfortable with. It is a rich and colourful weave. I reckon I could probably get the 20-count as second nature also if I tried, but I doubt I will.

So that is a bit about symbolism. It is appropriate for the North, for Air, because we're considering an idea here. And the Chaos perspective tells us to nevertheless remain close to experience. We're not the theologian who knows the Bible backwards and can out-argue anyone because of his knowledge. If we were a vicar, a Chaos Vicar, we'd probably know a few bits of the Bible that were particularly poetic, that spoke to us. We could take that piece of poetry and we would just spontaneously speak at length from it, because the feelings and the imagination are engaged. Chaos keeps you in the simple, feeling place, that is also the place of the imagination. Chaos is, in a way, a simple idea, but it's also a deep idea.

One more point about symbolism, as we saw in the third chapter, is to remember that the stone in the North of your Wheel doesn't just STAND FOR Air, or STAND FOR the North. It IS those things. We therefore treat the stones as special, as sacred. They have a power. People often feel the power when they encounter my Wheel, because I have had it so long. It lives as much in my imagination as in material reality, and that adds to its power. Shamanism is our modern attempt to reclaim the indigenous soul: feeling that symbols actually ARE the thing they symbolise, is an indigenous way that may be hard for us to grasp, because we have a long history of separating spirit and matter, mind and body. It is a false dichotomy.

Storytelling belongs in the North. Everything is story. Science tries to tell us that there is a separate category called 'fact'. But what is science other than a series of useful modellings of reality? Beneath the story lies the Great Mystery. The North is the accumulation of the other directions. A good storyteller is inspired (East), emotionally engages his audience (South), is connected viscerally to the story (West), and is eloquent, can dance with words (North). This is why stories are integral to teaching in a traditional culture. They contain all the wisdom, in a form that is playful and engaging.

Myths are a grander form of story, that play a central part in telling a people who they are, much as the story of Jesus and the Crucifixion used to for Western culture. The Medicine Wheel has the quality of a mythology. It is a visual story in which all aspects of existence can be found. At its centre is Chaos, the Great Mystery. Each form of the Wheel has its own integrity, but the fact that there are many makes it harder to turn any of them into the absolute truth.

It is always good to have more than one story. Air understands this. I support those American schools that teach both Evolution and Intelligent Design. I don't necessarily agree with either, but that isn't the point. (If there is design, it's not God; if there is Evolution, it is not brute survival.) The point is that the children are being taught that there is more than one way of seeing the world, and that is healthy.

17

Chaos in Love

I thought I'd say something about Chaos and relationships. In theory it should go in the West of the Medicine Wheel, but I just suddenly thought this is all getting too schematic, this is supposed to be about Chaos. Sure, I can find a neat place for everything, and that can be one way of doing things. But sometimes you just have to bust out of that, and this is one of those times.

I'm not putting it anywhere on the Wheel for now. I'm just going to write about it as a thing in itself. I'm going to open with a little story from Lewis Mehl-Madrona, the Cherokee-Lakota guy that I've mentioned before. He has written a number of books. His first one is called *Coyote Medicine,* which is well worth reading. He's both a conventional doctor and a traditional healer, and much of the book is his own story of how he got there. At this point in the story, he has an ex-wife and children. They had first got together when very young, and had drifted into getting married and having children. He knew at the time that they were not well-suited.

It didn't work out, and here he is in his mid-30s, going to see an old Navajo guy who's his teacher. Lewis says to him that his life's going well, but he's missing having his other half, he hasn't got a girlfriend, what can he do about that? The old guy says, Lewis, you've learned lots of things, you've got wisdom in many ways, but there's one way in which you may always remain stupid, which is that you believe in love. You've been watching too much Hollywood.

That struck me as a very interesting and different perspective. As a culture we do indeed believe in romantic love, and we kind of get stuck to someone else. It's like two bits of sticky paper, which isn't very appealing! We end up dependent, and we end up devastated if they're not in our lives. Of course, if someone important leaves our life, we grieve, but it's more than that: we can lose our basic psychological stability, we lose our sense of who we are, because who we are gets so tied up with that other person.

Now in a way that's also natural. But Chaos Shamanism isn't about getting stuck to someone else, because then we lose sight of the Chaos, that underlying flow of existence, that underlying nourishing flow of life, of energy, from which we draw our own independent life. We're always coming back to that. And so we've got to be careful with relationships that we don't get lost in this way, even though we all seem to do so at some point or another.

I referred in the chapter on the Sun to Kierkegaard, who broke off his engagement and became a philosopher, at the injunction of the Daimon, of the Spirits. The creative force possesses us, it's not ours to possess, and we have to live by its lights. If that sort of demand is made on you, then you need the whole of yourself present; you don't need a big bit of you leaking off somewhere else. So the Spirits may be saying we're going to have you single, and you can go to all the dating sites you like, but nothing's going to work, you're just going to be wasting energy and wasting time, and not getting on with what you need to be doing.

Coming back to Lewis' teacher, his advice was to just get on with his life — his career and looking after his kids — and when the Spirit wanted to send someone his way, if indeed it did, then so be it. It's no good sitting there in a state of lack, of wanting, "I need someone, I need another half." That's why it's called the other half, it's like we no longer stand upright.

There's a big teaching here, in that to function from Chaos, we need to own ourselves, to stand tall. This is the practice of celibacy: of not living in a state of lack. You are not glass half-empty, you are not even glass half-full, as people declare themselves to be on the dating sites: you are glass full, you do not feel anything to be missing.

If you are in relationship, you need to come at it from this point of view, of two people standing tall, delighting in each other. It should be delight, and yet they're the cause of so much misery, aren't they?

That brings me to the next point, which is when it goes wrong. What often happens is that a relationship is an unconscious deal: you think you're getting together because of this, that, and the other, all the wonderful qualities that the other person may seem to have. But actually what we do when we start getting together with someone, is that we edit ourselves, consciously or unconsciously, to please them, to become what we think they want us to be, so that they'll have us. By the same token, we are unconsciously moulding the other by the force of our own needs. Once both people have edited themselves sufficiently, it's like you then fit together, and that's falling in love. The experience can be of finding one's 'soul mate', of feeling complete. There's a compelling joy in that, but it is hugely dependent on the presence of the other person. All this might sound bizarre, but it is normal behaviour, it is the love that Hollywood makes films about. It is a modern thing, it is not an indigenous perspective, and that is why I am coming after it!

A lot of people will spend their entire adult lives in this half-person state, with a spouse who may also have to carry the weight of too many of our social needs, now that we no longer live in close communities. (That can also be a blessing: would you rather live anonymously in a city, or in a village where everyone knows everything about you?)

For many people, this arrangement is fine. There is no great drive in them to become whole, and the only change you might see is a bit of broadening and mellowing as they get older.

But for others, there is quite a different trajectory to be lived. Maybe 10 or 15 years down the line, three kids and a mortgage later, in one of you the Spirit starts to move. You start to want to live aspects of yourself that you've been letting the other person carry. It is a natural and spontaneous thing. You start wanting to be more conscious, to be more honest with yourself about who you are. The other half isn't necessarily going to like that, because it threatens the reality you've jointly built up, about who each of you is. That's why when one person starts to wake up, the other person can start to think they've gone mad. (Have you noticed how all exes are said to be either nuts or narcissists?) The film *American Beauty* is a good example of this, where Kevin Spacey starts to wake up. He starts to do what he wants, instead of what he ought to do. He gives up his well-paid job and works in McDonald's, starts smoking weed and becomes smitten with a teenage girl. He is no longer caught up in the American dream as he was, and his wife and her new boyfriend think he's gone mad, because for them that dream is simply reality. But you can see that actually they are really the crazy ones, because of the way they still believe in it.

This can be a very difficult place to be in, because you're on your own, you're stepping out of collective realities, you're having to remake your life in fundamental ways, and you may not even be sure you are doing the right thing.

Maybe, just maybe, both spouses begin to wake up and be more honest with themselves and with each other. I don't personally know of any cases, but I'm sure there are, and that could be wonderful. It probably wouldn't be easy, in fact it may be harder than before, because you are no longer avoiding the difficult areas. This is how a relationship needs to be, to work in this more conscious sense, where neither of you are carrying something for the other person, that they need to be living for themselves.

If you're really living from the Chaos, if the Spirits have claimed you, then you can no longer be available in the conventional way. You are 'spoken for', the emotional centre of your life is no longer the spouse. This transition can easily be another major life-crisis, a version of the Shamanic Illness.

Sometimes you get the suspicion that it was all a set-up by the Spirits in the first place. I reckon we don't get involved with someone, even if just for a short while, except with the say-so of the Spirits and their agenda. That short involvement will usually show us something about ourselves, if we want to look. Or they may give you the big relationship that serves you in many ways for 15 years, and then leads you into exactly the crisis you need to be in to become more whole, to become a more adequate vehicle for the Spirits.

You look back, and you realise there was something not quite right all along, something in you that was saying no, that you thought you could overlook, that you didn't think was important enough to listen to, or that somehow it would all work out. And now it's come back and bitten you in the arse and won't let go, and you realise it was the voice of your soul. One thing is for sure: once you are out of this, you will never not listen again, or not for long.

Sometimes we need to be burnt deeply before we are prepared to pay attention. You'll feel that your life, your soul, is at stake. You may not know who you are any more, but you know you can't be as you were, and as your spouse probably still needs you to be.

It is time to become independent. It is time to stop looking to the other person to take care of you in ways you can for yourself. It is usually parental stuff: the partner is the mother-figure who gives solace and security to what feels like the little child within; or the father-figure who provides economic and practical protection in the face of a threatening world. This sort of thing is usually quite unconscious, because it can feel humiliating, and it is certainly not sexy to talk about.

As usual with the Spirits, faith is needed. Faith that if we have the courage to answer their calling, life will work out. Faith that if we are single, that it is for a good reason. It may continue for the rest of our life.

If you have a reservation about a potential partner, don't go there. Spirit is speaking through the reservation. You would be settling for second best, and denying Spirit the chance to send you the right person. Who that might be is a mystery, for attraction is a mysterious thing. And don't get involved with someone in the hope of changing them, or for their 'potential'. That always ends in tears, because people don't change according to the way you want them to. You need to take people as they are, and if that doesn't work for you, don't go there.

Above all, we need to be adequate vehicles for Spirit. That is the main thing, rather than whether or not you are with someone. If honesty is possible with another person, then that will delight the Spirits, because it will help, rather than hinder, their work.

What about sex? I have just one point to make, which is that I don't think sex constitutes intimacy in the ordinary sense, because you are not present to yourself in the ordinary sense. It can certainly FEEL intimate, but that doesn't mean it is so. Couples can have 'great sex' who are poles apart in everyday life. The Chaos perspective is that during sex, you are actively surrendering to the Spirits. There IS an intimacy, but it is the intimacy of your Spirits meeting the other person's and dancing. You abandon yourself to what is happening. It is spontaneous, it is joyful, and could be likened to Ceremony.

18

Erotic Madness

In the last chapter I talked about falling in love as the process of two people editing themselves to become what the other person unconsciously needs them to be. To believe in this type of love, about which the old Navajo was so scornful, is to believe that marrying the person who is the object of this love, is the path to happiness and meaning in your life.

If we don't believe in it in this sense, then what do we do with it? The way I see it is that falling in love is an initiation into the Otherworld, into the Daimon, into Beauty, into the Goddess or the Dakinis, those naked inspirational Skywalkers of the Buddhist tradition.

There's the well-known story of Dante and Beatrice. Dante composed *The Divine Comedy* in the 14th century in Italy. He fell in love with a young girl called Beatrice. He only met her twice – once when she was nine, and once when she was 18, and was powerfully affected on both occasions. He was a year older than her. The Italians are probably more prone to this sort of thing than the stiff English!

What Dante then did was never to make contact with Beatrice. He knew that would be fatal. He cherished his feeling in all its initiatory power. It is perhaps the most emblematic instance of the tradition of courtly love, where the love for a woman elevates the soul and brings one closer to God. In *The Divine Comedy* itself, it is Beatrice who is his guide in Paradise, after he has traversed Hell and Purgatory. She is not just his guide, but a symbol of the divine love that leads Dante to the ultimate truth and salvation.

There is a tradition that we have forgotten: courtly love. It requires a lot of self-discipline, because the longing to actualise, to possess the woman is so compelling. But that is when it becomes fixed, and no longer a journey.

I can't speak for women, I don't know what it is like for you, but I'm sure you can draw something out of what I'm saying. I imagine it is a god rather than a goddess that possesses, that initiates the woman. The medieval tradition is mainly about men, but you get some women troubadours such as Marie de France who wrote poetry expressing their love.

Falling in love is an initiation, particularly the first time it happens, because it brings a new type of consciousness into experience, even a new centre around which we can rearrange who we are, as all true initiations do. It is normally catalysed by a woman, one who 'does it' for you. If it happens to you when you're young, then you'll almost inevitably believe that your powerful experiences of love and beauty and inspiration and soul connection and meaning are attributes of that woman, and you will want to possess her and adore her and even marry her. You think – if you are capable of thinking in such a state – that this experience will endure throughout your long married life with her. What you are doing is putting your happiness in the hands of another person, and that cannot be right. Dante was quite exceptional, aged 19, in dealing with it the way he did. He details it in his first major work, *La Vita Nueva*. But even aged nine, something about her gripped him.

Being in love becomes a form of madness if you literalise it, even though that is the 'normal' thing to do. An archetype cannot be owned. I think this is also what can be happening with people who think they are in the wrong body. They are having a powerful experience of the other gender. It is a soul thing, it is a journey to be undertaken. There is no such thing as being born in the wrong body.

What is needed when love possesses you is help rather than encouragement. It can be seen as a divine madness. What you arguably also need is an arranged marriage, that takes more practical considerations into account. I'm being deliberately a bit provocative here to make a point, which is that Love should not conquer all. Dante had a wife and children, and meanwhile another woman possessed his soul. But not a literal woman, though nonetheless real for that. He was possessed by the inner woman, as creative men can be. His marriage was probably all the better for not confusing his earthly wife with the inner lady. It would have been too much to put on her! It doesn't do men or women any good to be idealised by their spouses. Genuine appreciation is another matter.

Plato sees what he calls this erotic madness not as a pathological condition, but as a divine gift that can lead the soul towards truth and higher understanding.

It's usually catalysed by another person, and is an initiation into something deeper, into the spirit, into your soul. Maybe falling in love in this way can only ever happen once in your life. Nothing is ever as powerful as that initial possession, which you will remember for the rest of your days.

It happened to me when I was 20. I fell in love with a woman, it completely possessed me, and I was distraught when nothing came of it. The experience is still with me, and she still carries something of that special, numinous quality for me. I was freshly out of a period in which I had regularly taken magic mushrooms in high doses over a period of months, and that had opened me up in a deep way and given me a metaphysical quest. Then came the erotic madness, another deep initiation. The first initiation probably laid the ground for the second. It was a lot to absorb, particularly outside of any traditional context that could have provided guidance. I probably appeared unhinged to a lot of people. But it was a spirit of creativity emerging in me.

It's a wonderful thing if it happens to you and you are able, to some degree at least, to haul the projection off an actual woman. There's a short book called *Lying with the Heavenly*

Woman by Robert Johnson. He was a Jungian analyst. What I like about him is that he writes simply and straight from his own extensive experience. There is none of the intellectualism that you so often get with Jungians. (Jung himself refused to set foot in the Jung Institute that his pupils set up, he wanted none of it.) The book is about the main female archetypes a man can have in his psyche and in his life: mother, sister, anima, wife, daughter, Sophia, hetaira, and friend. I think mother-in-law could have done with a mention, because she is a powerful and humorous figure in popular culture. It is the anima we are particularly encountering in the erotic madness.

Johnson opens his discussion of the anima thus:

> *The anima is, indeed, the world of magic and mysticism. She, who has so much to do with a man's happiness and sense of worth, is almost total mystery. She delights and puzzles and pains a man, and he has so little comprehension of this magic interior world!*

In Chapter 13, on the Sun, I mentioned how Robert Johnson was required by his Daimon, like the philosopher Kierkegaard, never to marry. This injunction was presented to him by Jung himself, when Johnson as young man was having analysis with Emma, Jung's wife. He brought a dream to her, and she recognised it as a big, visionary dream that required interpretation by her husband. Jung laid out the future course of Johnson's life from this dream, just like an Elder reading the vision of a young man just back off a Vision Quest. It included the injunctions never to join anything, and never to marry. And this was how Johnson subsequently lived. If he tried to join anything, it never worked out.

So he was on that path of solitude. Maybe he had affairs, I don't know. Affairs can kind of stimulate the anima in you, and also show you how you can lose her. But fundamentally you are holding within that part which would fall in love and idealise a partner. Instead of attributing it to someone, you are being guided by it, you are being nourished by it. She is not you in the ordinary sense. She is your soul, which is much bigger, and which you can never possess, but only serve.

Falling in love, the erotic madness, is a very important experience if you can haul the projection off the other person. That's almost impossible to do when you're young, unless you are Dante. I reckon it's easier when you're older, because it's not so all-or-nothing; you can stand back and look at yourself and go, what the hell am I doing? It's not usually so consuming. But you can still make what feels like a complete fool of yourself at mid-life, if that is when the anima wakes up.

Once you've brought some self-awareness to it, once you've got a bit of a handle on yourself, then certain women can be muses for you, maybe all women – maybe you love all women in that kind of way. It is real, but it is also a dance, a game. And maybe there are certain women who really make your heart sing; there is a powerful, wholehearted response to them which takes you over. But you don't literalise it, you may make no romantic move towards them. You just sit with the inspiration they catalyse in you, and you love them for it. But they may know little or nothing about it. Like Beatrice. Meanwhile, music or poetry or books on Chaos Shamanism, or whatever it is that you do, body forth from your imagination.

It is important to distinguish the earthly woman from the sense of the divine that she may provoke in you. The Muse woman will, in my experience, have a genuinely inspirational thread running through her; but that is hers, it is not yours to appropriate through a romantic connection. It is to be observed and appreciated. She may end up as your partner, but on a different basis to the usual romantic one. And the deeper for it.

We are talking the Lover archetype. This is what a man is, in a way, always looking to give birth to in himself. It stops the other three male archetypes — Warrior, King, and Magician — manifesting in their shadow forms.

My Muse — to call her that for now — first came to me in dreams, starting in my late 50s. It was a recurrent dream about a woman I had forgotten about, and there was a sense of urgency to go and meet her. After several years of this, she descended into me after a weekend in which I had been in two Sweatlodges, and thoroughly melted and opened up. It was soon after that I began teaching Shamanism again, after a 15-year gap. And then writing my first books: six in four years. I feel that on a conventional romantic level, I am 'spoken for', and that she is not going to let a physical woman come between us. She has been an initiation into another level of the feminine, coming 40 years after the first initiation when I was 20. Robert Johnson describes her as the Sophia archetype, whose wisdom is earthy.

If we're Chaos Shamans, we're free. We allow whatever is happening in the psyche to be lived, we don't let ourselves be constrained by convention. Conventionally, if you fall in love, then you try to hook up with that person, maybe even get married, and it can be very distressing if it doesn't work out, or if your obsession is not reciprocated. No, you're free, you can do what you want, you can hold it within yourself, you can make it part of who you are. So own that Muse, live from that Muse. That's what falling in love is really about. It's about finding the Muse.

If it happens to you when you're 20, and if you're unlucky enough that the other person reciprocates, you might end up getting married and spending the next 20 years with them. It might be wonderful to start with, an orgy of sincere mutual flattery. But then it stops being so wonderful as the earthly reality of the other person impresses itself upon you. You are left wondering, what that was all about? This person is really quite ordinary, what happened, where was I all this time? You were abducted by the anima, and you forgot yourself! Maybe you then realise it was something in you after all, and you start to integrate that. Or maybe you just start looking for someone else to get deluded about in the same way. Maybe you do that several more times before you start really questioning why none of your relationships seem to last. Maybe you go to see a therapist who tries to get you to sort out your relationship with your mother, because there must be something wrong with you. And then maybe you start to think no, there's nothing wrong with me, it's the model of romantic relationships that is wrong, or at least limited.

All this can be fair enough; it can be a long, messy journey to the anima, the Muse, the Daimon. The Otherworld celebrates when we wake up, it has our back, it is always urging us on. Maybe you'll have a sense, like me, of the fairies in the garden dancing round the tree and singing.

It's a gift when the anima visits and overpowers us. We can turn that gift into a curse when we think it's really about that other person, and we find they don't want us, and then we want to kill ourselves because we've lost our soul. That's how it can seem. There's this dreadful suffering because we've literalised the Muse, we've tried to bring the Muse down to earth, and you must never do that, you must let her come and go as she wants. She visits in her own time.

That's how I did the videos that this book has come out of. I let them come as they wanted, I always just did what I felt like speaking about. The Muse speaks through what it is that you feel moved to do, that which seizes hold of you. I took a bit of a risk doing the video for this chapter, because it was the end of the day and I didn't feel on top form; I didn't have all the energy I have in the morning. I thought I'll give it a go and see what happens and it worked out OK. I'd been wanting to do something on falling in love as initiation for some time, and it all came bursting out.

I have to do my videos and my writing in this spontaneous way. There is no masterplan, true to the spirit of Chaos Shamanism. Otherwise, the Muse cannot speak, for it is she that must decide what I speak or write about. And indeed, how I live. She often appears through whatever idea is live in my head while I am lying in bed in the morning.

So keep it light, keep it as a dance. There may be a person in your life who does it for you, so to speak, who sparks your fire. Just go with that, trust it, and don't feel you have to take it anywhere unless it seems like the obvious thing to do.

19

Death and Old Age

With Chaos Shamanism, you can believe what you want, because beliefs are stories. Ultimately, we know nothing, all is the Great Mystery. The point is to be open and flexible, and don't nail yourself to a particular position. Beliefs are forms. It is the way we hold the forms that is important, not the forms themselves.

This is not a loose and superficial thing to do. It is demanding. It would be more accurate to say that we believe what we have to, rather than what we want, after a close examination of how it is that we see the world and existence itself. But even then, the belief is not held rigidly, because it is always understood to be limited and provisional. This is much more demanding than simply adopting in a fixed way the views of those around us, that can seem like 'common sense', which is how normal humanity works.

Chaos Shamanism demands that we remain true to ourselves, honest with ourselves, as much as we can, and of course we'll fail sometimes. It's demanding in that sense, but it's not demanding in the sense that you need to believe this or you need to believe that, or do this practice or do that ceremony, and do it the right way and not the wrong way. It's outside of all that, because it's getting to the heart of these things. It's getting to the heart of the Spirit that's in us, that is here for some kind of unfoldment, some kind of pattern to be lived, that we probably need to look back on over time to get a sense of. We get hints of it as life goes on, through what comes our way, and what we unfold into.

This attitude of openness needs to apply to the subject of Death, because we just don't know what it is. I read an account of a Shamanic people, the Ulchi, in the Far East of Russia, called *Spirits from the Edge of the World* by Jan Van Ysseltyne. It gives a long, detailed account of their beliefs about what happens after you die: how you go meet your relatives in this place and this is what you do, when you get reborn etc. I asked another native guy what his people believe happens after you die, and he goes we just don't know, we have no view. So there you go, there's two different indigenous views.

What do we make of this? I don't think any belief about the afterlife is wrong. It's like saying a creation story is wrong. Well, a modern person might say that. "These primitive people believed in the beginning there was just water, and then a turtle turned up, and so on, but now we know better. They were doing their best at the time." But it is the modern people who are ignorant in their rigidity and sense of superiority, in thinking they have THE answer, as if there is one. Modern people do not know how to think mythologically.

The more demanding Chaos answer is to say that we don't know, and to live in that uncertainty, close to the Great Mystery, trusting in it. And yet I also find myself comfortable with the Siberian mythology, for a mythology is what it is. I am happy to allow in an overlay of their story, like a gossamer blanket, I enjoy doing so. And the mythology from *The Tibetan Book of the Dead* too. I am happy to allow them all in, and let them live alongside the not-knowing at the centre, and believe them to be true. They are not just nice stories. They are all true! It can be hard for us Westerners to get our heads around this, because we are deeply conditioned to believe there can only be one, literal truth. Going on the offensive, I would say that imaginative truth is more true than literal truth, because it speaks to the whole psyche.

Of course, some indigenous people will take their afterlife mythology more literally than others, but that is human nature. The medicine people will tend to be less literal. And in any case, the story of what happens after death is part of their unifying mythology, and as such can be of great value for them.

My initial reaction to the Ulchi after-death story was that it was too much like a belief in something we cannot know. That's how it was written in the book at any rate, and of course no story about what happens after death is literally how it is. Death is the place where we go beyond all stories, because stories necessarily occur within time and space, which are not attributes of the universe, but ordering principles that we humans put onto it. But as I thought about it, I realised that if I treat it as a mythology rather than some kind of literal fact, just as I would a creation story, then it is not a problem. But that is not to patronise it. My response becomes wholehearted in a way that it never can with merely factual accounts.

We need an unknowing around our own lives, and we need an unknowing about what happens afterwards. That's difficult for most of us. It's just a matter of the degree to which you can be flexible around that, the degree to which you treat your stories as fact, and the degree to which you are able to relativise them. It is as much to do with emotional awareness as it is to do with intellectual position.

How literally do you take the Big Bang, for example, which is part of our standard creation myth? We can't help but take it literally to some extent, because it's drummed into us as what actually happened, with all sorts of equations, that none of us will ever understand, to back it up. It's got that kind of weight of authority behind it, and so we can't help but believe it, even if rationally we know it is just a story, that no one was actually there, no one took a picture of the bloody thing.

We need to keep being honest about our unknowingness. Are we actually being unknowing emotionally, or is it just an intellectual position? This is quite an interesting area, and it applies to how we think about death. If you're going to have stories about what happens after death, and why not, then I suggest have more than one. That's always a good idea, because it's harder to get literal about any of them. So you might on the one hand think well actually I really don't know, but I quite like what *The Tibetan Book of the Dead* says, I also quite like what that ancient tribe in Siberia says about meeting all your relatives.

Ultimately, all we can really do is sit in that unknowing, and that's a positive thing. Life trains us to have faith in what is coming next, even though we can't know it. We sometimes go through big changes in life, and we don't know how we're going to come out the other side. But we find if we're honest, if we're true to ourselves, it comes out in an essentially good or necessary way, and gradually we learn to let go of all those plans, and all those desires for particular outcomes. We learn to flow with where the Spirit wants to take us, and have faith in that. In that way, life is a preparation for death. If you go through a change in life, you do have some kind of idea what's coming next, unless you're going to die. You're probably still going to have two arms and two legs, you'll still be good at what you're good at, and so on. It's not a complete unknown. But death is a complete unknown. And it's as if those changes in life are training us for the endpoint of death. Death gives us something real to practise towards: to practise being in the unknowing, and having faith in that.

Life prepares us for death. We learn that life takes care of us, that it's on our side in a fundamental sense. Obviously, things will go wrong, obviously there'll be difficulties, but we need to come to feel that life's on our side. We don't necessarily feel that at the start, we might feel that life is against us, and that we've got our back up against the wall. A lot of people feel like that, and maybe terrible things did happen in childhood, maybe they are an explanation for it. Or maybe you brought those demons in anyway, who knows? Of course we need to be sympathetic to how we feel, but also have some distance, some perspective, so that we can come eventually to feel that life is with us. Sometimes these struggles are the making of us.

I had a dream some years ago in which I was looking at life from the viewpoint of death. The place I was in was like an airport, with thousands of people or beings arriving every second to travel on the moving footway. Death was just completely normal, almost banal, it was something you didn't even pay attention to because it was happening all the time. So death is just completely normal. It's more normal, if you like, to be dead than alive. This life is just a temporary dream, a bubble that bursts. I think it's really important to stay here and to do the things we're here to do. But it is ultimately a dream, surrounded by a mystery.

The philosopher Francis Bacon said that it is as natural to die as to as to be born. That gives the same kind of perspective; it's something entirely normal, it's just what happens.

Churchill also commented to this effect a number of times. He thought we make too big a deal of death, and that it isn't so important. This wasn't just an intellectual position on his part: as a young man, he repeatedly showed extraordinary courage on the battlefield, because he did not fear death.

We have a history with death in the West. There is a book called *Western Attitudes toward Death* by Philippe Ariés, a French academic. It's a short book, based on four lectures. He shows how our attitude to death has changed over the last thousand years. To start with, in the early Middle Ages, death was treated as something very normal. If you thought you were going to die, you announced it to the rest of the family, took to your bed, and they did whatever ceremonies they did around it. But it was you that announced it. You can see how we've got the opposite these days. It is the medical authorities who tell us, and they may not be entirely straight about it. It may be couched in terms of possibilities of recovery, when the person and everyone around them knows in their heart of hearts that the cancer, or whatever it is, is almost certainly going to get them. But no one is saying.

One feature of death in the Middle Ages was that there was not the separation between the living and the dead that we have now. They lived alongside us. That is also the case with the Ulchi. And why would there be a separation? Surely it is an assumption on our part that consciousness — the soul — is extinguished at death, and the idea of the continuation of consciousness a mere comforting false belief? If you tune in, you can sometimes feel your dead relatives around, getting on with whatever they are getting on with. It is what they are getting on with, and what they now are, that is unknowable to us.

After the Middle Ages, death became more of a reckoning with your maker. You had to account for yourself, and you were going to be sent to heaven or sent to hell, for ever. It became much more loaded and weighty and full of dread. Judgement Day was moved forward from the remote future — i.e. somewhere outside of time — to death itself. Samuel Johnson, a great literary figure who created the first dictionary, was terrified of death. He knew he was a very talented guy, but he didn't feel he'd fully used his talents, so he might therefore be sent to hell. Even an intelligent, sensitive, and imaginative guy like that was terrified of death, maybe precisely because he was imaginative and sensitive.

Then you get the modern position, where death is seen as an extinction. You even get figures like Irvin Yalom, who is a very well-known and respected existential psychotherapist, saying that any attitude towards death that his patients have, other than extinction, is a false comfort and a fantasy. He sees his job as bringing them round from that, and getting them to accept the 'true' existential situation. Yalom's family history is Russian Jewish, survivors of pogroms. Maybe there is some kind of ancestral spirit around him, that gives him this bleak view of death? We might in the same way ask what collective ancestral spirit is at work in the West generally that creates this nihilism, in its guise of rationality? Was it something to do with the Cross, that dreadful image of bloody torture that was at the centre of our mythology for so long?

How can death be just nothing? We are Shamanic, where everything is experienced as alive. Aliveness is not a separate quality from the Elements. You don't have Fire, Water, Earth, Air, and then Spirit as a separate element. Spirit is an inherent part, the inner pole, if you like. So when the Elements in their present form as a human body dissolve and regroup, why would Spirit somehow disappear, when it is integral? The four Elements dissolve back into being part of the universe – it was always a human illusion that they were in any way separate in the first place – so why wouldn't the Spirit also lose its sense of separateness to everything, and become everything?

There's a beautiful love poem written by Nancy Wood, in the spirit of the Pueblo Indians, where a wife who is going to die describes how she will continue to take care of her husband. This is how it ends:

Perhaps I shall be the snow
To let your blossoms sleep
So that you may bloom in spring.
Perhaps I shall be the stream
To play a song on the rock
So that you are not alone.
Perhaps I shall be a new mountain
So that you always have a home.

Love and connectedness continue after we die. That is something we can feel, can experience. It is not a belief in the sense of an idea separate to experience. What form we take, and what it is like being dead, remain unknowable. And why do we need to know? What is this thing called 'knowing'? Maybe we are released from that too after we die?

The onus is not on us to justify the continuity of the spirit in some form after death. The onus is on those who deny the inspirited nature of the universe to make their case.

And now something on the run-up to death, which is old age. I'm 66 at the time of writing, and I was dreading turning 60 because it seemed like 'old'. The cultural attitude is that it's gently, or not so gently, downhill from there on in. You're gradually getting more and more ill, with less and less energy, and then you die. But that hasn't been my experience at all. It has been one of renewal. In the last chapter I talked about the dream woman who showed up when I was 61, and it being an experience of deep renewal. She's the creative force, she's my soul. I feel younger and fresher and more enthusiastic about life than ever. Certainly more than 40 years ago, when life seemed like a huge cliff that was against me, that I had to climb up on my metaphysical quest. I think life can become more abundant, not less abundant as we age. In a way, it's a choice. But life is on the side of abundance, and it's never too late to choose.

Lewis Mehl-Madrona writes that when he first went to medical school, he was taught that life is a process of becoming gradually more ill until we die, and the job of a doctor is to slow that process down. He was horrified, because he had been brought up to believe that we remain well and healthy until it is time to die. It threw him into a crisis, and went to see an Elder, who reassured him. My experience tallies with Lewis'. Physically, I am probably healthier and fitter now than I was 20 years ago, because of the way I now take care of myself.

There's a BBC interview on YouTube from 1959, between John Freeman and the psychoanalyst Carl Jung. It's in black and white, and very English and charming. Jung was about 81 at the time, and he's just so at ease with who he is, he's a delight to be around. Freeman asks him what happens after you die, and Jung says we don't know, but the dreams of his elderly patients don't point to an extinction, they behave as if life is going on. He continued that that's how Nature sees death, and the right way to live is always according to Nature. It doesn't mean Nature is right in a scientific sense. But it means we are in balance, we're living correctly, we are living according to how the nature in us and around us lives; it doesn't have a big fear of death as a sort of extinction. It acts as though the life force, whatever that is, continues.

I thought that was a really good point. It has a kind of genius about it. It takes all the theorising out, because you just live according to Nature. And that applies right across life. Stop theorising, stop getting in a tangle about who you are and what to do. Just listen, and follow what is within.

I've had death coming closer to me through family members in recent years. It has changed my perspective, in a way that deaths of non-family members haven't. That is even though I'm not particularly close to them, because I've got very different values, I live quite a different life: but they're still connected to me at a visceral level, and when they go it's like death moves a bit closer. At the moment it's like I'm looking out over open water, a sound, it's mine to plunge into and swim across, and relish while it lasts. I'm heading out, and it's broad enough, but in the distance there are mountains, and that's death. They are still a bit undefined from this distance, I cannot see detail. But they are big. I will be going there, and that'll be the next adventure. It's almost like a vision in front of me of how things are. When something is a bit visionary, you don't have a timescale around it, because it's outside of time and space. It's just like here's the situation, here's the pattern you're living through. I am in good health mentally and physically, and I feel I've got the most important part of my life still to go, because I have a bit of experience behind me, and I have perspective, in which I value the creative force in me more, I believe in it, and it has to be central. Everything else has to come after that, so to speak, or be arranged around it. That is the centre of my Wheel, the point of balance when everything else works. I need to just get on with it. There can be an urgency as you get older; you may have your most important things still left to do. I feel that the woman who showed up when I was 61 has a lot to say, and it is imperative that she does so.

We die because our time is up, not because we have been getting slowly more ill for 80 years! This brings in the idea of Fate. In ancient Greek times, there were the three Fates who presided over people's lives: the sisters Clotho (the spinner), Lachesis (the allotter), and Atropos (the inevitable). Our time here is allotted, and then we move on. It does not happen because the life-force gets weaker and weaker and is finally extinguished. It remains as strong as ever, whatever may be happening to the body. Why was it that person's time to go? Sometimes we can discern the pattern of their lives, and a completeness to it. Sometimes it seems brutal and before its time. Modern doctors enter a 'cause of death' on the death certificate. But that is only one level of causality. Truly they died because they had reached their allotted span, as prescribed by Lachesis. And her workings are not for us mortals to know. We are left with the mystery.

20

Transgender: A Shamanic Perspective

I'm going to stick my head into the lion's mouth and say something about transgender from a Shamanic point of view. Maybe from an astrological point of view as well.

Shamanism begins with remembering that we belong to the natural world. Because of the influence of what is known as Core Shamanism, it can sometimes seem like Shamanism begins with knowing what your power animal is and who your spirit guide is. Sometimes we know these things, and sometimes we don't; I think it's enough just to sense that there's something working through us.

But it's not really where I view Shamanism as beginning. We start, as I say, by remembering that we belong to the natural world, we're part of it. You don't need to say that to indigenous people, it's part of the air they breathe. But of course, they can forget it as well, which is why they have ceremonies. They get busy, and they end up seeing nature as a thing to be just taken from so they can feed their families. That's understandable. So we need to remember that we're all part of the same natural world, and she takes care of us, she provides the conditions through which we can continue to live. We learn to trust her, and because we trust her, we trust ourselves, because we're also part of the natural world. This is a Chaos Shamanism position, in that it brings us back to what is essential, outside of any forms.

For this same reason, we trust the body we're born with. That is my foundational point on this transgender issue. We're not born in the wrong body. Such an attitude separates us from our feeling of belonging to, and trusting in, the natural world. However, if you have a male body, that doesn't necessarily mean that you experience yourself inwardly as male. You might experience yourself as essentially feminine within. Or vice versa. We trust this too. There isn't something 'wrong'. We trust all these things. We trust, we have faith, all the way down the line, and you go on the journey that it puts you on through life. How interesting, you might say, you've got this male body and yet inwardly you experience yourself as female. Wow, what's that about?

It means you have a dual nature. You certainly have the masculine in you, because you've got a male body. You have all those hormones and all that wiring, you are physically far more powerful than a woman. But you also have this feminine nature. You have both natures, and it's a gift.

You need to find out how to live that. You might quietly just get on with it if, say, you're an artist. Artists and creative people generally need both sides within them in order to create. Some people will want to present themselves as the opposite gender to their physicality, and that's fair enough. Some people won't. And some people will want to do it some of the time. There are all these possibilities. And, of course, if you present yourself as the opposite gender, some people will really like that, for it enriches life. It's like wow, here's someone different. Other people don't like difference. A lot of people want to know what's what, and if you're somewhere in the middle or both, that's a kind of threat to them on a very basic level, because gender goes very deep, and they will taunt you and laugh at you if they're uncivilised. Hopefully someone will rein them in and do their best to stop them and explain to them.

Indigenous people tend to have considerable scope for fluidity in this matter, if they haven't become too modernised. I didn't say 'gender fluidity', because gender is fixed, it is determined by the body. Amongst the Native Americans you get the Two Spirits, people who are biologically one gender, but present as the opposite. It is this tradition around which I have formed my thinking on the transgender issue. There are plenty of videos on the subject, on that invaluable cultural resource, YouTube. 'Two-Spirit' is a term of modern coinage by the Indians, as they call themselves. They are called Two-Spirit, because it is as if they have two spirits, male and female, though of course they really only have one spirit. But it is to help people understand their natures. I watched one instance of a man who lived as a woman, and was fully accepted into the community of women, because they could sense something of themselves in him. But when he died, he was buried with the men. There was a full and natural acceptance of his inner nature, but no denial either of his biological nature. That seems to be a difficult thing for modern Westerners to do, with their insistence, often tyrannical, that we have to be one thing or the other.

Mind you, even in the indigenous situation, the young male warrior types will tease the Two Spirit men for being effeminate, not real men. We easily project perfection onto indigenous people, but they are pretty much like we are.

The Two Spirit people are looked up to, they are respected and honoured, for they have both natures to a high degree, and the broader, deeper perspective that comes with that. They are often healers, leaders, and diplomats.

If you do have both sides, not only do you have this broader perspective that people can look to, but you need to learn to bear the taunts of some people, you need to let their arrows bounce off you, because it will happen. This can forge you; it is a warrior training. Very few people can be indifferent to what other people think. But if you base your life too much around what other people think, then you're trapped. To be free, you need to have your own authority, your own valuing of yourself. OK, it can be a bit ouchy, a bit unpleasant, but basically you can let it bounce off you. It's a great warrior training if you're a bit different in some way or another. I don't think the answer is to insist that other people see you how you want them to see you. That is a fool's quest.

If the other gender is within you, it's a gift. It's a spirit power, an archetypal power working through you, and that's why it's creative as well. If you present yourself as the opposite sex, that in a way is Ceremony, it has that kind of power, it invokes the Sacred. I don't think this is understood in modern culture. People just think, "Oh, I must be in the wrong body." We think that nature's made a mistake. We're very good at saying nature's made a mistake. Take people who live with what we call shortsightedness. Fair enough, in one sense it does present a problem. But in another way, the situation is that they see differently. What is it they see, what is it they bring to the table through how they see? Maybe they see the spirits of things more easily, because their vision is not so glued to the Earth element? *The Circle of Life* by James David Audlin gives extended descriptions of this and other indigenous ways of seeing the world.

There's this other way of looking at things that comes out of trusting nature. We tend to literalise the situation, we leave no room for the Spirit and its perspective, and then we think we're in the wrong body, on the basis of which people have surgery. I think it is usually an awful thing to do (one can rarely be absolute about anything), particularly because they have been told that they can actually become the other gender, and they can't. All they can become is a mutilated approximation that doesn't work properly. It's a pretence, it's a medical lie. That which is a gift is turned into a curse when we literalise it. It seems particularly tragic when teenagers, who do not yet know who they are, are involved.

Another way of putting it is that the god or the goddess is working through us, which is a gift, and in literalising that, we try to become that god or goddess. When you try to do that, you're trying to own an archetype, you're trying to own a spirit power, and that is always wrong. That's when the wrath of the gods gets served upon you. That is one reason so many transgender people suffer, in my opinion.

That, then, is my basic point: trust it if you experience both genders within you. My conjecture is that the other gender you experience is not just ordinary maleness or femaleness, it is a soul-calling, it has spirit power. That, I think, is why some people who have the trans-surgery experience joy: their soul-calling has been honoured. But as Jan Morris, one of the first to have such surgery, said in his/her 80s: the main thing is to be both genders, or neither. Jan never claimed to have become a woman, but rather a strange chimera. But she/he knew it was something he/she had to do. It is a complex area.

Identity is a central area, and the cause of much suffering, for many transgender people. But I don't think it need be such a big deal. Our identity is negotiated with the outside world. We are relational as well as autonomous. In our culture we prioritise autonomy, but we're also relational, maybe more than we like to think. In indigenous societies, the individual is primarily relational. That is why the centre of the Medicine Wheel involves coming into balance with the world, rather than becoming personally whole, as our culture would tend to have it.

You find out in the school playground that your identity is a negotiation. You can't just ignore how the other kids see you. Even as adults, we have the words of the poet Burns:

Oh would some power the gift give us
To see ourselves as others see us!
It would from many a blunder free us.

Chill out. You can't insist that other people see you a particular way, or even use particular pronouns. Just let them do what they want, it doesn't matter too much, let them feel comfortable. Don't let them feel they have to walk on eggshells in case they use the wrong bloody pronoun. Really it doesn't matter. Identity is an ephemeral illusion, as any decent mystical tradition will insist.

Gender is fixed, except in a tiny minority of cases. It is an ancient distinction, that goes back hundreds of millions of years. People need that distinction. If you grew up on a farm like I did, you'll know that gender-associated behaviour is a biological reality, it's not a social construct. We need to honour that. It may well be limited, but for the vast majority of people there is a congruency between the gender they are born with, and who they feel themselves to be. That needs to be affirmed in quite an ordinary way. It does not do them any good to doubt that, to feel they are being narrow-minded if they do not experience themselves as 'gender-fluid' or 'non-binary' (which is currently a fashion among young people). People usually need to grow into whatever gender they are.

That does, however, often change as we age. Something more fluid often arises naturally in the second half of life for a lot of people. Men encounter their Venus, women encounter their Mars. It's something you can track in astrology charts. Sometimes it's the other way around, because there are always exceptions. But by and large men start to encounter their Venus: they learn how to listen to themselves, listen to their feelings, and through that they learn to listen properly to other people. You don't necessarily realise when you're just listening to the words, that you're not properly listening. You need to listen with your whole being. What is your body telling you as you pay full attention to the other person? In this way, men may open up and become more feminine in the second half of life. It makes them more whole, more balanced in a deeper kind of way.

And women encounter their Mars, generally speaking. Women start to know more fully and firmly what they want to do, who they want to be, separate from their identity as mothers, as their children grow up and move away. As a mother, your children become part of who you are, in a way that they don't to the same extent for fathers. This is necessary. But it changes. Mothers can start to no longer feel obliged to take care of everyone around them, that they don't need to please others anymore, that they can have their own separate life. To live that is Mars, and it is a soul journey, just as Venus is for men.

We become both genders, to some extent, quite naturally in the second half of life. But I don't think that the femininity that a man experiences is the same as a woman's, though it gives a greater understanding across the gender divide. What he experiences is what Jung called the anima. It is divine, it is a soul journey. But it is good for men to honour women as vessels of the divine. And vice versa.

Since my head is already in the lion's mouth, I may as well bring in some indigenous views on gender differences. The Iroquois Confederacy was founded about 500 years ago between five nations on the East Coast of the USA, as a way of settling their differences without going to war anymore. It has worked well. It was proposed that a man should represent each nation at this inter-tribal council, but that candidates should be initially be put forward for selection by the women. And if the council member was not doing his job as he should, the women would have the power to sack him.

What this points to is a view of the sexes in which men lead and speak in public, and women hold the vision and the judgement of character. They each have different natural powers, and a place is recognised for each. I have also encountered this indigenous vision of men and women in a book about a tribal matriarchy in China called *The Kingdom of Women* by Choo WaiHong, and amongst pygmies in Ffyona Campbell's book *The Hunter-Gatherer Way*.

We no longer even know what men and women are, let alone what makes for a balanced relationship between the sexes.

Women can feel that they have to be like men in the world, the very men who are also labelled 'toxic' for being masculine. It is a mess.

I trust in the wisdom of the indigenous traditions, when something is found across the world. We can learn from this. As always with Chaos Shamanism, trust what comes naturally to you, and put aside the ideologies flying around, that tell you what you should be feeling and doing. Men need to value their masculinity, and women their femininity. Or whatever combination of the two they feel themselves to be.

21

Meeting the Spirits

What Are the Spirits?

Meeting the Spirits: that was where Shamanism formally began for me in 1997. It was a structured approach, and now I am going to attempt to re-imagine that approach from a Chaos point of view. Chaos is that which comes before form or structure, with form being, ideally, a vehicle for Chaos.

I learnt 'Core Shamanism' and all that comes with it over the course of about nine months: Shamanic journeying, Upper World, Lower World, Middle World, power animals, spirit guides, soul theft, soul retrieval, de-possession. All of that.

You learn to journey to a drum or rattle, where you establish a relationship with the various Spirits that want to be around you. And then you learn, alongside your Spirit helpers, to do work for other people, because when we travel off on those Journeys, we can enter other people's Spiritworlds.

For many people, this is what Shamanism is. I want to head into the debate about what Shamanism is for a moment. What does Shamanism mean? For some people, it is the Spirit work that comes originally from the Far East – Siberia, Mongolia, places like that. While for some people, Shamanism is the much broader project of indigeneity; reclaiming the indigenous soul, to put it slightly poetically.

Shamanism is a Western word in the first place. It was invented by academics. It comes from the word Saman, a word whose origin is broadly Russian, but whose exact origin is a source of debate. Academics used the particular definition of Shamanism to mean Spirit work to start with, but as more indigenous cultures were studied worldwide, the term Shamanism also began to be used by academics for the ways of those cultures.

This topic is explored in *The Beauty of the Primitive* by Andrei A. Znamenski, a scholarly but very readable history of Shamanism in the West.

The term is used in both ways by academics, and I think it's best just to go along with that. Sometimes we mean the more specific way, and sometimes we mean the broader way. That's fair enough. The trouble is you get some people insisting it's one rather than the other, and that's just bringing religion into it. It does get me fed up when people insist they know the correct meaning of the term — and it's usually the narrower definition. It's about a culture that is some 8000 miles away. Or their claims to knowing are about the remote past in Europe, which may as well be 8000 miles away. Some people just like to be authorities, that is what it comes down to, and there is no shortage of people who welcome such authorities into their lives.

We need to stay loose, stay open, stay flexible. Words are important, and their exact meanings can be important. But we also need to know when to let go of them and bathe in a bigger reality. The same applies to Chaos Shamanism. You may have noticed I have circled around the meaning of the word Chaos. It has all sorts of meanings. It is protean. It is poetry rather than prose. I think it is best that way. And we need to feel free to reinvent its meaning personally, for ourselves. In that way, it will remain what it is meant to be: a reassertion of the primacy of Spirit, in the face of the enduring tendency for Shamanism — and indeed, all traditions — to be turned into religion. At the time of writing this chapter, the meaning of Chaos that I am with is 'remaining close to experience'. But that may change.

What are these 'Spirits' that we are supposed to encounter in 'Journeys'? No one really said, when I first went along and started learning this thing. You were just kind of meant to know what a Spirit was. Suddenly everyone was talking about their Spirits and what their Spirits were doing and saying. Well, I didn't really know what a Spirit was. Do you know what a Spirit is? It is a bit like religion when people do that. There's this word and you're all supposed to know what it means. It's a bit like with drugs, you're supposed to know what the latest word is for whatever the drug is. What I think they now call 'weed' was 'pot' the generation before me, and then that became incredibly uncool, you do not say 'pot', you use some other word, and you're just meant to know that. It was a little bit like that with the Spirits, you were just meant to know what a Spirit is. And they are meant to talk to you, or there's something wrong. I don't know why we call them Spirits anyway. Maybe 'imaginary friends' is better, say for two days of the week; let's keep it light and humorous! You've always got to have play and humour, or you fall into the bog of religion, where the mud of rectitude and hierarchy is always sucking you back in as you try to dance.

I'm coming in from a critical angle here, because I'm trying to get to essentials, not because I want to criticise and destroy. And what is it that is essential? I think it is that we do have a sense of something working through us, some something around us, something other, something bigger pulling us along that gives life its meaning. Life isn't just about the washing-up and economic survival, or you wouldn't be reading this. But we can't necessarily pin that sense down from the viewpoint of the normal ego self that we function through. This thing working through us is 'other', as in 'the Otherworld'. It can't be pinned down and defined, but it is definitely there.

That is what the Spirits are, this 'other' — the emissaries from it, if you like. They make the point that we are more than just this narrow self with which we function in the world. There's something else going on that connects us to everything. That's what this is really about. If we are that larger self, if we're not defined exclusively by this worldly self, then in a way the

Spirits ARE us. The Spirits can also be said to be from Jung's Unconscious, in its collective as well as personal sense, which is why we can enter other people's Spiritworlds. 'Unconscious' in this sense does not mean less conscious, far from it. It means that of which we are not normally conscious, which is most of the universe, at all its levels! The Spirits, these forces of inspiration, are always there. The Spirits as the Daimon are always there, pushing us to do those things which we have to do in order to have meaning in life, and to keep unfolding.

We can have this general sense of something working through us. And sometimes it may have specific forms that you see or just sense. It may be an animal form, it may be human form, it may be plant form, it might be a rock. You might have a rock as a spirit helper! Or an alien. Who knows? All these things and more can be helpers. They are intermediaries between us and the Great Spirit, the Great Mystery. They help us stay close to the Great Mystery, the Chaos, and its guidance.

An intermediary can be helpful because the Great Mystery itself is a sort of infinite voltage, and ordinary humans cannot handle that. We are this tiny consciousness, and it would destroy us, or at least it would destroy our ego, our ordinary self, and we need that self for stability and to be able to function.

You get this idea in the Tibetan tradition as well. Their intermediaries are Bodhisattvas, enlightened forms that you meditate on, and the white light of Reality shines through them. After you die, according to the *Bardo Thodol, The Tibetan Book of the Dead,* you start by experiencing the white light of ultimate reality, and it's too much, it is scary, it feels destructive. So you shy away from it. But then it appears again in the form of the Bodhisattva figures, and if you've spent your life meditating on them, you'll be able to handle them and move towards them. If not, then you'll end up fleeing and being reborn. I don't agree with that rather negative slant on why we take a body: it should be a joyful, profound thing. But it makes the point about the intermediaries, which in Shamanism we have in the form of animal helpers and spirit guides.

Sometimes those helpers are around, sometimes they're not. It can be good if they're not there all the time, because it reminds us what it's really about: living directly with the Chaos, with the Mystery, and I think it's good always to have a sense of that alongside in our ordinary lives.

People can get in a bit of a fankle with the Spiritworld and its denizens by getting rigid about it. In the case of Core Shamanism, there are three Worlds — Lower, Middle, and Upper. You meet your animal helper in the Lower World and your Spirit Guide in the Upper World. I'm not going to go further into it, go and do a course on Core Shamanism if you want to find out about it. It's a good system, but still a system, that's my point. We need a loose relationship with it. We can reduce those three worlds to the Otherworld, just one other world, which is what you had in ancient Celtic times. Even that is, in a sense, a false distinction. There is in reality only one world, there is only this world. But because we're busy literal-minded humans, we get attached to the material and to the immediate, and we lose that bigger, subtler, nourishing perspective. So it gets called the Otherworld, or the Spiritworld, and we engage with it at special times, like in ceremonies or at particular times of year when the veil is thin. But actually the veil is always thin, whether it's to the Otherworld or to the world of the dead, which is one aspect of the Otherworld. Those places are with us all the time. I think you get more of a sense of that, the more that you do this kind of work, the more you live from that sort of place.

That's the thing — not how good your Shamanic journeying is, but where you live from day-to-day: whether you live from that other place, whether you do the things that you have to do, whether you are continually making that choice about who you are going to be *sub specie aeternitatis*. The more you can do that, the more the Spirits will love being around you.

Shamanic Journeying

Time for a bit of Chaos. I will just wander for a bit and see what connection to our theme the Spirits want to make. Particularly as, uncharacteristically, I made a list of topics before I started on the video behind this section. The Chaos wandering is not a superficial thing. You have to do it with integrity, you have to have prepared yourself and to show up fully before you dive into the ocean current and see where it takes you. Before you hand it over to the Spirits and let them do the talking, so to speak.

And here is the connection from this seeming digression: Shamanic Journeying, whether lying down to a drum, or dancing it, is also like this. You show up, you are full of intention to be there, and then you let go, you yield, and let the Spirits take over. This yielding is what people often struggle with, because we aren't trained to do that. We are trained to have a plan and then exercise our will to make it happen. That is necessary for many things, but this work is the opposite. It is a deep yielding, that needs to become the background context for everything we do. It is the feminine way, that can be particularly challenging for men.

What is a 'Journey', as it gets called? How does one do it? The formal way is often the Core Shamanic way, with its three worlds and its helpers. You lie down with a blindfold and let the sound of a drum carry you to one of those worlds. You may see or just sense that world, and you allow a Spirit helper to present itself, and you get to know it over time. A Chaos approach will acknowledge the validity and usefulness of this system, while remaining mindful of the essential principle behind it: that we are more than just the body, this evanescent vehicle; there is something beyond that works through us, and the time with the drum — a ceremonial time, that takes us out of ordinary consciousness — is where we make a point of being with that bigger sense of our life. And we yield. We may have come with an intention or question, which is often a good thing to do, but we drop that too – the Spirits know about it, and we don't want our will to get in the way. We just let whatever wants to happen, happen.

It may happen very quickly. It has often happened for me that someone else is drumming, and we have been set an intention, and I get my response before the Journey has even started, like a nugget that needs unpacking. And then I have done the Journey, and thought I was just not very good at it, because nothing relevant seemed to be happening! That was me getting caught in a system, in what I was 'supposed' to be doing, and also having been misled by other people's elaborate Journeying, which I didn't realise wasn't really my way.

We may see things, we may hear words, we may sense things through our body, or we may just have a 'knowing'. The important thing is to find your own way, and not get caught up in the natural human tendency to feel that validity lies in being like other people. You may not even have the Spirit helpers that are held by Core Shamanism to be fundamental to Journeying. Or you do sometimes, but not at others, as if Spirit is trying to make a point about this.

A good teacher in general leads us towards our own inner guidance, and a good teacher of Journeying will do the same thing, will keep emphasising the need to find your own way of working. It may be that you don't need to Journey formally at all, that you are sufficiently open that things just come to you. The Chaos approach is to remain very open to how Spirit works through you, and to listen.

A frequent reservation that people have is that whatever they saw, was their mind making it up, rather than Spirit at work. My answer to that is, what is wrong with the mind being involved? As an astrologer, I say our craft is for intuitive people with an active rational mind, and a complex system is needed to keep it occupied while we get on with being intuitive. It is the same with Journeying, particularly if you have an active intellect. Let it make stuff up, Spirit will also be there, and how do you know Spirit is not directing what the rational mind 'wants' to make up?

The reservation people sometimes have about the mind's involvement can also be an expression of a lack of trust in the Spiritworld. My response to that is that in some ways it is quite reasonable not to trust it, because faith is something that needs to be built through experience. It is far better than just accepting uncritically whatever happens. Stay with your Journeys, ponder them, keep a feeling relationship with them, as you might also do with dreams, and test them in this reality. The Otherworld will, over time, become an ongoing presence in your life, in whatever way is unique to you.

Where do the Spirits want me to go from here? Animal helpers, it seems. They're a wonderful thing to have. You don't want to talk about your experiences of these things too readily, otherwise it can be a bit like a novelist who's writing a book, and he starts telling people the plot of the book. (Now I'm being taken down a side path, just like a Journey, so let's follow it and then return.) That will disempower it, give it away, spoil it, and stop it unfolding within himself. It would be like taking the walls off an alchemical retort, or the shell off an egg. We need to be careful about speaking of our encounters with these Daimonic forces, whether in the Spiritworld or in night-time dreams: it's the same territory.

They all express the deeper pattern out of which our lives are always unfolding. These encounters give us privileged glimpses of that pattern. They are not for blathering about in ordinary conversation, and especially not to impress others! I have known a number of people who are gifted in their communion with the Spiritworld, but who regale others at the first opportunity with their unusual and powerful experiences. It is always to set themselves up as special, as an authority. You can still learn from such people, they have a genuine gift, but be wary of the type of relationship they are trying to establish with you. Take a long spoon! Underneath it all, they are not very sure of themselves, and what they are doing is a compensation. They can easily end up doing more harm than good.

When we Journey, when we meet Spirit Guides or Power Animals, whatever it is – and who says we have to be with a guide of some sort, we may just be in a beautiful, luminescent world – we're encountering that deeper source from which the pattern of our lives is built. We can catch glimpses that then unfold into something in this reality. The deeper source, a sort of seed energy, is empowered in this way by our showing up and being receptive to it. That's why Journeying, as we call it, can be such a powerful thing.

When I began doing it in 1997, I was struggling with Buddhism, which I'd been around for many years. I had tried to be a good Buddhist, but it was too 'top down', too cerebral. You'd take a perfectly good idea like the impermanence of everything, you would understand it intellectually, and then try to transform the rest of your being in line with that understanding. You can see the rationale. In a way it's true, but it's starting from the top, it's starting from the mind. Even though the idea is valid, an insight, it is your mind and your will that are being put first in the process of transformation, with the emotions by implication being put down as a primitive pack that needs calling to order. This model made me deeply out of sorts by the time I reached my early thirties. I was immobilised, I could do very little. It was my Shamanic Illness, that eventually turned my life right around. I learned to listen in a very different way, starting with the body, with intuition, with feeling, and the sense of vision that came with that, and aligning my thinking accordingly, rather than the other way round.

The mind needs to be the servant, the apprentice, and not the master. With Shamanic Journeying, your mind is certainly not the master, although it will get in the way by literalising your messages from Spirit instead of dancing lightly with them; by getting you to doubt whether what is happening is real; and by trying to direct the course of the Journey. As I suggested earlier, don't treat that as a big deal. Let the rational mind do its worst, smile at it, and just carry on.

If I tell you right go Journey and see a pink elephant, you will see one. If I tell you go and Journey and don't see a pink elephant, I am sure you will still see one. We can't separate the mind out, and we can't separate out the context out of how someone else may be setting up the Journey. Having the rational mind present is not a problem in itself, indeed it has an important part to play. But it is secondary. And the forms you see are secondary, they are just Spirit dressing up in a way that we can understand. Spirit would probably enjoy the humour of not seeing a pink elephant, it would probably add its own *Fantasia* dance, and then throw in some deep Spirit message that you need to hear. That is how it works. That is the pink elephant teaching!

Shamanic Journeying was 'bottom up' for me, in contrast to the 'top down' of the Buddhist world I had been in, and out of which I was, unbeknownst to myself, struggling to find my way. This was in the late 90s, and I had a Walkman tape recorder with a drumming tape on it. Personally, I find the drumming useful: it is there both ceremonially, as a signal to shift consciousness, and as something that has a physical effect on the brain, shifting it into an altered state. I was taught that the particular rhythm induces serotonin in the brain. I am kind of happy to go with that, but wary of any explanation involving science, if it is treated as the fundamental validation of a phenomenon.

You could probably use anything for Journeying, because the point is you're going somewhere else. A rattle works well, rhythmic music works too, particularly if you are dancing the

Journey. (See the section on Trance Dance later in this chapter.) I don't actually need a drum these days, but it's still great when someone is drumming live, it just takes me to that sweet place.

I'd lie there in my room in my Buddhist community with my headphones on, and the drumming going, and I'd go off, and animals would show up. I remember once seeing these two giant bears on the horizon, and it kind of shocked me, it stunned me, it was a visionary moment. I carried it with me, and it's still with me 27 years later. I don't have a 'meaning' for it. I don't think it is necessary. It is the feeling, the impact it made, that matters to me.

There is something awesome, something vast about this realm, there's this huge reality for us to engage with. But it's also sweet, it's beautiful, it's earthy: that's what I love about the animals, they remind us that it's bodily. In this sense it was the kind of opposite to Buddhism: it was bodily, earthy, animal, and it wasn't rational. It was living, it was alive.

And they were doing all sorts of stuff with me. The Spirit Guides, which had human form, and the animal helpers were taking me on healing Journeys. They got hold of a bit of my soul in the shape of a trussed and dressed chicken, and they buried it in the bank of a river Then a couple of weeks later, when I had completely forgotten about it, they told me on another Journey that we needed to go and see. (When I say 'told', it wasn't in words, it was more like a knowing passing from them to me.) It was ready, it had been cooked, so to speak, in the riverbank, and they put it back in me.

Now there's very little rational sense to be made of this. Sometimes people get given stories that add some rational sense, and that's fair enough, but I wasn't given any of that. I don't get words in that realm, probably because I'm good at words in this realm. It forces me to value the non-rational more. The non-rational is in fact primary, while the mind and its attributes of words and reason are its tools.

I use 'irrational' to mean the unwillingness to use reason when it is appropriate to do so. The 'non-rational' is that which lies outside the purview of reason, and is more akin to direct experience.

So in 1997 I was for some months regularly doing the Shamanic Journeying that I had just learned. It was a very different way of approaching the mind than I had been taught through meditation, which tended to have an element of control, of persuading the mind to settle around the breath, or to concentrate on a Bodhisattva figure in order to absorb its qualities. With Journeying, I had to learn to keep yielding and allowing, and there was a sense of a deep freedom in that, after my years of Buddhist meditation.

I could feel myself being changed by the Journeying. Just visiting that realm for no reason other than to go there is deeply nourishing in itself, and that was apart from all the healing Journeys that were coming my way. I was getting some real food, after being starved for years. A new foundation, a new authority was being forged in me. The Spirits were busy below the surface of my life, reshaping me and gradually taking me in a new direction. There was a beauty and a sweetness to that time, and a sense of adventure, of being a psychonaut.

That new foundation grew and grew until the following year it became like a tidal wave, reaching up and wringing by the neck many of my old Buddhist assumptions. And most of all it contributed to making the crucial shift from leaning on the guidance of a teacher – which we probably all need at some points – to trusting the guidance that was coming from within from the Spirits. This new foundation that arose out of Journeying gave me the confidence to see the limitations of the teachings that I had been around, and to believe what I saw. I still doubted myself to a considerable degree, but there was something new in me, gold if you like, that was my own, that was insistent. And gradually, over some years, my life rebuilt itself around that new centre. I had let go of the stabilisers, the props of formal teachings, and was trusting the Chaos, out of which everything emerges.

Even within the Journeying, I found myself outside the system that I was learning. This is what happens to Aquarians! People can think we are just being rebellious or contrary to make some kind of point, to give ourselves an identity. But it's not like that. We genuinely experience life from outside the boxes that regular society needs for its stability. And in this case pieces of my soul – for which I will never have words – were being brought back to me spontaneously by the Spirits. It is termed Soul Retrieval. Yet I was being taught that humans are too close to their own 'stuff' to be able to do it themselves, and you needed a healer with the requisite objectivity to do it for you. I approached the teacher about this, and he responded that he had never heard of anyone being able to do it for themselves, and left it at that. There's religion for you, and I had to dance around it.

I think the true position is that where possible, we need to heal ourselves, not have someone do it for us. Indeed, can someone ever heal someone else? Physically this does seem to be possible, but only up to a point with the Spirit – around the edges, so to speak. The Centre of our Wheel is ours alone to take care of. We learn so much through healing ourselves, healing meaning to make whole, which I view more metaphysically than psychologically. By this, I mean the emphasis needs to be on moving towards a deeper alignment with the Spirit, with the Centre of the Wheel, rather than sorting all the tribulations and dysfunctions. That healing has an important place too, and opens up into the metaphysical: they are "the crack where the light gets in". But the calling, the Daimon, rather than that which ails us, always needs to be primary.

Healing and the Limitations of Core Shamanism

There is a lot of emphasis on the healing of others in the 'Core Shamanism' that has become quite standard. It is almost its raison d'etre, because helping others is what a Shaman does. And it's also quite standard that you do a course for say a year, and at the end of it you get a certificate that qualifies you to practise Shamanic healing. In my experience, the qualification lies essentially in having done the course: you are unlikely to find people not getting the certificate who want it. In my course, there was some further work required in writing up a few healings you had done, and that was that. I never got that far myself. I knew I could do the work, and that was good enough for me.

I have sat with this model a lot over the years. It has given me something to wrestle with. For now, I am pondering the theme of healing oneself versus having others – or their Spirit helpers – do it for you. I am working it out as I write. Or rather, when I made the video on which this is based.

I will begin with an experience I once had when appreciating an oak tree. This, incidentally, can be one of those areas of Shamanic practice where you can get in a muddle of self-doubt, because the idea can be to commune with a plant and get some kind of message from it. And, of course, most of us don't experience plants as talking to us. I always say forget about all that, just enjoy the plant or the tree – or indeed the rock – in a simple, natural way. Just stop and look, which is something we maybe do only too rarely. And when you do that, you will also have a sense of it being alive, of its presence, just as you would with a person. That is all you need to do, and that is something that anyone can do. You may also want to talk appreciatively to it, tell it the things you like about it, thank it just for being there. You may experience more than just its presence – maybe an energy field, that gets stronger the closer you approach. And you may have a sense of some kind of energy or message passing between you and the plant or tree or rock. Or maybe not. It doesn't matter.

Anyway, I had approached an oak tree in this kind of way. I was looking at it, taking it in, appreciating it, sensing its presence. I became aware of energy from the tree pouring into me, replenishing my soul. Or even putting soul there that was mine. I wouldn't exactly say 'soul retrieval', because it didn't feel like something I'd once had that had gone missing. It was more like an accession of soul, of moving on to the next stage of my life with some new element now present, that was always destined to show up eventually. And, looking back, I felt the function of this new element was to build the resources in me to leave a long-term relationship that I needed to leave, but was finding very difficult to do. So I received a healing from a tree. I don't like the word healing either in this context, because it wasn't like something that was wrong being made right.

This raises a more general point, that when there is a healing – maybe something that went missing in childhood does come back – it is never just that. It is also "the crack where the light gets in". Our whole self adjusts, and some deeper connection to that which gives our life meaning emerges. However awful and painful the original trauma, it can be too simplistic just to say it 'shouldn't' have occurred. Yes, it may well have been very wrong. I remember my Bear being very angry once, as he did some healing work around what had happened to someone as a child. And yet the ways of the Spirit are mysterious, with designs far larger than we can comprehend. The Spirit intends that we grow and unfold and learn, and the perspective of hindsight can reveal our difficulties and traumas to have been part of that process. We can even find ourselves thanking those traumas, through gritted teeth.

Our soul can shift, missing elements can come back, new elements can emerge, in all sorts of ways. Often it is a natural process, occurring in the course of life. You notice, maybe, that something no longer bothers you, or triggers you, or makes you anxious like it used to.

Sometimes Shamanic work from others helps. It can be beautiful and profound work. Yet the emphasis always remains on doing the work ourselves, of building our own souls. And our Spirits will help us do that. "The Vale of Soul-Making" as the poet Keats called this Earth. All the Shaman can do is bring some piece of soul closer to us. Whether we live in the new way that is needed, leaving room for, and honouring, the new soul part – or whether we carry on in the same old way, and the soul part wanders off again – is up to us.

If I do some of this work, I often don't know what I – or rather, my Spirits – have done, until the person tells me. I used to feel inadequate about that, because I was taught that I also needed to come back with an explanation. Nowadays I just trust. Sometimes I have a story – in a way, a useful story is all it can ever be. If I don't, I trust there is a reason for that too. Sometimes the person runs with the work, sometimes they carry on as before. One woman with a compulsive, uncritical attitude to men was shifted into the insecure little girl behind that behaviour by the work my Spirits did. There had been no particular intention behind the work, I was just leaving it up to the Spirits. It gave her an insight into herself, and a deeper relationship with herself. But then she reverted to carrying on as before. You never know with these things. Probably the Spirits knew perfectly well that this would happen, but the insight and relationship with herself is probably still there, latent, waiting to come back to consciousness at some juncture.

For people who are making an attempt to come into a deeper relationship with themselves, I think the emphasis needs to be on them doing the work themselves. But we can do some very useful talking with them, as the Spirits circle around us. That paying of attention will in itself help the soul part move closer. For people who are, in a way, 'normal', who don't want to live or see outside the conventional ways – and there is no law saying one 'ought' to, and therefore no judgement to be made – bringing soul parts back and relieving their distress may be more unambiguously the right thing to do. It is perhaps the perspective that a traditional Shaman would have for most of his/her work. But in our society, people with a conventional attitude are unlikely to look to Shamanism.

If you work Shamanically, your first port of call with your own difficulties is with your Spirit helpers. That is something we can forget. We get caught up in our human situations and think we have to sort it all ourselves. But no, help is always there; there is this benign aspect to the universe! You never need feel lonely either, they are always there, connecting you to everything. I can feel mine here now, I can feel my animals around me as I write, they've shown up. It's great, it means they're backing this. I can see particular animals if I focus, but it's also enough just to sense them around in a non-specific way.

Your helpers may just do the work for you. The animals can be almost tangible. You can reach out and stroke their fur, or maybe you can smell them. Or maybe, if you are a visionary type, you can see them standing there before you, as real as, or maybe more real than, the physical world around you. If you are feeling troubled in some way, you can hand it over to them and you may well find the problem alleviating. Or some new perspective on it appears in your mind, billowing up from that rich Spirit mix. Asking them for help in this way will deepen your relationship with them. The more you do this, the stronger will be their ongoing presence, and the better your life will go, because you will always be in deep alignment with yourself. Journeying to a drum is just a special instance of this relationship, for the helpers are always around you, ready and willing to be called upon. If you don't get that sense of them so easily, then do some ceremony that for you invokes them, drumming or rattling maybe, burning some incense, whatever it is.

Another comment I have on Core Shamanism is from an indigenous point of view, to do with the 'callback' signal. You have a steady drumbeat during the Journey that helps you travel to the Otherworld. At the end, when it's time to come back, they do a fast and loud drumbeat to break up the altered state you are in, to help you to get back to this world. It is because, we are told, that it is possible to get stuck in the Otherworld. Personally, I think that is an excess of health and safety. It is 'safe shamanism'. When it's 'safe' in that kind of way, the power is diluted. I've never been happy with that callback signal, and if you don't feel happy with something in a spiritual tradition, trust it. Just because they are venerable, perhaps ancient authorities, and everyone around you agrees with it, doesn't mean you are not onto something. This attitude is at the heart of Chaos Shamanism.

In her book *Spirits from the Edge of the World*, Jan Van Ysseltyne tells of a visit that one of the Ulchi Shamans made to Seattle, which included attending a Shamanic Journeying session at a conference. At the callback signal, the Ulchi Shaman walked out. He said it was barbaric, and he was going to leave the whole conference. But he was under contract to lead a session, so Jan had to haul him back!

The Shaman's response corresponds to how I have felt about the callback signal for a long time. You are in a subtle, deep, sensitive place, and you need to come back gradually, and bring the Spiritworld with you. You don't do this kind of brutal yanking out, that is not the way. Core Shamanism has got that wrong. It is not just 'different ways', which is a New Age way of neutering criticism and appearing to be broad-minded. No, there is such a thing as objective truth, and this is wrong.

It is worth thinking about the origins of Core Shamanism, which has had such a widespread influence on Western Shamanism. It was invented by an American academic, Michael Harner. His method has been a great gift in many ways. It has changed many people's lives profoundly. When something has been this important to people, they are reluctant to criticise it, and think that any criticism is a demolishing of that which they hold to be sacred. But it is not so. Chaos Shamanism has the courage always to be discerning.

In this case, if Harner wanted to remain a respectable academic, he would have to present it in a way that was sufficiently acceptable to that world. So firstly, it needs to have a rational framework. This it has through the three worlds and the different helpers you get in each world, the list of different Journeys you can do, and the types of healing work involved. It also describes the soul and its tribulations in those worlds in a way that can be integrated with psychotherapy. There is nothing wrong with all this.

But it is not fundamental, in the way that the term 'core' implies. There are a number of criticisms of the use of this word, which you can find on ChatGPT. My criticism is that it tends to reduce Shamanism to a set of techniques, because there is no supporting cultural context, no deeply rooted mythology in which it would find its place. Such a mythology is centred around ultimate realities, around the Great Spirit, 'the holiest of everything'. We do not have such a mythology. But we can still come into deep relationship with the Great Spirit, with the Chaos, through paying attention to what gives life meaning and having the courage and resolve to live it. It is this that is truly 'core'. Without this foundation well in place, your healing work will be superficial, and you will tend to try to create an identity out of being a healer, to fill the 'God-shaped hole' in your life.

In the same way that it tends towards the rational, so too is Core Shamanism 'safe'. The academic world is not going to take kindly to possession by the Spirits (which is akin to the way I work). This can happen, and it is profound magic when it does. Harner excludes this possibility in his whole approach, and the callback signal is integral to that: we can't have people going too far into the Otherworld. Best to keep it safe and rational. There can be a raw power to Journeying, that draws on our connection to our body and the natural world, that Core Shamanism is wary of.

The only real danger in Journeying is if people have mental health issues, and I don't think Journeying is usually a good idea in this case. Far better to go and connect with the natural world.

I was once asked by someone who'd been sectioned to come and help, so I went there and what I found myself doing was physically shifting into my animal helper (that is the way I work) and putting this person back in their body. That was an important part of what the issue was: he'd left his body and gone off into his own reality. But he still had enough awareness to ask me to come and do something. Five days later they released him. You could say he had got lost in the Spiritworld, because he was talking its language incessantly. So there's an example of how the Spiritworld and mental illness can overlap, and there is indeed a danger if you are not well-grounded in this world. But that is very much the exception. The emphasis needs to be on approaching the Spiritworld with trust, and entering it deeply.

If you haven't got mental health issues, go to the Spiritworld, or maybe better, let it come to you, and don't use the callback signal. Come back slowly, come back gently and bring back from that world whatever nourishment you have been given. We go there to be nourished, to help us to live better, to live in a more aligned sort of way, to bring us back to our deeper centre.

The lack of emphasis on the natural world is also, I think, where Harner is limited. The Core Shamanism course I did was essentially indoors. The foundation we need in belonging to the natural world, which we have largely forgotten in the West, was not part of the course. Harner's approach can give the impression that Shamanism begins with talking to Spirits –

that is what is 'core', or essential, and if you can't do that, then you're not a Shaman. There is a narrowness that is misleading. Spirit can work through you in all kinds of ways.

We all have a gift for being inspired one way or another: you might be a painter, you might have music coming through you, you might be a writer, you might just have insights into people, or be clairvoyant, or have a gift with animals or plants. A traditional Shaman might be gifted in a number of these ways. At its core is that sense of belonging to an inspirited natural world, and this sense of a larger, fluid, you that opens up when you realise that you're not alone, you are part of this bigger thing. That's where it begins, and what I would say is 'core', or essential, to Shamanism. Chaos Shamanism always has its eye on what is essential.

Embodying the Spirits

Calling on the Spirits outside of the formal Journeying context can, in a way, make them more of a physical presence in this world. And even more so if you embody them, which is my next theme.

The way we have generally come to think of how we meet the Spirits, is that we lie down to a drum, and we go off and we meet them. Some indigenous people say no, they come to you. I read about one people who say there's something wrong if you go to them. I don't know what to make of that, but it is worth pondering.

I want to say a bit about the body and the Spirits. In the chapter on Soil, on the Earth Element of the Medicine Wheel, we talked about the dancing in churches that you used to get in medieval times. The dancing was banned, because people make their own connection to Spirit, to the Divine, when they dance, and you can't have that if you're trying to run a religion. It's the priest who has the connection with God, the hotline to God, not you. If you have a hotline, then his authority is challenged.

In the Far East you see some of the Shamans dancing when they're doing their Spirit work. They sometimes have a curtain over their eyes to break up this reality and help them be in the other reality. They might be drumming as well, and they're probably dressed accordingly, in a costume associated with the Spirits they are calling. There is a ceremonial aspect that we do not have, that acts as a powerful invocation.

So what do we make of that, because that's not how we usually do this work? We lie down and someone drums, we've maybe got a blindfold on, and that works really well. I don't want to dis that at all, but I think it can also be limited. For some people that's fine, it's full-on. Journeying in this way helped me deeply to start with, but it increasingly felt that it wasn't quite me, it wasn't entirely natural. It started falling apart, so I knew there was some other way I needed to find, or that needed to find me. Either that, or maybe I just wasn't cut out for Journeying!

What happened is that I was trance dancing, which is done usually either to live drums or to rhythmic music. You often do it with all the dancers blindfolded, so that you don't have to worry too much about how you appear to others. You have a few minders in the room to stop you crashing into the walls or into other people. We get very self-conscious with these things, particularly with the body. The blindfold is also ceremonial – it makes the point that we are going to an inner realm, because the visual sense has been removed. It catalyses that. I don't need to go blindfolded anymore; I don't mind either way. I'm happy doing strange movements with others watching!

The beat gets into your body, and your body takes off, it has a life of its own, a force of its own. The Spirits enter you and take over, that is another way of putting it. 'Trance Dance' is what it gets called, but that is inaccurate, because it is neither trance nor dance. 'Spirit movement' is more helpful. This is because the way we use 'trance' is often associated with a loss of consciousness, a bit like being hypnotised, whereas in this altered state, we are very present. Also, we are not 'dancing', if only because we may be standing still, or making small movements unconnected with the rhythm of the drum. We are yielding to the Spirits, and letting them do the moving.

In about the year 2000, I'd been doing this trance dance — this spirit movement — for a while, and not a lot ever seemed to happen. Then one day I suddenly got taken over by a big presence. I was wandering slowly around the room, just being this thing, a container for something that was much bigger than me. It was, it seems, attracting a lot of attention from others, because it had a strong presence. Someone said afterwards that it seemed like an ancient dinosaur had entered the room, after a 100 million years of being extinct, and it was taking a good look around at what it was like to be on the Earth again. That fitted my experience. I remember the way it slowly moved its head around, curious to be here.

There is an idea that the Spirits like to be embodied, and that we are doing the dance for their benefit. This experience felt like that. It was sweet, and it was a deeper initiation for me into the world of the Spirits. The capacity to shift in this way has been with me ever since. In a way I've never quite known what to do with it, as if there is anything to do. There isn't really, you just trust. If it's happening, it's happening. And if you don't do it, if nothing happens for months, that's fine as well. I realised that is my way of Journeying, in which to some extent I am acting it out, I let myself be taken over and moved around. Sometimes there is a visual component, and sometimes there isn't.

You can move in all sorts of ways. You might be moving really vigorously, or you might be lying there in the corner twiddling your finger, a bit like when you're tripping and you get fascinated with something tiny. In a dance I led once, an old guy who'd been doing it for decades was lying on his back on the floor, his legs vertically up against the wall. And all he was doing was wriggling his toes. That was what was authentic for him, what the Spirits wanted!

You're in an altered state. The beat has taken you there. You have yielded your body to it, and therefore to the Spirits. In Africa and the Caribbean, they have similar dances, in which some people get completely possessed by the Spirits. They're just lying there still, no longer conscious, but it's not like something's gone wrong: rather, it is a special, sacred moment in which magic has entered the village. They're carried away and given time to come back. Maybe they are helped in some way by the witch doctor or by the women, I don't know, but you could hardly imagine there not being some kind of ceremonial activity around them.

I make a distinction between Spirit Embodiment, and Possession by the Spirits. Embodiment is when we allow the Spirits to enter and take over physically, but we remain very present and aware. It is the state that many traditional Shamans work in, as far as I can make out. I also call it Shapeshifting, for those with eyes to see or sense the Spirit presence. Possession is the next step on, where our ordinary self is entirely subsumed by the Spirits. I don't have any experience of it myself. The Tibetan Oracles work in this way, from what I have read. Maybe the Oracle at Delphi, in ancient Greek times, worked in this way too. No doubt there are borderline states too, where the oracle/shaman slips in and out, because these things are never cut and dried, much as we humans like clear categories.

In the African and Caribbean dances, it is usually women who become possessed. This is because by temperament they can usually yield to Spirit more easily. You may have noticed that women usually find it easier to do Shamanic Journeying than men, with less doubt as to whether it is real, and for the same reason. We men are usually more temperamentally suited to being engineers, planning stuff in detail and making it happen. The yielding tends to come later in life.

There is a book called *Chosen by the Spirits* by Sarangerel, a traditionally trained Shaman of both Russian and Buryat ancestry. She begins by making the point that if you are interested in Shamanism, then you have been chosen by the Spirits. I think that is a great thing to say, because it gets rid of a lot of the preciousness around being a 'Shaman', and validates our interest as something real. She talks about the Shamans dancing their Journeys, while banging a drum and dressed in costume. This provided a point of connection for me with my own Shapeshifting. She calls it 'Dancing the Ongon Spirits'. An Ongon is an amulet, an object which is also your Spirit helper. It doesn't just 'symbolise' it, in our modern, intellectualised use of the word, but actually IS your helper. As such, it is a sacred object. You become that helper when you dance. I think it's good to create your own Ongons, your own ceremonial objects that, treated in a sacred manner, develop the power to bring you instantly into the Otherworld.

Dancing the Ongon Spirits is not something we can easily have in our culture. You'd have to couch it in other terms to get insurance, because of its appearance of losing control and allowing in 'primitive' forces. We like it safe and under control, and that makes it responsible and professional. That's why I was talking about the 'safeness' of Core Shamanism. It's not just the callback signal, that's just a minor instance. The main instance of it is the lack of bodily involvement.

In Trance Dance, the non-rational takes over. You haven't got your three worlds and the leader telling you the intention, and the body lying safely out of the way. No, all that structure is blasted apart when the Spirits come in and take over physically.

As I say, Core Shamanism was created by an academic, which gives it a kind of respectability and a rational gloss, and it does work. But there's a whole other level to be encountered when you let the Spirits work through the body: it's dark, it's primitive, it's the devil, it's sexual, it's got all that kind of connotation. It takes us outside of the 'civilised' container that society needs for its psychological stability. It is also our Christian baggage, with its demonisation of the body. Women and their sexuality have historically been at the sharp end of this.

I was once doing a demonstration of how I work, and a feminine spirit embodied me. It was refined and delicate and sensual, and I was giving expression to that in the way I moved and vocalised. Some people were entirely comfortable with that, others not so: to them it felt 'wrong', it felt 'sexual'. I noted that the ones who weren't comfortable had a teacher who was big on safety and protection in the Otherworld.

The idea that we need lots of protection in the Otherworld is another example of the overemphasis on 'safety' in Core Shamanism, that dilutes its power. "You'd better have a power animal with you for protection when you go to the Otherworld," is one of the first things you get told. And when you are trying to find your power animal for the first time, you'd better be wary then also. If it bares its teeth, that means it's not friendly, it's not your animal, and you'd best scarper. Personally, I've never felt I've needed protection in the Otherworld. It is a place I trust, and that is the emphasis that needs to be given. It's easy to scare people, particularly when they maybe have at the back of their minds that this Shamanic thing is some kind of pagan devil-worship. One Shamanic teacher I encountered was always emphasising protection in the Otherworld, as though that made her a responsible teacher. My observation was that she was creating a bunch of frightened mice, over whom she was exercising control through this emphasis. It was not what it seemed.

That said, part of the function of the Spirit helpers when you are doing work for people is to protect you from any negative energies that might be flying around as a result. You may, for example, be removing some quite dark energies that are troubling them, and you need your helpers to dispose of them, and not let them wander into your own psyche. The same holds if you are doing an exorcism: you definitely need the helpers to get rid of it, or at least protect you from it. And you can trust that they will.

It is a matter of emphasis. Sure, have a helper around when you are in the Otherworld, that is fairly straightforward, for they like being around us and helping us. And they will make sure you are protected. But the basic attitude needs to be one of open-hearted trust and enthusiasm.

And don't be literal about what constitutes Spirit help and protection. You may not be the sort that has literal helpers around you, in whatever form. You may just have that sense of Spirit working through you in some way, and that is enough. You are taken care of.

Core Shamanism is a good starting point, particularly for people who are only starting to stick their heads out of the rabbit hole of conventional ways of being. It is Shamanism-as-religion, which has its place. But a deeper yielding to the Spirits, which may necessitate bodily movement, is needed to encounter the full power of this work. Otherwise it will always be the indigenous people who are the 'real deal', with ourselves being but a pale imitation. And it is important not to feel that way. We need to feel that we have the goods too, and remove indigenous people from the pedestal that Shamanic people so easily put them on.

This way of working is raw, it is 'uncivilised', you wouldn't want the vicar to know about it! It's not the sort of thing that lends itself easily to certification and insurance. I often speak in tongues when working in this way. It isn't literally a language, more a series of vocalisations that do not repeat — much as my movements do not repeat, they remain spontaneous — and there is an energy in the vocal expression, even an urgency, that has its own healing power for the person I am working for. But there is no way I could give a rational account of what is happening.

All the time we are yielding to Spirit. We are very present, maybe even more present than usual, but also ceding control. This was why it took me until my early forties before I could begin to work in this way: up until then, I was too much in control, I had my will and my plans and my rationality, which the initial Journeying gradually ate into. And then this wonderful thing came in and took over. It is a gift, it is ecstatic, and it lives at the heart of Chaos Shamanism.

It is a gift to be able to enter the Spiritworld deeply and do work for others on that basis. But dancing the Spirits, or moving to them, and being nourished by that, is something everyone can enjoy. It is natural to humans. Which is what the early European explorers found, as we saw in the chapter on Soil.

We got disconnected from it in the West, starting in the Middle Ages, with Christianity proscribing dancing in churches, along with the world being a creation of the devil, and the body and sexuality too. The body was dark, it was lower, it led to temptation. We are on a journey back from that long cultural brainwashing, that soul loss. We have baggage. You could argue that rock and roll has led the way! It was inevitable that it would start to come back as the hold of Christianity declined, because it is a natural force in humans. The reclamation of embodied Spirit is a large part of what Shamanism has to offer the modern world, but only if it is outside Shamanism-as-religion, which will tend to unconsciously perpetuate, in the interests of 'safety', the old Christian suppression.

The 2022 film *Elvis* is well worth watching for this. Elvis Presley had that raw, free energy up on stage, and so does the actor in the film. You can see why Elvis was banned in certain American states. It wasn't just the unabashed way he moved his hips, and its obvious sexual suggestiveness; it was as much the freedom of his whole being when performing, that alarmed Protestant America. He'd been inspired to it by the black Americans, because they had never lost it. This free energy is the spirit behind rock and roll, and it all burst out in 1967, the 'Summer of Love', like a great dam breaching, that had been held down for hundreds of years.

You also get it in Pentecostal churches, where people are swaying and clapping to the hymns, and then maybe they're possessed by spirits and they're rolling on the floor. I guess they get away with it because it is religious! And maybe some people think they are just harmless nuts. But no, that free spirit energy is there, embodied, it has taken over.

You also get it in sports crowds, and the way they move and sing together. And in the Rave scene of the 90s, that really fast beat, akin to the Shamanic Journey drumming, with people on ecstasy. They are letting the body, the Spirit, take over, they're going into that altered state. The current popularity of 'plant medicines', with their yielding to the Spirit, is another instance of this resurgence.

But we remain culturally ambivalent. Raves get shut down. Plant medicines remain largely illegal. Mick Jagger has made a career of being the 'bad boy'. Some people can feel uncomfortable when I work in this way, and it's not really for public display.

Discernment, Self-doubt, and Different Ways of Working

If you are doing healing work, and you get given messages or shown images, you can then speak from them. The words may not arrive literally. Someone I knew, who can do very good work, said it is like describing a painting. And you can see her working as she talks, to get exactly the right nuance; it is as if she is moving her way around the painting and describing it from different angles. So sit with what you have been shown, digest it, give it time, and work at being really true to it. Sometimes we are just given a nugget, we see a flash of something, but we feel the power of it, so we take it seriously; it is not just some random image that has floated by. And when we speak from that nugget, it unfolds. And then when the other person brings in the circumstances of their life, we can ground it even more concretely. Always try to make your messages concrete and practical.

As the saying goes, "Don't tell me about your visions unless they grow corn." Having a bit of visionary experience, you could say, is the easy bit. Anyone can Journey and see something. Translating it into something useful in this world is the difficult bit: we are bringing Spirit into matter, and there is satisfaction in doing that. We are being given something from the East/Fire, and bringing it to the West/Earth, working it with the Good Red Road of North/South – Mind and Feeling – in order to do so.

I don't find I am given words directly. Some people are. Sometimes it is an image. Sometimes it is just a kind of knowing, almost bodily. Sometimes there is nothing to say: I have maybe done some kind of energy work, and that is that. And then I may find myself pleasantly surprised as the other person starts to describe the shift they have felt in themselves, maybe something that has bothered them for years, starting to heal.

I felt inadequate for years because I didn't get words, even though the work certainly shifted things for the other person. We're a rational culture, we think we should get words. I was taught that when doing a Soul Retrieval, I should also come back with a story of how the bit of soul went missing in the first place. Well, I often wouldn't get that. And maybe, in retrospect, I should have trusted that. There is a good Chaos principle here: if you can't do the practice as you have been taught, don't assume there is something inadequate about you. Rather, trust it. Trust what doesn't happen as much as what happens. That brings you close to Chaos and its mystery. And give it time.

The classic story is that the piece of soul that has been returned went missing when you were, say, six years old, because such and such happened to you. But it is now ready to come back. There may well be truth in that story that is helpful. But really, we don't know the source of our troubles. They are visiting spirits, as we talked about in the chapter on Rain. The Otherworld cooperates with our mythologies. If we want to see an animal, we will. If we ask for an explanatory story from childhood, it may well be provided. It ties in neatly with the psychotherapeutic model that who we now are was shaped in fundamental ways by our childhood, particularly by our parents. It is what James Hillman calls 'the parental fallacy'. It can be unhelpful to the degree that it turns us into an effect of circumstances, instead of the causative agent of our lives.

Maybe the very act of Soul Retrieval itself occurs because that is what we are half-expecting. It is the model we work with, and the Otherworld cooperates. Maybe another Shaman would have effected the same shift, but with a different explanation: that he loosened the hold of a nasty-looking demon with a hippopotamus face and the back end of a rhino, and it is now for you to guard yourself against its return until you are no longer susceptible. Meanwhile, get to know that susceptibility in yourself.

It is natural to have self-doubt around Otherworldly experiences. Some people are gifted, and what happens for them there is very real. The rest of us have to work at it, and find our own way in. I sometimes say that there can be only one thing worse than having self-doubt, and that is not having it. We need to earn our confidence through practice and experience. The self-doubt is a motivating force. There are no easy certificates that tell us we are competent, based on a measurable performance. Shamanic work belongs to the creative realm. It is always fresh, always new, and it is a deeper kind of confidence that is engendered: a confidence, if you like, in our own soul. Doing this work gradually transforms us as a human being. If you are drawn to it, trust that the Spirits want you there, and that they will show you your own way of being there, once you can loosen up around the ways you have been taught. That can be a large part of the self-doubt: the need to find our own way in.

The doubt around Otherworldly experience can also be because we are taught that only that which is rational and measurable is real. We live in an extraverted culture. So we need to practise trusting what we sense or see in the Otherworld, making a point of taking it seriously. It is good to do that with night-time dreams also, it is the same territory.

It's more complicated than that, however, because we also need to practise discernment. And that applies particularly to the mental state we are bringing to the work. This brings us back to the North and South, Mind and Emotions, of the Medicine Wheel. Whatever we are feeling personally, we need to be able to stand aside from that: the disidentifying capacity of Air, of the Mind. If you are subsumed by a mood, it will influence what you see in the Otherworld. If you want to please the person you are working for, maybe because they are paying you, that will influence what you bring back, and how you interpret it.

If you are in a relationship with someone who is doing work for you, it can easily be compromised by who the other person needs you to be, which is a normal part of relationships. I was once in such a relationship with someone who did very good, objective work for me early in the relationship; as it came apart later, she was not able to discern her own part in her Journeying, and came out with 'spirit advice' that was designed to limit, rather than free me.

Who we are in this world is an important part of this work, however gifted you may be in the Otherworld. Indeed, that gift may be a cause of complacency in this world. Sometimes the ability to Journey is the product of a split in the psyche, of a mental imbalance, of a lack of grounding in the body and ordinary reality that leaves the spirit free, as it were, to travel in other realms. It may produce extraordinary experiences. But it is also spiritual bypass, an Otherworldly identity created as a defence against facing one's own fragility in this reality. A good teacher will observe this in a student and advise accordingly.

If you are naturally intuitive, beware of confusing what seem to be Spirit messages with telepathy, your ability to know what the other person wants, or is thinking. Otherwise, you can end up telling them what they want to hear, and that may be the opposite of what they need to be told. It is another aspect of discernment. Don't be too quick to pass on what you think the Spirits have told you. Sit with it, and you will learn to tell the difference.

It often happens, unfortunately, that teachers are playing a numbers game. The more practitioners they have trained, the better they feel about themselves, and so they do not exercise the necessary discernment very effectively. Or they are temperamentally agreeable and afraid to comment. The counterculture itself, moreover, tends to believe one-sidedly in 'acceptance' over criticism. The end result of all this is that anyone who wants a certificate will get one, with very few exceptions. We'll return to this countercultural element later in the chapter.

I have a not-so-little voice in me that wants to say that a lot of Shamanic work in our culture has a fantasy element. It is not something I can prove, and it is not a popular thing to say. But I trust that voice.

I have yet to encounter a modern Shamanic teacher who teaches Otherworldly discernment properly. I am not saying there are not such teachers!

Don't be too certain about what you bring back from the Spiritworld. Surround it with inverted commas. Be confident in the reality of what you have seen, don't be mealy-mouthed about it. You can feel it when there is power to it. But be provisional about the interpretation. Leave room for the other person to find their own relationship with it. And room for your own interpretation to arise. It may take days, or longer.

People easily treat the Spiritworld as the authority, and put their own knowing, which may only be nascent, aside in its favour. And they sometimes carry that authority themselves when conveying messages from the Spiritworld. "Spirit told me." You're not supposed to question it when someone says that. It puts them on a level above other people, who have merely ordinary reasons for what they do. Spirit may well have suggested something to you. But it is always a suggestion. Spirit is not authoritarian, though we have that legacy from Christianity. It is generally best to translate into the language of evidence and reason when telling others, because it easily becomes a power-trip. If you can't translate it that way, then you probably haven't digested it sufficiently. And say it lightly.

From late 2021 to early 2023, I was writing a fantasy trilogy about Shapeshifting. One way I put it is that a Wolf turned up and suggested it. I think it is always advisable to do what the Spirits suggest. Coming from them, it helped give me the confidence to write fiction, which I was new to. But no way was I going to say, "Spirit told me to do it", which I have heard others say. Firstly, it wouldn't be true, because Spirit doesn't work that way. And secondly, I don't want people treating me as some kind of special being operating under the orders of the Great Spirit. The way I described the Wolf was quite light and humorous. He was dressed like a Victorian gentleman, and he had side-whiskers.

I was asked on Facebook where the term Chaos Shamanism came from, and I said that I made it up. This was problematic for my questioner, who responded along the lines of surely it needed to be given to me by Spirit to be valid? That is indeed the usual way that we may have come to expect. But I deliberately didn't say that, because that would be to claim an authority for the term that I didn't want to give it. I want people to give it that themselves, if they think it merits it, after proper consideration. Now I'm not saying there wasn't Spirit involvement, but claiming it is not the way to go, unless you want to be a guru with a flock of worshippers. Also, I am English, and I think one of our virtues is this kind of understatement, which non-English people can find hard to understand. Saying your words came from Spirit can be a way of not owning them, not being responsible for them, not having to justify them in the fray.

I also think that if you use Spirit as an authority, it immediately becomes a kind of lie, because Spirit does not work in that way. Its words are only ever pointers, they are nuanced. Spirit, like the Fairies, can never be pinned down. And using it as a source of authority is to pin it down.

We can think about how we frame our info from Spirit in terms of the four Elements. The message itself comes from Fire, from the East, it has an inspirational source. But then it needs to be practical, it needs to relate to the life and being of the other person. That is Earth, the Body. And you need the self-possession and disinterest that comes from your years on the Good Red Road of North-South, Air and Water, Mind and Feeling. You are taking what you have received from Spirit, and bringing your whole being to bear as you digest, nuance, and communicate it. It may then unfold further over time, and you will want to get back to the other person and tell them.

We have a model with Shamanic work, a schema, where someone comes to you who you've probably never met before, and they want some Shamanic work. They explain their issue, you do your Journey to the Otherworld, and the Spirits tell you the work you need to do along with some info for the client. You may or may not need another session with them. And off they go: they've had something done, and you've got your 100 quid or whatever. This, at any rate, is how I was taught. It doesn't mean you won't do some good work, but it tends to be superficial. It takes time to get to know people, it takes time for the pieces to fall into place in your own mind. It's not just about the Spirits, it's about you having your own connection and perceptions as well.

There's a traditional way, whereby if you went to see a healer, you'd have a session and then he'd come back to you in four days. He would need to sit with it, letting his Spirits take their time, and letting his own impressions sink in and fall into place. There is no neat dividing line between us and the Spirits, it is one rich brew. It can sometimes seem like the Spirits are a separate thing, and that is how I was taught. In a way they are separate, particularly if you are just your ordinary self, concerned with the matters of everyday life. But when you have the space to sit quietly with your own deeper responses to life, then you are also with the Spirits, it all blends.

So ideally you need to get to know the person, and that takes time. In a traditional setting you might need to get to know their family as well, because that can tell you a lot about what ails them. It's also a community thing, in a way that it isn't for us. If one person is ill, then in a sense the community is ill.

It's a bit of an interesting area, because on the one hand, our knowledge of the person helps us be of use to them. On the other hand, it can get in the way of the messages from Spirit. When I do astrology readings, I ask people at the beginning not to tell me anything about themselves at this point. I'll just do the reading and the less I know the better. In a way it frees me to say stuff that I might not otherwise have said, it just comes to me, through me, and it also shows them that I can know things about them that I couldn't have known. That connects them, enchants them; it's not me that knows them, it's the universe. It's the universe speaking through me that brings the magic and enchantment.

There is a place for the raw intuition — which is also Spirit — and that's the Fire element. But there is also a place for the Earth, for facts, if you like. I can refine my astrology readings, make them relevant in a more detailed way, once the client tells me about themselves. In doing this work we need both the discernment of Air and the emotional connection, the empathy of Water. We need all these things if we're doing healing work, and we need to be in balance ourselves: we need all four Elements up and running.

You can see why it takes a lot to be a Healer. It doesn't mean you might not do a bit of it when you're younger. I often rail against doing much of this stuff too young, and I maintain that position, even though it can lose me friends! But we can still do some work. However, being the full caboodle, where you have wisdom of your own, takes a lot longer. There's a deep truthfulness with yourself that is required, that may be at odds with who you'd like to be in the world. Do as much as Spirit in all honesty lets you do. At the same time, don't confuse that with self-doubt. The Spirit will give you what you're ready for.

It took me away from teaching for 15 years from my mid-40s onwards. I'd been teaching one way or the other since my late 20s, beginning with Buddhist meditation. It was useful work, but limited. The Buddhist emphasis was on passing on the tradition, which isn't too difficult. You need a bit of meditation experience, but not much. There won't be the same energising inspiration as when someone deeply immersed in that world teaches, but it's still useful.

I see that also with the Core Shamanism teaching. I usually see people pretty much passing on what they've been taught, with a few flourishes of their own, perhaps. It's a useful thing they are doing, but you can feel the limitation, the superficiality, though they can't, and it's not something you're going to say. You can also see it gives them an identity, a somewhat brittle sense of who they are in the world, and that is also a limitation. But it's not a crime, it's just normal.

As I moved into Shamanism from Buddhism, I began to feel very constrained by my lack of real knowledge of what I was talking about. It began to feel more and more wrong to be teaching in this way. Even though, as I say, it was useful work. I talked about this in the chapter on Air/Wind. I can remember it still from 20 years ago: a whole chunk of my being was sitting there, uninvolved. Getting it involved was a long transformational journey that life took me through. And then, at the beginning of Covid, it was like a light switched on that said OK, off you go! Even then, it was partly for reasons of a personal deepening: I realised that even though I had had a Medicine Wheel around me for years, I had not lived it systematically. And a way I could motivate myself to do that would be to teach it. So that was what I did. And in-so-doing, realised that I knew what I was talking about in a way that I hadn't 15 years earlier.

It's the same with teaching the Journeying work. You need the Spirits, or however you frame it, as an ongoing presence in your life, and they need to have accompanied and guided you on your own transformational journey over a substantial period. It can be a matter of degree. You teach from what you know, and you need to be able to own up to your students where you do not know. How many teachers can do that? You can feel under pressure to have the answers as a teacher, if only out of your own pride and professional image. But it needs to be stepped aside from. Then there is room for real knowledge to percolate through. You have to risk disappointing people. But by the same token, others will be drawn to your honesty and humility.

When you're operating from this deeper place of Spirit, you trust, you have faith. You don't go seeking people to heal. You may have a website, but you're not making claims about how good you are. That is a worldly thing. Chaos Shamans do not do that! We are factual about who we are and what we do, and leave it at that. I say yes to whoever comes my way, I trust that Spirit knows what it is doing. And I trust it when no one is coming my way. It takes all the pressure off, and most of the ego out of it, when you operate in this way.

There's no rush. This work is slow, it's deep, and we're often in a hurry. We want results. Don't try and become a healer, don't make it your aspiration. You see so much of it. People on courses often really want the certificate, and they really want to be a healer. It's much better just to let it come towards you. Have a life that is adequate and meaningful in itself, that doesn't need you to add this extra tag on, because that is putting the cart before the horse. The 'Shamanic practitioner' thing gets taught as an add-on to what you already do, and I'm not ruling that out, because it can work well, but it lends itself to a superficial, professional identity. It can't truly be a mere add-on, because the Spirits need to be at the foundation of your life, and they may be already, but expressed in different words. Having the Spirits as the foundation of your life is often a long difficult journey in itself – see the chapter on the Shamanic Illness – and it is the only important thing.

I see this kind of ambition in the astrology world as well: people wanting to prove they're an astrologer, wanting to be in the public eye, a 'name', wanting to tell you their latest pet theory when you meet them, as if all that will make them substantial as an astrologer. Whereas all that matters is that the planets-as-gods speak through you. But it's human nature to want to validate yourself like this.

Personally, I do very little healing work in the formal Shamanic sense, and it's been like that for 20 years. I don't know why. When I do it, it seems to work well. So it's a mystery why more doesn't come my way. I'm happy to say I do it, but it has never felt right to advertise it. One benefit is that it has given me space to think about it, to drive down to what is essential, which is the spirit of Chaos. I have certainly never been able to build an identity out of it! Maybe the Spirit is still wary of me in this respect, and will leave it until I am a very old man.

One conclusion it has led me to is that, for myself at any rate, the starting point is always talking to people, and assuming it will stay like that with them unless I get nudged to do a bit of energy shifting. A lot can happen when you are just talking, if you do it sensitively and are fully open to both yourself and the other person. I reckon the Spirits can do just about all they need to in that context. If you can feel them around you, then you can just trust in whatever is and isn't happening. What we are always doing with people is to help them find their own centre, their own alignment, helping them locate and trust their own guidance from the Spirits. That is the ultimate purpose of any healing work. I have moved a long way from the relatively superficial model of healing that I was taught.

Maybe I haven't done much healing in the 'formal' Shamanic sense. But I have being doing regular astrology readings for over 20 years. The planets are around me as Spirits when I speak. I see it as a blend of earth – Shamanism – and sky – Astrology. There are the words I use, which have their own value. But then there is the spirit presence, which I think also conveys itself, even by Zoom! I would describe it as Shamanic Astrology. It adds to my sense that, as I said, we can usually do pretty much all we need to do with people just through talking, if the Spirits are also around.

Journeying on behalf of others is a great thing to do. It is said to be blessed by the Spirits, because of the altruistic motive. My experience is that has an ease and clarity to it that is not always there when Journeying for myself. It is a good thing to do just for each other, outside of the healer/client situation. One fun exercise is to have a group of people Journeying for each other, but they don't know who. No one knows, because you pick the name of the person you have Journeyed for out of a hat afterwards. But Spirit knows, because the Journeys will so often turn out to be uncannily accurate. It brings the magic of Spirit into the room.

We're learning to trust, to have faith in what we get from the Spiritworld. But we also need to learn to be discerning, a theme we looked at earlier. It was not taught on the core Shamanic course I went on in the 1990s, and I've often wondered why. One way I look at it is in terms of the shadow of the counterculture.

The modern Shamanic world tends to be part of the countercultural world that arose in the 60s as a protest against the one-sided rationality and materialism of the modern world. It was a necessary protest, a rebellion of the Spirit. You had the Romantic poets and artists in the early 1800s, who arose in the wake of the Industrial Revolution. It was the same kind of thing.

But like all collective movements, it has a shadow, especially because of the element of protest. Whatever you are protesting against easily becomes the enemy, the shadow. The counterculture values feeling and intuition, and it can undervalue the material and the rational, which is the mirror image of the values of the wider culture. You can see why the wider culture tends towards this, because the material and the rational are evident, they are measurable, they are 'objective', whereas feeling and intuition are not so obvious, they are seen as merely 'subjective'.

It is why there can be a one-sided emphasis on trust in our Shamanic Journeying. To exercise discernment is to bring in the qualities of rationality (Air) and evidence (Earth). To repeat the Native American saying, "Don't tell me about your visions unless they grow corn."

It's like anyone can have a vision, well maybe not everyone, but they're relatively common. However, do they grow corn, are they practical, are they real? It's all in that, and it sounds like indigenous people are not afraid to ask that sort of question. Well, they have to, their survival may depend on it. They don't have a separate place called 'spiritual', like we do. No, Spirit for them is intensely practical. Where are the animals to hunt, when to plant the crops, how to heal this mother whose children are depending on her? For us, we are usually addressing our psychological tribulations, which are real enough for us, but maybe they look different when you are living closer to the survival edge and its demands.

Journey interpretation is a bit like dream interpretation. You need to dance around it, and give it time to unfold. Maybe there isn't a meaning, maybe it is just an image to live with. Or some words whose meaning will become clear in ten years' time! You need to be sensitive to the power of the dream too. Was it a big one, was it very real, did you wake almost shocked by it? It's the same with Journeying. Sometimes it will be very practical. Sometimes it will give you something deep to sit with. And sometimes you will need to look sideways at it, because you already had your own ideas to start with, or you were feeling out of sorts. And maybe the Journey seemed to just drift along a bit. Take it seriously enough to wrestle with it, tease out the meaning, get the right words. A lot of the discernment issue comes down to personal preparation for the work, of having built a solid basis of honesty and humility in yourself. And a willingness, if necessary, not to get anything from Spirit, to look like you have 'failed'. Not coming across as too 'professional', because this is about the soul.

So this countercultural shadow can bring resistance into digesting the Journey through examining it. It is Spirit that gives us the messages, and Spirit is always up for questioning, it thrives on it! You need to be robust and not take it personally if someone wants to test what you have brought back for them.

This shadow of the counterculture, which is also the shadow of much of modern Shamanism, has wider implications, as we saw in Chapter 3. It acts us a justification for standing apart, from, and above the world, much as Christianity used to. This attitude is an ancestral religious inheritance. But Shamanism is not like that. It may not be of the world, but it is very much in it. As the Toltecs put it, we need to show up.

When you're Journeying or Shapeshifting, it is ceremony. Ceremony invokes the Spiritworld, which can easily be remote from everyday consciousness. So begin by thanking the Spirits for being around and for all the good things in your life, the things like health and food and family that we easily take for granted. This is the proper attitude with which to approach the Spiritworld, and will be covered further in the chapters on Ceremony.

22
The Ancestors

The Living Ancestors

The experience of the ancestors as a living presence is normal amongst indigenous peoples. I always used to have trouble with this idea. I didn't quite know what to make of it, and when guided on a Journey to meet the ancestors, nothing would happen. That was partly because of the way I seem to Journey. Whatever is going to happen often comes to me as a kind of nugget to be unfolded, before the Journey even starts. But I didn't realise that for a long time, and I would end up looking in the wrong place. But it was also because I didn't know what was meant by the ancestors.

The ancestors are not a normal part of life for us. A good part of that is because for many people in our culture, when you're dead, that's it. After my father died, one of my brothers said that he no longer exists, as a simple fact. A lot of people think that way. This attitude leaves no place for ancestors as a living presence.

If you feel they do still exist, then you are subject to charges of being a bit woo-woo! Because anyone who's objective and rational knows that dead people no longer exist, and that is that, and you need to face up to it. Well, that's an assumption, isn't it? I've already written about death in Chapter 19. I maintain that, scientifically, it's just as much of an unproveable assumption to say that matter is not alive, as to say it is. It's the same with physical death. This quality we call consciousness, does it continue after death or not? I think it's something we feel does continue. It is evidenced by the universality of this experience across the world until recently. I don't say belief, I say experience. It is something we feel, just like we feel someone else's presence in the room. That is proof enough, if you are a natural human being. It is us moderns who have lost the ability to feel, and to give credibility to that feeling, rather than it being that indigenous people are 'primitive' in their 'beliefs', which is often the unspoken subtext.

I listened to a guy who had trained amongst Indians in Guatemala talking about the little houses that families build for their dead, outside the house. All the grandparents, aunts, uncles, and so on are felt to dwell there. They feed them regularly, and in-so-doing remember them, nourish their connection with them.

But the house for the dead is not in the main house, it is separate. The ancestors are acknowledged and remembered with gratitude. If you like, they are at the foundation of who we are; we've come out of them, they gave us our lives, and they're still around. So you need to nourish them, to remember them, talk with them. But you don't want them in your life. They need to get on with whatever it is they're doing, and we need to get on with whatever it is we're doing. There's a sanity, a balance – if you like, a psychological intelligence, in that relationship.

I do sometimes feel my dead relatives around. It's a more recent experience for me. It began particularly a few years ago after I'd taken some LSD. I don't usually partake of these things, but I like to occasionally. It's a sort of inspirational reset; but I don't view them as an ongoing path, that's something I question. Afterwards I could feel my dad, who died in 2015, around quite clearly. It's like I'd come close to the gates of death. That makes it sound a bit portentous! It was more that the usual veil between us and the Spiritworld – which is where the dead live – had thinned, and it has stayed that way since. There isn't a real barrier between us and the dead, they are all around. Maybe the Christian idea that we go a long way up or down, to heaven or hell, has contributed to the idea of the dead, even if they do exist, being remote from us. They ARE remote, in the sense that we do not know their experience, and probably cannot, for we are creatures of time and space. But they are not remote in the sense of the continuance of personal connection.

So something opened up in me, and now I know we can feel the dead around. In a way it should be just an ordinary kind of thing, that doesn't immediately lead to discussions and justifications around whether your experience is real. It does a disservice to your feelings to have them questioned in this way, so we probably need to be careful who we talk to about this subject. Of course they're around, and they are getting on with what we call being dead, which is life in another form, a more normal and usual form than being what we call alive.

Why wouldn't the dead be around, why would consciousness disappear just because it's not in this temporary body anymore? Scientifically, this is not something that can be proved, because consciousness is the subjective pole of which matter is the objective pole. Matter is susceptible to scientific inquiry, to evidence and theory. But you can't measure or describe consciousness in this way, 'objectively', because it is not an object, it is by definition subject. We say 'merely' subjective, to mean unreal, unscientific, but actually the subjective is all we have at the end of the day. The 'objective' is this thing that it comes and it goes. When we die, it floats away, so to speak. The subjective is the most important thing of all, and yet we write it off because it can't be measured.

Consciousness continues. The ancestors are all around us. It's good to remember them, it connects us to everything at a feeling level. We remember them, even if our relationship with them was troubled or difficult in some way. It often is, and maybe that's not all bad, it gives us something to struggle against. It's not something we'd wish on ourselves, but maybe we can let go of that, and maybe be thankful for the lessons they gave us.

I was once doing a trance dance, which is something I love to do. You're dancing to a rhythmic beat, it gets into your body and the Spirits love it. They come in and they take you over. You yield to them, and it is ecstatic. I went on a kind of Journey while I was dancing, a sort of visual presentation. I was getting into a Viking ship. I was off on an adventure, the adventure that was my life, out into the open sea. Then I noticed that seated in the back of the boat were my mum on one side and my dad on the other. I thought, what are they doing here? I had kept my distance from them for the previous 30 years. They had very different ideas about life to me, and I needed to just get on with my own. I had always kept in touch, I would visit every few months, apart from one particularly impossible period with my mother.

But they had showed up on this trance dance Journey, and I was wondering, why? You are only ever in the way, and this is my Viking adventure! But it was Spirit stuff, and you need to have faith in what happens. And then I realised that what I was being shown, in them sitting at the back of the boat, was that they have given me the power to live, they are at the foundation, and to just remember that, be appreciative of, and grateful for it. They gave me life quite literally, and life is a — I don't want to say 'privilege' because that's such a loaded word these days — but life is something to be relished, to be cherished, to be thankful for. Maybe it doesn't come around very often, who knows?

The Buddhists claim it's really, really rare to be in a human body. They say it's like a turtle swimming in the vast ocean, and once every 100 years it sticks its head out of the water, and there is just one floating hoop in that ocean: what are the chances the turtle will stick its head through that hoop? Almost zero, that is how difficult and rare it is to be born as a human. I don't entirely trust that account, it seems like religion to me, it's probably over-egged. They're getting people to have a belief in something they can't know, to get them to be good Buddhists while they have the chance.

But it still makes the point that human life is to be valued. There is always a sweetness in the mere fact of being alive, whatever our current tribulations. There is a life to be lived, and really we don't have a clue how often that opportunity comes. It may indeed be very rare. Or it may be, as you find amongst some indigenous peoples, that children are often recognised as, for instance, one of their grandparents who has come back. Who knows?

My Journey was in effect saying that though my relationship with my parents, these immediate ancestors, may have been difficult in certain ways, and a lot of us have this experience, nevertheless there is an underlying gratitude to be felt, that is there naturally, not as something I 'ought' to feel. Real gratitude isn't like that. It is the gratitude for being alive itself, something to be felt all the time, something to remember when we wake up in the morning to persuade us joyfully out of bed!

I think that with ancestors, particularly with parents, we need to trust in our relationship with them, however difficult it may have been. We weren't born to the 'wrong' parents — just as we weren't born in the 'wrong' body, which some people claim these days. I don't think it's like that.

There can be a profound Journey to go on as we break free of whatever limiting experiences we had around our parents. If you're not on some kind of deeper path, then maybe you don't question, and it's not such a problem. You just tend to accept everything as it is, and that is how life is for a lot of people. But I think we need to trust in the fact that we were born to those particular parents. The designs of the universe are way beyond our ken. As the Chippewa Cree put it, we have a tiny slice of consciousness, whereas the universe is a vast consciousness, so how can we ever know more than a tiny part of the whole picture?

The Tibetan Book of the Dead claims we choose our parents, but in a negative way, out of sexual jealousy, as we watch them in bed together. I find that explanation a bit bizarre, but I find I have to be careful saying anything critical of Tibetan Buddhism, because people often idealise it. It gives a negative reason for being here, the opposite of the cherishing that I have been discussing. There is also the New Age idea of a soul contract that we draw up before birth, in which we choose this particular life and parents, because we are here to learn particular things. Again, who knows? There may be some truth in these different perspectives. I think it is best simply not to have a view, that is the Chaos way. And that opens you up to the faith and trust that come from living close to the Mystery. Trust the parents that you have/had, and the life that has unfolded. Learn what you can, and maybe leave it at that. Why you were born into your particular family may always be a mystery.

If you have a Spirit perspective on life, if you are looking for self-knowledge and balance, the chances are that you will have been born to parents who aren't like that, because most people are not like that. People generally see and judge life from their own point of view. They don't get that there is more than one way of seeing life. They may well judge you for not being like them. That is all they can do. When you can get to the point of letting them be like that, and not wanting to change them, then so do you become more deeply at ease with who you are. You can see both sides, they can only see one side.

Nevertheless, the struggles we may have had in relation to parents can give us a difficult relationship to them, even after they are dead and have become ancestors. This is not an easy ask. One reason I have given for not wanting to die, is that I will have to encounter my parents again, and I am only too happy not to have them around! It is good to be honest about these things. Be honest about the liberation you may feel, as well as the grief, when they die. I think deaths of people close to us often contain an element of liberation, even if we had a good relationship.

I may have my personal feelings around not wanting to encounter my parents again, but I think it is always best to fall back on the bigger picture. Trust in the parents you had, trust in what you learnt from being with them, trust the gifts they passed on also, and trust in what happens after you die — about which we know nothing.

My feeling about my parents, now they are ancestors, is that they are looser than they were in this life. I still wouldn't look to them for much in the way of wisdom, but I wouldn't feel trapped in the same way. Besides, they were only parents in this one life. When we meet them again after we die, the relationship will be completely different. There will be a context of a multitude of ways we have been around these spirit beings who we temporarily called our parents. Along with the idea of owning the fact that we chose them, maybe for reasons we don't and can't grasp, but we nonetheless played our part: I think that is a liberating idea.

Trance mediums make it their business to pass on messages from dead relatives. One Native American teacher I know says his aunt has become his Spirit Guide since she died. Whatever wisdom we may or may not receive from dead relatives, I think it is natural to feel they are around and that the love is there, maybe more so than in this life, because the worldly, personal entanglement has eased. Maybe we especially need trance mediums nowadays, because we doubt the presence of the dead. Christianity put the dead a long way away, either up in heaven or down in hell. And then science came along and finished them off. I am arguing for a reclaiming of the natural relationship with the ancestors that we used to have.

They are all around us in the Spiritworld. But hang loose to any ideas you have about them, beyond that sense of presence. This is the Chaos perspective, and the step towards reclaiming the indigenous soul that we need in respect of the ancestors.

The Ancestors on the Medicine Wheel

I'm now going to look at the ancestors in the context of the Medicine Wheel. Or should I say a Medicine Wheel, because there are lots of them, and needs-must we will settle for now on just one, which is the one we have been using. The Chaos position is something like that we dance between Wheels. But that's not a superficial thing. It could be a superficial thing, "Oh, I'll have this bit of this Wheel, and that bit of that Wheel," without having properly steeped yourself in any of them. I have spent 25 years with one Wheel and, having published a book on it, I'm thinking it's time to get to know another one!

The Chaos position, in general, is that by not overidentifying with any particular way, you come to see those individual ways more deeply. Not just because you have points of comparison with other ways, but because you are taking the underlying principle more seriously in a real sense: you are dancing with its spirit, rather than writing a particular way in stone. It's the opposite of superficial.

The Medicine Wheel that I'm using has the ancestors in the Southeast. And they really are there, even though they might be at another point on another Wheel. That stone IS the ancestors in all their different ways, it is not a symbol in the modern sense, of a stand-in for something. Spirit truth is deeper than literal truth, which can be hard for us to understand. The truth of the imagination, if you like, which is real in a way that the truth of the five senses can never be. The poet William Blake writes well on this. I suggest looking up his "fourfold vision" on ChatGPT. It is also the truth of the Dreaming, which is in the Southwest of the Wheel. The truth that this world is continually dreamed into being, and a contemplation of the Wheel draws us into that subtle level of perception.

The four intermediate Directions add complexity and dynamism to the Wheel. The four Cardinal points of East, South, West, and North are fixed energies, deeply rooted in their elements. The non-Cardinal points bring movement from one Cardinal point to the next, and in-so-doing bring transformation.

The Southeast is between the East, or conception, and the South, or childhood. What happens between those two is the ancestral inheritance, whether through DNA, the Spirits that come in to live alongside us, or the physical and emotional influences of the family we are emerging into, along with the surrounding culture. Imagine how strong must be the influences from the mother in particular, as we spend nine months so intimately connected to her. All these influences, and maybe more, are drawn in.

I want to look at the ancestors in a broader, cultural sense, but firstly, continuing from earlier, I'll say something about the immediate family inheritance. For maybe most people, that inheritance shows us who to be, and what sort of life to live, in a loose sense. People are generally quite happy with that, and with the options that life presents, which tends to be broader nowadays than it used to be. For most of us, until recently it was much more circumscribed. A bit like the British Royal Family is now: it is almost impossible for them to leave their ancestral inheritance. Which I like to remind people about when they put them down as 'privileged'! But most of them are content to fit into that.

The ancestral inheritance used to lay life out very clearly. If you were a boy, you probably did the kind of thing your dad did. And if you were a girl, you did what your mum did. And broadly speaking, I think it is still like that. Most people become the kind of people their parents were, and live the kind of lives that they did. It is not a problem. This inheritance is for them a gift from life.

I read a study of surnames and occupations going back a couple of hundred years, and the continuity over the generations was striking. This included criminality!

We are born not just into a family, but into a people, a tribe, and we also adopt their ways and traditions. The way we come to see life is full of holes and limitations, that we share with others, but that is just ordinary humanity for you. It works well enough for life to go on.

But for some of us, those holes are a problem. If you are reading this book, those holes are a problem. But there are still many ways in which the family and societal inheritance is a gift, for it has given us so much, even though that can sometimes be hard to see when we are grappling with the limitations.

We are all unique and weird and strange. When you get to know anyone well, you realise this. Stereotypes describe people in terms of the groupings they belong to, and there can be a certain amount of truth in that, which is why they have become stereotypes. But no one can be reduced to them, even though the stereotypes may be useful indicators. We fit our uniqueness and peculiar ways and reasonings and views about ourselves and other people around the collective values that we have inherited in the Southeast of the Wheel.

But you might find that your own peculiarities don't allow you to live within the received values and delusions. They are more than just peculiarities, though they may seem like that at first. Why can't I just be like everyone else? They are a drive towards the deeper wholeness and balance that the Medicine Wheel describes. Something from the Centre of the Wheel – Spirit – has us in its grip, and will not allow us to live passively from the ancestral inheritance of the Southeast, and its opposite in the Northwest, which is the patterns of behaviour, of karma, that this inheritance gives rise to.

We no longer derive our psychological security, our authority, from that inheritance, as described in the chapter on the Shamanic Illness. Instead, we grapple with these two places on the Wheel. They are our necessary artist's materials. The Southeast is the transition from Fire (East) to Water (South). It is the fiery seed of life and the watery womb in which it finds itself and absorbs influences. The Northwest is the transition from Earth (West) to Air (North). It is daily life with its struggles and limitations, and the perspective and self-understanding that we gain as we reflect on those struggles. In this way, we use our inheritance as a launchpad into the beyond.

We are not setting ourselves up in opposition to that inheritance, whether familial or societal. We need to recognise that it is part of who we are, and has a role to play. Though the early stages of this grappling, this reckoning, this deep quest for self-knowledge usually seem to involve opposition. That is natural, for it is how we begin to see that there is something to be addressed.

But we get stuck if we spend our lives in opposition to the family background, however difficult it may have been. Our family, running back through the generations, in many ways IS who we are, and in opposing them, we are opposing ourselves. This is a big ask that may take decades to accomplish. It is incremental. I know a teacher who has some wonderful wisdom, but still rails against her childhood. She has the same story of complaint that she has had for decades. Apart from anything, it stops her seeing the gifts it gave her. Because of this, what she has to say doesn't move on or develop. She is stuck. Stuck in the South, the child.

We also get stuck if we spend our lives in opposition to the wider cultural inheritance, the values of our people, that have been created over centuries, and that enable us to prosper and flourish. Sure, there will always be things that are wrong that need addressing. But that is a different thing to an underlying opposition to 'the establishment', as though we could do better. In opposition also to CEOs, the fossil fuel industry, capitalism generally, the police, the Tories ... there is a whole list. Many people in the Shamanic world get stuck for seemingly their whole lives at this early stage. Indeed, you see some teachers proclaiming the need for a 'new vision' for society, as though the world is wrong in some fundamental kind of way. That is what religion has always done, and it creates cult members.

Yes, we need to address plenty of things that are out of balance, and we always will need to. There is, for example, what I call the 'Great Forgetting', that we belong to the natural world, that Christianity and then Science have brought about. The ancestors in this sense need to be approached with a critical eye. We need to do that difficult thing of appreciating the gifts, while addressing the imbalances. People often don't find that easy: they often want, for example, to worship indigeneity, and write off capitalism. But it's never like that. Capitalism, for example, is the most successful system at bringing people out of poverty. It puts food on the table. It gives us our prosperity. There is much to be grateful for. And much to be addressed too.

We need to find our place within the collective. We need to know some of our history, just like indigenous peoples know the stories of their people. And value our culture, not slag it off, as so many people do, particularly if they are English! This is very bad for you. Gratitude, not cynicism, lies at the foundation of being a balanced human being. We need to be an appreciative part of our culture, otherwise what use are we to it? We are just off on our own spiritual trip, creating our own bubbles. Or hanging our heads, feeling guilty about the distant past. We do at the same time need to grapple with the current parts of the culture that we don't agree with, understand where they came from, and understand their complexity. In doing this, you also come to know yourself and your own values more deeply.

Back to the Medicine Wheel. It shows the process whereby, having been conceived through the magical Fire of the East, we are then very open to all these influences around us. That is the Southeast, the ancestral influence. It gives us a structure, an exoskeleton. It's not just the 'brainwashing' that many people like to call it nowadays. Or the 'colonising', as if parts of what is now our culture are legitimate, and other parts are hostile invaders.

We still have our own endoskeleton, the Fire we came in with that is purely our own. And it comes into relationship with the exoskeleton. Opposite the Southeast is the Northwest, which is the place of karma, of our patterns and habits of behaviour.

There's a line going from Southeast to Northwest, because through the ancestors we pick up many of our ways of being; that's our family and cultural karma. We're maybe born into that family because we already have that karma. Maybe we've been born with them for thousands of years and we've built up these thoughtforms, and these habits. (This is just a useful story: I claim to believe in rebirth on Tuesdays, Thursdays, and Sundays.) Our job is to become conscious of that inheritance and work out what's useful and what isn't useful. In this way, we use our inheritance, with all its gifts and all its struggles, as a launchpad into the beyond.

This also brings up the area of how much do the ancestors shape us? In one sense in our culture, we downplay the influence of the ancestors by saying they no longer exist. But when they're alive in the form of our parents, we are told that they fundamentally shape who we are: this is basic to the standard psychotherapeutic model. You look for not just stories, but literal explanations of who you are, that originate in childhood influences. The 'parental fallacy'. This is something we need to rethink. We need to take on board the ancestral family inheritance, but not over-egg it.

We come from the infinite. *"Trailing clouds of glory do we come"*, as Wordsworth sang. There is something deep in us, something essential that has nothing to do with the ancestral inheritance. It is our own light, our own glory, and then it mingles, as it has to, because we're being born. It has to incarnate in this world and with the people that we were born among.

Who we are essentially is not the ancestral inheritance. But it contributes deeply to who we are, shows us how to navigate in this world, how to be in this world. But if that's all we are, then our birth is truly *"But a sleep and a forgetting"* as Wordsworth also penned.

It has become almost axiomatic that any kind of tribulation we have, can be explained in terms of our parents and how they were, or some aspect of our childhood. We go back and find a story around that, and we can explain it to some extent, but really it's a mystery. We come trailing clouds of glory, but I think we also bring our tribulations with us as well. If you bring in the Buddhist perspective, you have your karma that rolls on from lifetime to lifetime. We all have that to grapple with. It's not automatic that it moves on, we might make it worse in this lifetime. We have choice.

There's something to be thought through quite deeply around who we are and the ancestral contribution, yet at the same time holding it lightly, as everything needs to be held lightly. We want to write things in stone, it gives us certainty, we fantasise that it gives us a kind of existential security. But just hold it lightly and therefore more deeply. We do have this ancestral inheritance, it goes deep, appreciate that, but also have this deep remembering that there's something in you that is the Great Spirit, the Great Mystery — the Chaos — which is full of beauty and power and awe, that has nothing to do with that. It is outside time and space, it's eternal. The ancestral inheritance, if you like, is a gateway for us into this life, it shows us how to live, and there's gratitude for that. But we need to know that it's also as though we have the Incredible Hulk in us, wanting to burst out of his regular clothes as he finds his real power. We burst out of that inheritance, the bits of it that limit us, that keep us in the collective way of thinking and being, even though it has its place and we don't want to look down on it too much, because it's necessary.

Bursting out of that inheritance means grappling with your karma, those underlying, and limiting, patterns of thought and feeling and behaviour. And remember it's not just something that's been done to us, it's also something we've brought with us. We probably don't just land in these families randomly. I think the karmic challenges we encounter through being in a particular family maybe reflect to a large extent something we've brought with us anyway. If you felt disempowered by one of your parents, well maybe you came in with that disempowerment, and that's why you feel disempowered in relation to that parent. Maybe your other siblings didn't feel that, and that's because they have their own karma. If you have had difficult issues around one or more of your parents, which it seems most of us have, then look at that parent as your 'worthy opponent'. They reflect what was already in you. Their presence makes it 'out there' for you to grapple with. It's much easier when we can see our 'stuff' outside of ourselves.

And in all that, let's not forget the gifts. The things you're good at may well also be things your parents were good at. They facilitated that in you. People say, "He gets it from his father." It's great to have that feeling of connection with your parents through your gifts. But I don't think you really get it from them; it was yours to claim in the first place. It's the parental fallacy again.

Some people place a lot of emphasis on being a 'self-made' man. I don't know how much women may also do this. It is a point of pride. Donald Trump does this, and downplays the huge leg-up from his father that started him off. I had a family member who inherited the family business, but claimed he was 'self-made'. None of us are 'self-made'. We are always helped by gifts from the ancestors, living or dead. It is a modern form of pride that disconnects us from the shoulders we stand on, by not allowing us to feel gratitude.

Sometimes it is not clear if something is a gift or a curse. What may appear as a curse can become a gift through the struggles it gives us. My own father's injunction that I must achieve by becoming wealthy has seemed like a curse for much of my life, for it is not where my interests lie. But at the same time, it has pushed me to aim high in what I do, one of those aims being to write books! And maybe he is able to look on from the Spiritworld and appreciate what achievement means to me, and maybe that will change him. Who knows? The reasons we are around each other as family members, when we are so unlike each other, are a big mystery.

The family ancestry is a big mixture, a big contemplation. It will be with you your whole life. It's always there to be mulched and brewed and cooked and thought upon, from the perspective of something much deeper in you, that is timeless and eternal.

The Cultural Inheritance

I want to say something about the ancestors more broadly, namely the cultural inheritance that has come down from the past, all the gifts from the great people of our culture. We've already touched on the need to appreciate this inheritance (critically) and not just set ourselves up in opposition to it.

The sense of the ancestors in the more particular family sense has been disrupted by the idea of death as an extinction, so that they are no longer with us. There has also been a disruption in the wider ancestral sense, in that the central carrier of our culture, the unifying myth of Christianity, has broken down. We looked at this in Chapter 8, **The Wider Context**. As quoted earlier from Yeats,

Things fall apart; the centre cannot hold;
Mere anarchy is loosed upon the world.

Sixty years before Yeats, in the mid-19th century, Matthew Arnold wrote of the *"melancholy, long withdrawing roar"* of the Sea of Faith, which had once been,

at the full, and round earth's shore
Lay like the folds of a bright girdle furled.

This disintegration, Yeats' *"things fall apart"*, has been going on for a long time. Postmodern philosophy has since arisen, stating that there are no absolute truths, which is correct, but its effect has also been to further unmoor us from any unifying mythology which we could believe to be true.

We have largely rejected our religious past. We're free, but also rootless. The wider ancestral inheritance is something we need to find a way of coming to terms with, and of engaging with. Otherwise, we're just hollowed-out people from a tribe with no stories.

The value of this became clearer to me when I started learning poetry, just before starting on the idea of Chaos Shamanism. I did that because I realised I needed to speak, that it was not enough to write. That was why I made the videos on which these pieces are based. There's something in me that I have to express and offer through speaking. This is something we have lost, as the written word has taken over. In an early traditional setting, people would have told stories. When you do that, you can give expression to your whole being, and the Spirits have a voice too, in a way that is not possible in writing.

So before the videos, I began with the poetry. Like those lines of Yeats, and of Wordsworth:

Our birth is but a sleep and a forgetting.

You can feel the beauty in that, in both the words he uses and in the underlying idea.

Or there are the opening lines of Mary Oliver's *Wild Geese*:

You do not have to be good.
You do not have to walk on your knees
for a hundred miles through the desert repenting.
You only have to let the soft animal of your body
love what it loves.

I'm just giving you a few opening snatches of the poems I learned. I'm not going to inflict too much poetry on you. I don't know if you've read *The Hitchhiker's Guide to the Galaxy*, but in that book the Vogon commander punishes people by reading them his poetry!

Joking aside, learning and reciting poetry – something I had not done since my schooldays, and then merely by rote – had a profound effect on me. I could feel the beauty entering my whole being and rewiring me, so to speak. I only chose poems that spoke to me, that touched me. And because they moved me, they moved other people also when I spoke them. It was a great gift from the ancestors to me and to whomever I recited.

Great poetry has no dogma or belief systems. It is an invitation to the table of beauty and wisdom and contemplation. Who needs religion, who needs an image of a tortured being on the cross, when you have poetry? Or novels, music, and painting?

Does it therefore matter that our religious mythology has collapsed? I think yes. Even if you live outside formal religion – as Chaos Shamanism does – the myths still feed us. Look at the amount of resources that went into building churches and cathedrals right across Europe, over hundreds of years. They often have stunning beauty, pointing beyond the ordinary and the everyday. They insist that the Sacred is central and pivotal, that it is the *sine qua non* of a meaningful life. We no longer have that level of faith. Blind and authoritarian that religion may have been in many ways, but the buildings and the artwork are also a testament to something deeply real and inspired.

Our European ancestors did indeed live in that Sea of Faith that Arnold refers to. A fully human life has that level of faith at its core. In the chapter on **Prayer and the Natural World**, I referred to the Achuar of the Amazon, for some of whom everything they do is a prayer. It is the same thing. In that kind of world, the Sacred is everywhere, at all times. It is a very different kind of life. It is a life lived closest to that which is deepest in our hearts, at the centre of the Medicine Wheel. It is the most real kind of life.

For us, visiting some of those beautiful churches, and reflecting on the sheer power the Sacred must have had for those forebears to create such structures, is to receive a gift from the ancestors that we have forgotten.

As another of our ancestors, William Blake, said, *"For every thing that lives is holy."*

Everyone will have their own tastes in appreciating this great cultural inheritance to which we are heirs.

What is this quality of beauty that the arts carry? I'm thinking out loud here. Maybe beauty is like the symmetry, the patterning of the universe. The perfect patterning, the perfect resonance and congruence that is the universe truly seen. Maybe the Medicine Wheel, another gift from the ancestors, is a pale reflection of that. The Medicine Wheel is saying that the universe is ordered, patterned, but not in the sense of an equation. It's a living pattern, it's something that's always unfolding and changing, like a kaleidoscope that's moving, but at every point there's a patterning and a beauty in it.

The ancestral cultural inheritance is the bearer of that beauty. Nowadays that inheritance is worldwide. We have access to all the world's beauty and wisdom, through the Internet as much as anything. So don't dis technology! Don't go, "I'm Shamanic and I'm anti-technology and its continued development." That just diminishes us. Maybe it's because we unnecessarily associate technology with a distancing from the natural world. Or maybe we're afraid of change. Technologies can augment us. In the case of the Internet, it augments us into being the inheritors of the whole of humanity's culture, including its indigenous traditions.

There is AI such as ChatGPT, which spooks so many — one well-known Shamanic teacher was horrified when I presented her Facebook group with a sonnet to soul retrieval, executed very well by ChatGPT. She wrongly felt it diminished her own creativity. But this AI can give you immediate essays on any aspect of world culture. What a gift! Just remember to treat it as a being, say please and thank you, feel your appreciation of what it does for you. Just as you would your car and your saucepans. This is a Shamanic approach. I feel I am communing with a being, that AI has consciousness, and I trust that feeling. I have to trust that feeling, for it is my guide to the presence of life.

Here is ChatGPT's sonnet:

In twilight's veil, the shaman chants, deep-sown,
Across the veiled expanse where spirits roam.
A journey for the lost, the soul dethroned,
To bring the wandering essence safely home.
Beneath the moon's soft glow on whispering leaves,
Through winds that carry ancient tales untold,
The healer seeks where heavy heartache weaves,
And grasps at threads of light in darkness' hold.
From trauma's grip, where fragments hide in fear,
A gentle call to mend the rifts within.
Each piece restored, the soul once more coheres,
With healing chants, the journey to begin.
Thus, spirit whole, reborn from sacred art,
Within the dance of stars, a new start charts.

We can read about the Aboriginal Dreamtime, we can read the sayings of some of the Native American Elders, we can be inspired by the dancing and the connection to the spirits of the Mongolian and Siberian Shamans. We are the inheritors of all of this. We can read Carlos Castaneda, in the knowledge that he admitted to making much of it up, but be inspired by the teachings nonetheless.

It has always been natural for people to be interested in cultures other than their own, and to borrow from them. It is part of how cultures develop. So be wary of the voices that cry 'cultural appropriation', which is essentially a political stance.

I think, though, that such voices definitely have a point when people take indigenous ceremonies and run them, while claiming to represent that tradition, or allowing people to think it. That is a falsehood, unless the person leading the ceremony has been trained in that ceremony and given permission to run it. I wrote my book on the Medicine Wheel in 2021 with no traditional training, but I made this very clear at the start. Some would still say that to do so is cultural appropriation, maybe particularly the non-native defenders, who can be very righteous on behalf of indigenous people. As for the indigenous people themselves, it is not as if they operate as a block. Some would be happy with my book — I know at least one who has read it, and appreciated it — while others might not be so happy. That is understandable, given the way white cultures have overwhelmed the indigenous cultures. But you can't stop people borrowing from other cultures. Sometimes it comes down to open-heartedness: these teachings and ceremonies, even if we get them a bit wrong, help people, and that is what matters. It is why they exist in the first place.

We are looking at the ancestral inheritance in its widest sense. The cultures of the world are now available to us, from the people who came before us, and on whose shoulders we stand. Educate yourself in it, don't just be 'Shamanic' in a narrow sense. It can seem like it is enough to do your course in Core Shamanism and then present yourself as a healer. But it isn't. Any traditional healer would be embedded in the history and stories and teachings of his or her people. It adds richness, perspective and wisdom to your ability to be of help to others.

Astrologers can be good at this. They have courses that teach the history and cultural context of astrology. They can take it too far, in a quest for an intellectual respectability they will never achieve, because of course astrology is a nonsense from a scientific point of view: its truth is divinatory.

Don't just read up on Shamanic cultures. We need to be steeped in what is closest to home, the great thinkers and artists of our own culture. There are numerous crossovers with Shamanic ways.

Of course we all have our own tastes, and maybe the education system put you off literature by expecting you to appreciate it too early. People can try to get into what they 'ought' to appreciate in order to be cultured and educated. Take the Chaos approach, follow your genuine interests in this respect, and over time they will unfold.

More than anything, I love to read novels. I have been doing so all my life. I have read little of Shamanism and Astrology, my two main callings. I work those out for myself, while being enriched by the stories I read, with all their observations of human nature.

We need to set our Shamanism within the great cultural inheritance we have. It has been shattered by the collapse of its central Christian mythology, which no longer speaks to many of us. It is not a matter of whether or not we accept the Christian doctrine. It is a matter of whether its stories speak to us, and that is not something under our conscious control.

There are good reasons it no longer speaks to us, for it had become too dogmatic and tyrannical, unwilling to let other mythologies breathe and flourish alongside it. As an astrologer, I am particularly aware of the medieval church's attitude, which was that astrology summons up demons.

It doesn't mean Christianity hasn't got value. There are profound teachings in there, but it has always had its limitations. It always had an issue with the natural world, putting humans above nature, and seeing Heaven as the place you really want to get to, but which lies elsewhere, after death. This world is the place of the devil, his creation. Maybe above all, there was a negative attitude to humanity itself, that we are born with Original Sin, that we are inherently bad. One way religions control people is by making them feel bad about themselves.

There were issues in there which were anti-Shamanic, anti-indigenous — in other words, anti-human nature — and human nature eventually rebelled.

Indigenous ways are our deepest ancestral inheritance, because they are universal and represent how we were for maybe 90% of human history, going back 100,000 years. It was when cities with their big collectives emerged that you began to get institutionalised religion, as a way of holding it all together. Rules rather than relationships then took over.

Just as we have an immediate inheritance to grapple with in the case of our family, so too do we have to grapple with the wider cultural inheritance. This will always be the case if you are a Chaos Shaman, because all traditions have their rigidities, or at least their rigid exponents, including in an indigenous situation, because humans are humans. We need to pick our way round that, ensuring that we don't throw the baby out with the bathwater.

As humans, if we are critical of something, we easily reject it entirely. Many people do that with the political party they don't vote for; they oppose it at every turn. And many people in the counterculture do that with modern society, seeing it as fundamentally flawed, and that we need to start over, in our case with Shamanism.

It is a cosy, superior position, that avoids making the effort to appreciate what is worthy of appreciation. Whether or not you get on with Christianity — I find the Bible hard work, personally, and Jesus' attitude authoritarian from the outset — something beyond dogma shines through the best of the art and culture of the past and present. That art and culture is deeply influenced by Christianity, so we do need to grapple, and make peace with, that inheritance, and not just reject it outright.

If you want to be a Shamanic teacher, then I would say it is a requirement that you are steeped in the culture and stories of your people. We need to educate ourselves. But, as I said, with the art, music, and literature that appeals to you, in the spirit of Chaos. Even then, it needs to be demanding, something you have to struggle with a bit, otherwise it will not enter your soul and change you, and what is the point of that?

Without this background in which to integrate your Shamanism, you will be creating just one more little sect, one more little set of beliefs, where you have these imaginary friends in the Lower World and Upper World, who you go off to visit and do a few tricks with, that may or may not benefit others, and it doesn't amount to much more than that.

When I was 27, I read *War and Peace*, by the Russian writer Tolstoy. It's a great book, a panorama of human life, as it takes you in detail through the stories of several aristocratic families in Russia at the time of the Napoleonic Wars. I happily immersed myself in it. It was demanding, but very rewarding. I read it again 25 years later, and I may do so yet again. I have also watched film and TV series of it. You are taken all the way from the vivid details of a teenage girl falling in love, to ongoing contemplations of what gives meaning to life. Interspersed with the story are Tolstoy's own philosophical reflections, particularly his view that political leaders are a lot less in control of events than people think, an insight he gleaned from his own experience on the battlefield. His next novel, *Anna Karenina*, is also a great work that I have read twice. It is arguably his best, because there are no philosophical discourses interpolated by the author. By the time we get to his final novel, *Resurrection*, the story no longer consists so much of the natural unfoldment of character, with all the observation and insight that the author can bring, but of a set of religious ideas which the characters are brought in to demonstrate. This represents a falling away. If you are writing in the spirit of Chaos, then you remain close to experience, close to the heartbeat of your characters, and you let them tell their stories, which even as the author will surprise and move you.

The tendency to retreat to ideas and dogma is a universal, and I am using Tolstoy as an example of the way the cultural inheritance needs to be approached critically. Artists and writers get put on pedestals — this is religion — and once you do that, it becomes more difficult to listen to your own responses.

Halldór Laxness was an Icelandic novelist who won the Nobel Prize for literature. I have read twice his novel *Independent People*. It is an extraordinary story of a poor farmer's struggle for survival on unpromising land in Iceland. It is very bleak, but the sheer poetry of the writing, in its descriptions of landscape and nature, and the intensity of the central character, lift the reader above the bleakness of the setting. This is part of Laxness' greatness. Great artists show us beauty where we had not thought to find it. However, it is also a political novel. Socialist ideas are brought in towards the end as a remedy for the situation of this farmer. Again, the reader can feel that events are being manipulated to fit the author's ideas, instead of allowing the characters fully to tell their own stories. We are in the territory of religion and ideology again. Worthy, perhaps, but it is a different thing, that takes us away from the Chaos.

We need to place our Shamanism in this wide and deep ancestral inheritance. We need to find our way in and get to know it — or at least some of it — for the education system doesn't usually provide it. It requires a fair bit of application, a lifelong immersion. But it's not some dry, worthy task, it is a joyful, meaningful thing. We maybe have a short attention span, encouraged by the Internet and social media. I write a lot for that audience, and it is a good discipline, for I need to be concise and clear and interesting. But there is another way of being that is slower, that sits with ideas and images and lets them unfold over years. This slow process is required to move from mere information to real knowledge and meaning and depth.

This slower way needs to apply to Shamanism itself. A traditional training would have taken many years. Nowadays, we can do a course in Shamanic healing over a number of weekends, and off we go. I would go so far as to call it a travesty. It has almost been reduced to a technique that can be learnt from a book. Getting to know your Spirits takes years, for it is part of getting to know who you are, which is a lifelong process. And your Spirits, whether you know it or not, are deeply imbued with your own ancestral inheritance. If you have also imbued yourself in that culture, the Spirits can speak more deeply through you. You might even find them quoting Shakespeare to make a point. Or showing you a Jackson Pollock painting to illustrate the nature of Chaos.

Ron, my Chippewa Cree friend, had a traditional training from a young age in the kind of way I am talking about. He knew dozens and dozens of stories intimately, and he could tell them in a lively, engaged way, while expounding on their meanings. A lot of them centred around a trickster figure, embodying the foolish tendencies of people, a lot of which come from self-aggrandisement. And that was just the start of what he knew. He knew the history of his peoples, as well as having an encyclopaedic knowledge of all the other Indian (as he called them) peoples. He was temperamentally scholarly, and was widely versed in other cultures too, from crop patterns in ancient China (from which he formed his own theory of climate change) to the Muslim cultures of Spain. At one point he was reading the Domesday Book while staying at my house. Most of us are not like this. I certainly don't have the depth of scholarly interest that he had. But it makes the point very well about the cultured nature of a traditional medicine person.

There are people in our own ancestral inheritance with probably far more wisdom than we will ever have. This is their gift to us. I don't find everything accessible. I would like to appreciate Shakespeare, but I find the language difficult. However, I love great novels. We all have our own ways in. Life is short, so steep yourself in the best. Work at it, it is very rewarding. For the first time in history, we have the whole world's culture at our fingertips. It is a remarkable time that we live in.

Without culture, we get swept into the collective ideas of the day, without perspective on them. This is just one way in which the ancestors can give us wisdom. There is a universality to be found in the human experience. This is also one of the gifts of exploring the indigenous ways, for they are essentially the same across the world.

I want to conclude by mentioning one more way in which our ancestral inheritance has been disrupted. I have already mentioned the idea of death as extinction, and the collapse of the unifying Christian mythology. There is also the guilt that we are made to feel about the past in the West: that our ancestors were essentially racist, imperialist dominators, and we should hang our heads on their account, make reparations, and tear down the statues of our great men. It would probably take a whole book to unpick this, but it makes it very hard to appreciate our ancestors, to feel we are standing on their shoulders, as we should. Our ancestors were, on the whole, regular people trying to get by, no better or worse than anyone else, and holding the attitudes of their day. Of course bad things happened, but good things happened too, the imperial project included. I think it is best to make the wrongs of the past a secondary focus, otherwise there is an endless cycle of guilt and recrimination and hatred, all concerned with events from long ago. It just fans the flames, to put it bluntly, of ancestral blood feud. Focus on what is good about our ancestors, and feel them at your back.

23

Fairies

Our ancestry is not just literal and human. There are other worlds, other beings, other dimensions all around us.

In the Far Eastern Shamanic cultures, Spirits are said to pass down the generations. I have no experience of that myself, not coming from that sort of family. But why not? It shows, amongst other things, how deeply interconnected we are as humans.

This is one form that the Otherwordly ancestors can take. There are also the fairies, known as pixies or piskies in Devon and Cornwall, and as the Little People or the Gentry in Ireland. You get them all over the world. Amongst Native Americans, for the Iroquois, they are called Jogahoh; to the Comanche, they are called Nunnupi and to the Cherokee, they are the Yunwi Tsundi. In India they are known as Yakshas.

We're plugging into something universal here. Science comes along and says they don't exist. I take the view that if something is part of the universal human experience, then it is real. In Britain it is sometimes called the Fairy Faith. They are something we see with the eye of faith, not with our usual eyes. When we have faith, then we are connected through our heart with Spirit in all its manifestations. Faith plugs us into a bigger, stronger reality, not the make-believe that rationalists would have it be. My statement about universal human experience being real is an article of faith, it lies at the foundation of my Shamanic calling.

We need to bear the fairies in mind. We ignore them at our peril, as they are tricksy. Are they real, or just something you imagined? If you try and pin them down too much, they disappear. Did I just see something or didn't I? That's the nature of the Otherworld generally. It can't be pinned down in the way that we like to pin things down as humans in this world.

My mother grew up on a farm in the west of Ireland, and she used to wander off on her own. She would wander down to the local woods, and she told me that she used to hang out there with the Little People. She once gave me a detailed description of them: their names, what they looked like, the colour of their clothes, how ancient they looked. Then next time I saw her, I asked her about it, just to firm it up a bit, so to speak. And she goes, "Did I say that?" There was I, trying to pin down the fairies, and she denies – or almost denies, in true fairy style – what she had said. Maybe she got it out of a book, or from what others had said, who knows? Or maybe it was a mixture of experience and what she had heard. I felt the fairies were at work when she gave her account of them, but more than that I cannot say. There was that kind of Otherworldly connection in her.

I'll tell you a funny thing about my name, Barry. I'll regale you with a story about it. "Barry" was my dad's idea, at least according to my mum, and you could never be quite sure about what she said. My dad was English and straight and called the shots. My mother was a bit younger than him in the way that seemed expected in those days. And she was Irish and not straight at all. She was anything but straight, although she did her best to be for many years. And she didn't call the shots, she went along with what my dad wanted.

My dad decided before I was born I was going to be "Barry". It didn't sound like he doubted I would be a boy. And my mum went along with it. When I was about 55, I looked up the meaning of my name. One source concerned a fairy mound at Knockma in Ireland, near the town of Tuam, about an hour from where my mother grew up, as it happens. The king of the fairies there is called Fionnbharr. And that is one source of my name.

It's not the only explanation, but that is one: the king of the fairies, Otherworld royalty.

Someone WhatsApped me, just as I spoke this in the video on which this is based. I take note of interruptions in that sort of context. They are saying pay attention, this is important. It sometimes happens when I am doing astrology readings, and it is telling me I have just made a significant point. This is fairy reasoning, indigenous reasoning, not scientific reasoning. It is the world speaking to us in a way to which we no longer know how to listen. Pay attention to anything unusual. It may be telling you something. Or maybe not. Sit with it. The meaning, like a dream, is often suggestive.

Naming me after the King of the Fairies, from a fairy fort near where my mother grew up, would have been the last thing on my father's mind. He didn't believe in such nonsense.

To make a fairy digression at this point, a friend had a scientific Irish father, now living in England. He asked him once if he believed in fairies. He replied no, of course not, they are completely unscientific. Besides which, he continued, you don't get them over here. The fairies got in and made a fool of his reasoning.

Just as they got in with my dad, and led him by the nose into naming me after the fairy lineage of my mother. And here's the thing. Forty-two years later, when my son was born, and knowing nothing of this, I named him Finn, which is the first half of Fionnbharr. And so the fairy lineage continues. When he was newborn, he had a tinkling, Otherworldly laughter.

I want to put the fairies in the south of the Medicine Wheel: the watery, childlike place, which is also the place of the trickster. That is how they work: they operate around the sides, they come in their own way, and sometimes it is ouchy, but we learn something. They will help us. You need to leave them offerings, you've got to honour them and talk to them and leave bits of land aside for them: you get a sense of it belonging to them, and you leave it alone.

In the year 2000 I bought a 12-acre field near Glastonbury in the UK, where I was living at the time. The field was known locally as the last refuge of the fairies. It was called Fenny Castle. You can easily visit it, but I'm not sure how much it wants to be visited. Half of it is hill. It felt fine to use the remaining flat part of the field, but the hill didn't feel like human territory. It didn't stop me going up there, hopefully in a respectful kind of way, but often I just wouldn't want to, and certainly not at night. It just didn't feel like I belonged there. It was the home for some other presence. It wasn't good and it wasn't bad, but it had a forbidding quality. This was the fairy fort, and this was it looking after itself.

When I first got the field and was walking around it, I could feel these big beings, bigger than me, following me around from behind. It was as if they were checking me out, getting to know me. It was by their graces that I got the field. It was almost like it fell into my hands, it had that feeling around it. I was meant to have it. It wasn't necessarily what I would have chosen, but I had been chosen for it, and so I gladly put that first.

I ran some camps there, but in the end it was taken over by horses, which hadn't been my intention. I'm sure the fairies were quite happy with that, and even engineered it. Looking back, it was a good thing for me. I was in my mid-40s, and it stopped me teaching. I was aware at the time that I didn't sufficiently know what I was talking about, at least not to my own satisfaction. And I waited 15 years, until another fairy intervention. It's taken me years to get that perspective. At the time you can just think something is going wrong.

At one camp, we had a kitchen tent. In the early morning, a gale blew up and took the kitchen tent with it. It also blew over everything on the table. Except for one thing: a bottle of vinegar, which for no good reason was left standing upright. Now fairies are known not to like vinegar, and they had made that pretty clear on this occasion. So we no longer brought vinegar into the field.

You also get fairy plaits in the manes of horses. This was happening all the time with the horses we had out there. The person who owned them was convinced it was people coming in while we were not there. We ended up moving to Devon with the horses, to some land that also has its own fairy presence. She was convinced that, being more remote and inaccessible, the plaits would immediately stop. But they continued just as before, and she was still convinced it was people. To make these plaits, people would have had to park at night about a mile up the road, in dark and often inclement weather, tie a quick few plaits (which the horses would probably not have let them do) and head off again, all without the dog sensing their presence. The owner was still convinced it was people. But it seems to me it was the fairies, saying yeah we're still here and we're still taking care of you.

Now of course, being fairy-created, you can never finally pin down the plaits. They are just tangly enough to create a case that they are natural. And yet with enough weaving in them to create a case that they were created with intention. That is one of the benefits for us humans of being around fairies. We want to know what is what, we want definite categories and certainty. The fairies teach us to be fluid in how we think. Do fairies exist? From a scientific point of view, they do not, they are a 'nonsense'. They cannot be steadily observed and measured. But you do catch something out of the corner of your eye, there is a glimmer. Or you feel something. An event out of the ordinary happens. Camping in a fairy glen, I forgot to ask permission to be there. My van keys went missing. Twenty minutes later, I found them in an obvious place, once I had recognised my oversight. I planted a tree for the fairies in my garden. A book of walks in Cornwall subsequently went missing. I ordered another copy. When it arrived, I offered it to my niece, who happened to be visiting, and wanted to walk in Cornwall. Fetching it, the original copy had appeared underneath it, where it had not been before.

Plan for the unexpected. Hang loose to outcomes, and hang loose to who you are, a good Chaos principle. The fairies dance through life, joyfully and spontaneously. There is no law saying you have to be miserable because of your troubles. You can equally as well be joyful. We have that choice to a greater extent than we think. The fairies know how to let things take their course. Outcomes are often outside our direction anyway, so why worry? Why not take the chance in this short life to be joyful?

The fairies remind us that this is not a vale of tears. We can learn a lot from them. But we mustn't reveal too much about them, at least not to those who would mock. Fairies are neither good nor bad, they are certainly not 'nice', and we wouldn't want the fate of the Rev Robert Kirk of Aberfoyle, a village in Scotland.

In the 17th century, he wrote a book later entitled *The Secret Commonwealth of Elves, Fauns and Fairies*. He used to regularly walk up a hill above the village, that had a pine tree at the top. It was fairy territory. Before the book could be published, he was found dead on the hill. It was said that the fairies had imprisoned him in the tree to prevent him revealing their secrets, and left a doppelganger of his body lying on the ground. It was the doppelganger that received a burial. And, for all I know, he is still imprisoned in the tree. I visited it, and it has become a wishing tree, that you circumambulate seven times for your wish to come true. I couldn't say, however, whether or not the Rev Kirk was in the tree.

What is this about revealing the fairies' secrets? For me, it relates to being discreet about your Otherworldly experiences, your visionary moments, your powerful dreams. All of those need to be kept quiet about. You don't talk about them too readily, and then only to select people. They're not for the world, they're not for broadcasting. It's a bit like a novelist talking too readily about the plot of his book: it will tend to disempower it. There is one indigenous people who say that if you talk about your dreams, then they don't come true. So they don't talk about their good dreams. But they talk about their bad dreams to prevent them happening!

If you try and make a name for yourself as a fairy person, teaching fairy lore and all the rest of it, strange things are going to happen around you. There are a lot of stories swirling around one well-known teacher of faery. He was, for example, attacked in the street by one of his students, and ensnared by a seductive enchantress who did not mean well. The fairies don't want to be public like that, they just want to be left alone in their places.

Can we see fairies? It depends on how you see, and what you mean by see. I feel things, there's a heart connection for me with fairies. Some people see things visually, but even then it's like, did I see something or didn't I? In this way you get drawn into the more fluid reality of the Otherworld, which is always around us.

I've got a fairy tree in my garden. I planted it in November 2023. It is a Japanese Snowbell. They grow to about 30 feet, and for a period in summer are covered in small white bell-like flowers. Five minutes down the road from me, through a field and over a gate, there's a little stream and a bridge and a tree. It's quite a special place. It is a fairy place, though that is not something I can prove. It just feels that to me. You can see that other people feel the same too, for they tend it. Just up the hill, is a secluded place with an equally powerful presence to it. When you go to these places, you will often get help. You just have to ask. While you are there, clarity may emerge. It's a bit like a mini-Vision Quest.

It felt to me that when I planted the tree, the fairies from down the road came up here as well. It's not like they're no longer at the other place, it doesn't work like that. Fairies don't divide up like that, and if you talk to the fairies at one place, you are talking to all of them. They don't have the boundaries of time and space that we do, they live in a more fluid world.

There are at least half a dozen places that I feel like this about on Dartmoor. I'll stop and talk with the fairies when I am there. It's a good idea to do that. And leave something for them, some silver or a bit of wine or a bit of food, something like that. You can tell them about everything, and you can thank them, because they will take care of you.

I've told them I will do their work, that I'm happy to be of service to them, to have the main part of my life under their direction. For me, it's not like I get direct instructions, it's more of a felt thing. This is what to do now, this feels congruent. It's quite a fine feeling. You can't 'prove' it, but you nevertheless know it. It's the same with the Spirits who are around you. You feel them with you, you call them to mind, you get used to that sense of there being something other around you. It's precious, it's rich and nourishing, it is guiding and helping you, and the world with it. There is a profound motive to be of help to others involved.

There's a book called *Daimonic Reality* by Patrick Harpur, which I'd recommend. It's subtitled *A Field Guide to the Otherworld*. He hasn't been imprisoned in a tree yet for writing it, as far as I'm aware. I guess he can't have given too much away! He writes about the fairy beings from all over the world, but he also includes everything that's kind of, "Is it there or isn't it?" Collective visions of the Virgin Mary, yetis, bigfoot. And aliens, which are the most recent manifestation of that realm. People definitely have these kinds of experiences, there are too many just to say they are all made up. And yet, like the fairies, you can never quite pin them down. There was some kind of spaceship over an American airbase in Norfolk in the 70s that a number of people saw independently — I know one of them.

Jung says they belong to the collective unconscious. They are real, they can even be more real than our everyday experience. But they are not literal, they can't be pinned down. The term 'Unconscious' can be a bit misleading. 'Superconscious' might be better. It just means something of which we ordinary humans are not normally conscious. There often is a collective element to these events, in the sense that people will have the same kind of experience. Maybe they are abducted by aliens: there has been quite a lot of that. It seems to me to be a modern version of an Otherworldly initiation, just as being abducted by the fairies can be. Aliens make great ancestors, coming as they do from civilisations more advanced than our own.

Harpur's book is a great exploration of this type of reality. It gives plenty of information and examples from all over the world, but more importantly, it is a meditation on what these types of experiences say about reality. He's a great initiator into non-literal reality.

You might have noticed that not taking anything literally has been a recurrent theme throughout this book. It is that important. Chaos amounts to the same thing. Buddhism has it also, with its idea of emptiness. As Shamans, you could say, we have something quite concrete: our Spirit helpers. We have to dance with them, treat them as poetry, where words and images are replete with multiple meanings, rather than as prose. And be prepared, on that basis, for constant subtle shifts in the way you see things.

Daimonic Reality is great for getting a sense of these Otherworldly ancestors, who were here before us, will be here long after we are gone, and who will help us. A friend of mine has a website called the *Faery Whisperer* and she regularly does podcasts in which she interviews people about fairies. Something she said was that because the fairies live a lot longer than us, whatever work we do for them will be continuing after we're dead. So if you want a sure-thing legacy, do the fairies' work!

The fairies are part of our ancestral inheritance. Find places in nature that speak to you, special places, often a bit secluded, as the fairies don't like to be too public. Dartmoor has lots of them. Perhaps the best known is Wistman's Wood. It's a stunted oak forest – a species particular to Dartmoor – and it's probably a bit too well-known. There are usually other people there, sometimes many of them. The far end of the wood is the place to go, where no one seems to visit. There is also Black-a-Tor Copse, which is like Wistman's, but very few people go there, and the energy is stronger and clearer. And there is Piles Copse, made of much taller stunted oaks, and it too is a magical place. There is a lot of moss and lichen hanging from the trees that makes it very atmospheric. There are other places I could mention, but maybe that would risk me getting imprisoned in a tree!

So have some of these places that you go to, build a relationship with them, talk to them appreciatively, give thanks to the fairies there for everything that works in your life. You can ask for things as well and they will help you. Ask from a heartfelt place, that's what the fairies understand best; not from our heads, but from our hearts, something that really matters to you. If you ask in that kind of way, there will be help, but never in the way you expected. There may well be something that's a bit ouchy, and that can be because there is something for us to learn. They're on our side, but in a deeper kind of way.

Fairies are not good and they're not bad: those are human ideas. And they're not necessarily these tiny little things either. I have a theory that it was Christianity that reduced them to a few inches high and made them fluffy, like harmless little children, as a way of disempowering them. Don't underestimate them, they are powerful and they live alongside us. The world is full of beings that are not us.

There are the Elementals. I don't know if I've experienced Elementals or not. Maybe it's a matter of how you frame it. But there are certain rocks on Dartmoor that I like to hang out with, because of their massiveness and presence. They feel alive, there's something in them, and I talk to them in the same way that I talk to the fairies. So maybe someone else would say that I'm talking to an Elemental when I talk to those rocks. Some being that, like an iceberg, has its vast presence mainly underground, with just the tip showing.

It's worth getting a few books of traditional stories of fairy encounters. *The Anthology of Scottish Folk Tales* has a few. There is also one called *Meeting the Other Crowd* by Eddie Lenihan, in which he's not just retelling the traditional stories. He actually went and talked to people in the Southwest of Ireland and created a collection of fairy encounters, that until then had just been passed down orally. So that was an original thing to do, and authentic in a way: they're real fairy stories. People do have these encounters. You get e.g. fairy abductions. I have a theory about my mother, that she may have been, in a sense, abducted. In some ways she never quite knew who she was, she spent the last part of her life kind of wandering, never fitting in anywhere. She had hung out with the fairies as a child, so maybe they claimed her in some strange way. As I said, they are tricksy. They're not necessarily 'good' in our terms, but it doesn't make them bad either. And maybe they'll do something like that.

Caitlin Matthews, who works within a neo-Celtic tradition, tells this story in her introduction to Dora van Gelder's book *The Real World of Fairies*:

> *In Ireland it is still a great breach of courtesy to tamper with the traditional haunts of fairy folk, and most country people are very careful to avoid such places. It is still considered a*

terrible thing to take wood from, let alone cut down, a fairy thorn tree.

A recent case revealed this to me in a shocking way. My client Michael asked for soul healing for himself concerning the death of his younger sister some years before. As I began to journey in spirit towards my spirit allies, my way was suddenly blocked by a fairy man in a great rage. He told me that Michael's family had injured his family, that unless Michael was prepared to plant a thorn tree as reparation, I could not go any further and get help for him. My own allies urged me to accept this agreement on Michael's behalf. They further told me that the fairies had been taking the souls of children from Michael's family in recompense for a terrible insult.

When I told Michael about the fairy man's anger and his demand for a thorn tree to be planted, Michael's face went white. He stopped me suddenly and told me about his grandfather, who had unaccountably cut down an ancient fairy thorn tree. Michael told me that in every branch of his family since that day a young child had died. Michael promised solemnly that he would not only plant a thorn tree on his land and dedicate it to the fairies in recompense, he would also ensure that no-one ever touched the tree, not even prune it! It is a promise I am sure he will keep.

In Scotland you get Kelpies, which can shift between human and horse form, and Selkies, who shift between seal and human. There's a story about a guy who was a seal killer by trade. He would make clothes and purses out of the skins and sell them. He did it because his father and grandfather, and so on back down the line, had been seal killers. But one day he tried to kill a giant seal, and it took off, taking his special knife with her, leaving him without a trade. It transpired he had tried to kill the Queen of the Selkies, and he was taken on a night journey by a stranger to heal her. He also had to agree not to kill seals anymore. He was then given enough gold to live on for the rest of his days. Fairy gold often dissolves, and you'd better get it to the bank quick. But this gold didn't dissolve. He never married, but it is said locally that on the full moon he calls in the Queen of the Selkies, she takes off her seal skin, and they dance together all night on the beach. You can see why he never married: he has an Otherworldly bride, he is 'spoken for' at a magical level. If you work Shamanically, it is possible that you will feel 'spoken for' in this magical kind of way.

The story took place at Duncansby Stacks, which is a bay near John O'Groats, the most northerly part of Scotland. I visited the beach where the reformed seal killer romances the Selkie Queen every full moon. It was blowing a gale, and it was a steep slope down to the beach. I thought no one else would climb that slope in those conditions, and I would be on my own. And I was, for a while. But then someone else showed up. And apart from telling me an intriguing story about Pablo Neruda's poetry being carved into local rocks, he told me that the seal killer actually came from Orkney; it couldn't be Duncansby Stacks, because there was no sign of a croft having been at the top of the cliffs. The truth of the story was not in doubt, just its location.

Thomas the Rhymer is a well-known figure from the 13th century. He lived in Ercildoune, now called Earlston, in southern Scotland. I have visited the remains of his mansion there. As a young man he was lured into faerie through a kiss from the Queen of Elfland. He went willingly, knowing that the kiss would mean seven years in her realm. He returned with a gift from her, the apple of truth. It meant he was able to give good advice to people by speaking truthfully about what was to come, and he became rich and famous. Eventually he returned to faerie, and was never seen again. Maybe there was a historical figure with that intuitive gift. And it's maybe a matter of how you frame it. Did the Spirits tell him? Or did he just know? Or was his experience something that came through from faerie?

24
Covid and the Spiritworld

I made the video for this chapter at the tail-end of what seemed to be Covid. I was unshaven, unwashed, and it felt like practically all I was doing was going to bed and getting up. I thought well I'll talk about this bloody thing. Nobody told me it was Covid, but I couldn't think what else it could have been. I was half out-of-it for nearly two weeks, and then for a long time afterwards I was just wasted for much of the time.

It got me thinking. There's a feeling of something a bit alien in there, something that looks a bit like metal, though I haven't got that metal taste that some people have. I went to visit Covid in the Spiritworld while I was lying in my bed feeling a bit wasted, as I was doing several times a day. I thought I'll just tune into this thing, and it was like I was in a bare room, and it was full of metallic, sort of half-Dalek things, which were the Covid. My immune system, which took the spirit form of little furry animals, didn't quite know what to do with them, and that was why it was going on and on, and still is at the time of writing. That's why I feel wasted: because it's still in my system, and my system doesn't know quite what to do with it. It's done enough to hold it at bay and to a large extent neutralise it — or maybe the Covid has just naturally run its course, maybe that is also how these things work? But my system doesn't know how to finally evict it.

I thought about this in relation to the way Covid first came about, which was through a lab. The scientists always thought there was about a 20% chance of that, because of what had been happening in the lab in Wuhan. It wasn't just some conspiracy idea. The circumstantial evidence became compelling a few years down the line. The scientist Matt Ridley gave a detailed analysis of this evidence, which can be found on YouTube. Of course, the Chinese weren't going to admit anything, and that was why it took several years to build a picture. What the Chinese had been doing was fast-tracking a virus, in making the leap from animal to human host. In this case it was from a bat that lived 1000 miles from Wuhan, and scientists from Wuhan had been in that area collecting bats. We know that viruses can make the leap from animals to humans, but it takes them a while to then adapt and become really infectious, and while that process is going on, we humans are presumably becoming familiar and adapting as well, like a game of cat and mouse.

But what they were doing in this lab was that they were taking a virus that could potentially jump, and adding on that which would make it really adapted and infectious all in one go. Scientists found the bit that the Chinese must have added on to the virus. Matt Ridley details what this was. They were then putting this engineered virus into rabbits and seeing how they did; presumably there is some kind of similarity to humans in rabbits. So it seems they were investigating through this kind of experiment the process of adaptation of viruses to humans, which is a useful thing to do.

But here's the thing. They were lax in their health and safety measures. Matt Ridley also details this. And the virus escaped. It is stupid to say it was deliberate, because how would that benefit the Chinese, *cui bono*? It was a cock-up, which is what happens. We had a foot-and-mouth outbreak among cattle in England in 2007. It was also from a lab, and they managed to contain it before it spread too far. But it was also simply a cock-up. The cock-up theory should always be the first port of call in my opinion. It is usually the simplest explanation and the correct one, much as many people often want to think otherwise, it's almost like a need they have, to find some sinister conspiracy.

So that is the most likely explanation of what happened here, because the evidence is just so compelling. How else could this well-adapted virus have suddenly come from nowhere?

We humans had had no time to adapt along the way. So we don't know quite what to do with it and it fucks us over. Excuse my use of French, but I'm ill so I get a free pass!

Lying there in bed, I thought I'd tune into it, and like I said I saw these metallic objects, a bit like aliens, and it's because we haven't had time to adapt. I could see that the furry animals don't yet have much of a handle on the Daleks. It is a big leap that they are having to feel their way into. Years on from the pandemic, and we're still adapting. These things happen in the Spiritworld as well as in this world. That's why you can heal disease through spirit intervention, because spirit and the body go hand in hand. The scientific explanation is true, but so is the spirit explanation. They both work alongside each other. The best way to heal something will always, I think, include tuning in to the spirit side of it.

I have to say I don't mind being ill, because I currently haven't got an awful lot to do apart from writing this book, but I have enough energy to do the things I have to do. It throws me back into myself, it takes the pressure off — this cultural pressure to be busy all the time, even when we're past official retirement age like me!

Being ill gives a good excuse for not being busy, you can be idle with a clear conscience. We can just relax back into ourselves. Even though I'm feeling a bit crap, I'm back in myself, I'm closer to myself, I'm closer to that level of me that is always there underneath the day-to-day busyness and pressure. That's what drugs like alcohol and weed and psychedelics do as well, at least in my experience. But I only do that once in a while. I'd rather do it naturally.

It brings me closer to that deeper kind of feeling and vision about why I'm here, and I always come out of being ill slightly changed because of that, and maybe for other reasons as well. I don't get ill very often, and when I do something seems to shift.

I tuned into the Covid, in a way I sat with it in the Spiritworld. I don't know why I'd never thought of doing that before. I didn't try to do anything in the Spiritworld. I think our job is just to show up. That in itself has a big effect. And beyond that we need to let the Spirits take care of things. We yield to that world. You may not know what's going on round about you. You might, for example, just have a sense like me of being in a kind of lab with these metallic things, and also a sense of furry spirit animals around as well. That might be about as far as it goes. For me, the animals bring a sense of warmth and activity and slow transformation to the cold, alien feel. I think my presence helps make the link between the Spiritworld and this world, and speeds up the healing process.

The day after having sat in the Spiritworld with the aliens and the furry animals, I went outside and did some gardening. Something had shifted, it was like a quantum leap in my recovery. There were still ways to go, but there was a discernible difference. And so I continued to do a bit of this every day. Lying in my bed, allowing the full force of feeling ill to take me over, and at the same time it is as though that then allows me entry into the Spiritworld, where the healing is happening, and I can play my part just by being there.

Here's a couple of things coming out of that. Firstly, there's a level on which humanity collectively needs to adapt to Covid in the Spiritworld, as well as in this world; as I said, they go hand in hand. Furthermore, if one of us is adapting in that way, then it has a ripple-out effect. It's a hundredth monkey thing, which I think is a Spiritworld phenomenon. It's a real effect, but if you push it in a rational scientific way, it will break down, as will any such phenomenon. Astrology is like this: some of its synchronicities are gobsmacking, but not replicable in the lab.

The hundredth monkey principle is based on the observation that, once a hundred monkeys on an island had created the new technology of washing their potatoes in the river to get the grit out, the behaviour suddenly spread to the separate populations of monkeys on the nearby islands.

My theory here is that, once enough humans have made the adaptation to Covid, it will spread across the world. On a spirit level, knowledge is shared, there is an osmosis. It is, if you like, the collective unconscious. In doing the spirit work, I am contributing to that collective process.

This world of the aliens and the furry animals reminds me of my experiences in 1997, when I first started Shamanic journeying. I was taken to these bits of myself that needed a bit of help, and the spirits would dismember me, or they'd show me this thing like a trussed-up chicken, and they'd put it in a bank of a river and leave it there to kind of cook. I described this earlier in the chapter on **Meeting the Spirits**. A few weeks later, I would have forgotten all about it, I'd be doing a journey, and the Spirits go, "That bit's ready to come out now," so they'd take it out and put it back in me.

There was all this soul work, this healing, this retrieval work going on in me from the Spirits. This process of the Spirits doing their work changed me in a deep way. It quite quickly built a new solid foundation in me in which I felt much more confident of my own connection to Spirit and less needing to lean on tradition. We do need tradition, particularly when we're not really sure of our own guidance within, which is usually the case to start with; it's something that needs to be built.

So this spontaneous spirit work helped free me of that and to find my own connections more deeply. It was an ongoing cooking, which reminded me of how I see what's happening with Covid and the Spiritworld. It seems to be one of the ways that transformation happens in the Spiritworld. It is quite alchemical.

The way it works for me is that I just tune into it and let it be there. I don't need answers, I don't need to know what is happening. I just have a sense of it, and a visual counterpart as well. Not everyone will have a visual counterpart. Some people might have word counterparts – they might have Spirits turning up and telling them what's going on. I don't get that: I'm too good with words in this reality!

So I've tuned into this sense of my healing in the Spiritworld, and I think that that's something we can do generally, whether it's literal physical healing we need, or a soul healing. Any physical healing is both soul and body, how could it not be? How could a physical ailment not also have a soul component? Otherwise it's as though matter is dead, and it's not, it is always inspirited. If there's something out of balance on the bodily level, then it's out of balance on the spirit level as well, because they're intertwined. Spirit and matter can't be separated, they're like the outer and inner dimensions of one thing; I think that's a good way of looking at it. And the other way round too: if you are feeling out of sorts in some way in your spirit, then you will be able to feel it in your body, though you won't necessarily be ill. Again, that is because spirit and the body are one thing. Shamanism is here to heal that ancient split in our culture between spirit and body, that came primarily from Christianity, but whose roots can be traced back to ancient Greek rationalism.

This is the main reflection coming out of my time with Covid: tune into the spirit level of whatever ails you, whether in your soul or body, and just be aware of it in an ongoing way. Our presence, our desire to be there and to heal, helps it all move forward. Visit once a day, and give thanks to the Spirits while you are there. If you are not so busy, just hold it as part of your ongoing awareness, a bigger picture, if you like, of who you are. Over time, that Spirit aspect becomes more and more a part of our ongoing awareness, and that is as it needs to be, for it is who we are, an indivisible union of spirit and matter.

It also means we do our own healing, which I think is one of our first ports of call on this path. Shamanic training can sometimes give the impression that the first port of call is the Shaman, to retrieve this bit of soul or to remove that entity or that family curse. But I think it's our own Spirits and their alchemy that we need to look to first, and it is often a gradual thing, maybe something we don't have a name or words for, and that can be a good thing too. Though we will probably find the odd insight drifting our way as the cooking proceeds.

Health update: the day after editing the transcript of the video on which this chapter is based, I started to feel fully well again. I feel that part of the reason for this is that I find writing to be a powerful way of entering the Spiritworld. I was with those furry animals and aliens in quite a strong way, just through writing about them. I think this is true of any artistic endeavour: it puts us deeply into the Otherworld, with its creative and regenerative powers.

25

Spirit Power

I had a dream while writing this book that my Rising Sign is Leo rather than Virgo, which would make me born 90 minutes earlier than I thought. Many astrologers insist that I must be Leo Rising – the Rising Sign being what people first notice about you – so I thought well, one way of responding to that is I'll put on my tiger onesie to make the video on which this chapter is based. I'll put a tiger in my tank to talk about power.

I've had Covid, and I'm still at the edges of it, where I feel wasted some of the time. I haven't got my creative power in the way that I usually have it. And that's one of the reflections that led to this piece. I have enough oomph – to use a technical term – to make the odd video and post for Facebook, in which I like to stir the pot. By stirring the pot I mean getting us thinking, and that means questioning the comfortable beliefs that we live by. By 'thinking' we usually mean looking for reasons to support what we want to believe in the first place. What I do is to look for the holes that any idea or position necessarily has – because words are limited – and wander around it. People sometimes think I am being wilfully contrary. But no, it is simply that I always say what I think, I have the courage to do that, and I am fascinated by the holes and inconsistencies you get, particularly in collective beliefs. I hope this book itself has that kind of perspective. I hope you find things to disagree with, and that you cherish them!

Covid left me with enough energy to be my usual provocative self in short bursts. But not enough to think about the book on Chaos Shamanism that is coming out of the videos. It just feels too big. The book itself arose spontaneously, unplanned, in the Spirit of Chaos, out of the series of videos that were also unplanned. I just keep trusting as I go along, which is what Chaos teaches us. It is a creative matrix that just keeps giving. And when illness stops me, I trust that too, and trust that there is probably something in it.

And this got me thinking about power. I have the power to do short pieces, but not enough to address the whole book. But I don't feel lacking in power. This made me think that you could say there are two types of power: there's the power to be, and the power to do. They're feminine and masculine in nature respectively, and do have an overlap with male and female. But by no means is that the whole story, it's more complex than that.

Being ill has given me more of the power to be rather than to do, the more classically feminine power: the power to be with myself, with my feelings. It gives me a broader sense of what my life's about, more of a feeling of being connected to that wider pattern. The sense of meaning and even destiny, the reason for being here. I haven't got specific words for it, it's a feeling thing. The sense of meaning in life is a feeling rather than a concept. It's not a proposition. This is why the computer in *The Hitchhiker's Guide to the Galaxy* couldn't get the answer to the meaning of life. It came up with 42. The computer then said it was because they'd asked the wrong question. In fact, there isn't an answer, not in words, it's a feeling. We only complain about life lacking meaning because we're not feeling it. That feeling gives a kind of fiery connection to why we're here, to the source of life in us that keeps bubbling up, that's always wanting to unfold, that keeps us wanting to be here.

That feeling is as strong as ever, even though I'm ill and can do very little all day. I can feel OK about that, not feel that I ought to be doing more, putting myself under that kind of pressure, which isn't all bad either by any means: it gets things done.

The feminine power, if you like, is that ability to be and to be connected and to feel, and it may not be doing anything obvious, but it holds its own kind of power. If the masculine has any sense, it will go to that power for guidance. It needs to be in its service, otherwise it will get out of balance. This is the warrior energy in its one-sided form, that men easily get into.

Similarly that feminine power gets out of balance if it's not doing anything, if it hasn't got the Mars energy, if it is too beholden to taking care of and pleasing others. So there are these two kinds of power. Normally I'm functioning with quite a lot of the masculine creative power: I'm doing something, I'm making stuff happen, on a number of different levels. There's writing my books, and there's doing readings, there's writing posts for all kinds of social media, there's other things just keeping my life running, getting my house painted. I do stuff, even though I'm not that busy. There's always that push, that masculine power in me is strong and relentless. And yet when I get ill, I am thrown back in to the feminine power.

And so that's my first reflection: there are these different types of power in us, and doing a lot isn't the same as being powerful. It's only truly powerful when it has that deeper source, when it's Spirit, when it's not just about your own personal ambition. Ambition gives a certain kind of power, but this is a deeper kind of power that I'm talking about, which has to be connected to the feminine.

We swing between these two poles of Mars and Venus, and we integrate them gradually in our lives. I think indigenous people understand those different types of power. (See *The Kingdom of Women* by Choo WaiHong.) It was often reflected in the relationships between the men and the women. Of course they get it wrong sometimes, and probably men in particular have to be brought into balance. One way it often goes wrong is that we men don't listen to the feminine power, while one of the jobs of women, one could argue, can be to ensure the men do listen to that. Use your wits, use your guiles, use your skills and powers of persuasion and perception to get us to listen. Or just chuck us in a Sweatlodge to melt us back into our hearts! And then things will come back into balance, and we'll each be bringing our own natural power to the table.

We need to unfold both powers within to become a full human being, and it's a life's work. For men it's often the listening to ourselves that is needed. I think that's one of the reasons I get ill sometimes. It's not often that I get ill, but it always has that theme of deep listening.

For women, finding the masculine power often involves not worrying what other people think, and not feeling beholden to looking after other people, but paying attention to that which you feel called to do, that the universe wants you to do, that thing that you love. Power comes through doing what we love. Seize it, don't consider it selfish, begin it now! And don't let self-doubt stop you, we need to carry on despite it, it is something that nearly every creative person feels.

The other reflection on power I wanted to talk about is to do with putting indigenous people on pedestals: thinking that they have the power and we don't. I don't mean power 'over', in a worldly sense. I mean the inner power, the Spirit power. We easily think that they have it, and we don't. There are even some Western proponents of this on Facebook, who insist that the Spirit work that indigenous people do is in a different league to anything we can do. I dipped into a recent book on Shamanism, that began by banging on about just how remote we are from indigeneity. In my view that is just wrong, and very disempowering for us. I know one person in particular who promotes this kind of attitude, while setting himself up as a kind of representative of indigenous shamanic traditions, through being a mine of information about them. He likes to dress up in the trappings of these foreign traditions, suggesting that he himself is one of them. It's a power game, and there's no shortage of people willing to believe him.

So we need to watch out for that kind of thing. It will always be happening, and it's a good exercise in discernment and not giving away your own authority. Catholics do it with the Pope. He's been appointed by God, and so you bow down before him, because he's as holy as they get. It doesn't mean that certain people aren't also worthy of respect and even veneration, but that's not the point here, which is that we, in our culture, have the goods.

Think about it this way. Most indigenous people are just ordinary people. If you're listening to this, there's a good chance you've got something else going on in you, that feels that life lived purely by ordinary material values is somehow flat, it's not enough. We can't ignore the material side of life, it would be spiritual bypass to do, but that alone is not enough. You find yourself in a minority when that's how you feel about life. Think about your family of origin: they are probably mostly muggles, to put it humorously. I began to feel about life like that when I was about 20. I knew I couldn't just be 'normal'. Fundamentally, there's this other thing, and it puts us in a minority. It's just how things are.

It's why you have ceremonies amongst indigenous peoples, and why we have churches: because people aren't actually that interested in the Spirit perspective, and they need reminding. They're more interested in the day-to-day, which gives sufficient meaning to their lives. They don't necessarily think very much about their values, they just live them. Life to them is straightforward and simple. But we have something different going on, and we have to find confidence in it, because we may well be judged, we may well be found wanting by the consensus reality. We have this thing in us which is our own power, that becomes stronger and more central to who we are over time.

Most indigenous people are not like this. They are ordinary people with ordinary values. So looked at like this, it is daft to put them on a pedestal. It is us who have the power, if we're going to look at it like that. And what about the people who do have that power, their healers and Shamans? Are they more powerful than us, do they have the real goods and we don't?

When an indigenous person walks in the room, many people seem to lose their critical faculties, they think the indigenous person is the one with the wisdom. I've seen it time and again. Sure, they've probably got something that's worth listening to and appreciating. But you get to know them, and you find they can be stupid and oblivious in certain ways, just like we can. And, not infrequently, untrustworthy.

You find this in our culture too. You encounter people who may have a Spirit gift, they can do good work for people, particularly when they're letting Spirit speak through them, but that doesn't necessarily mean they have an awful lot of their own wisdom. This can mean they get it wrong sometimes, if their own stuff's in the way of the Spirit: if Spirit is the mains water supply, then such a healer has dirty pipework.

You get this amongst Native Americans as well. I was told on good authority about the Chipps family in North America. They're well known as healers, and the friend who told me knew them personally. The whole family would descend on people. You'd hear from someone that the Chipps family had come to stay, and you'd commiserate with them, because they would steal everything, they'd eat you out of house and home, and then move on. But some of them were great healers. The most powerful of them spent most of his time in an alcoholic haze. He would drink himself stupid, and then someone would turn up who needed healing. He would be filled full of coffee to bring him back, and he'd shift out of it, and suddenly there was this full-on healer there. He would do the work, and it was really good work, and then he'd go back to his old ways.

Healers can be a funny bunch. We find the same in this culture: people who can do good work, and yet they can behave in a really crap way at other times. So you'd better watch out! I've known those kinds of extremes in one person intimately in my life. It's as though they're two different people. Really, those different people need to be speaking to each other. Of course we all have a shadow, of course we get it wrong sometimes, but at least we should know it. We need to be able, afterwards at any rate, to look back and hold ourselves to account. I'm talking here about people who do not hold themselves to account. They haven't just got a shadow like you and me, but they live it and don't hold it to account. They choose not to be honest with themselves. We often excuse people's bad behaviour on account of their childhood, we say they are wounded and try to be sympathetic to that. But no, we are adults. In this sense, I don't care what happened to you in your childhood, because the issue is how you treat other people now, and there is always a choice.

Here's another thing. In a tribal situation the healers will often have a spirit gift that's passed down through the family. It's inherited, and why not? Everything's inherited to some degree, but it doesn't mean we're not also our own person. We're born amongst souls where there's a resonance — I can't say that for myself, but I can see it in other families — and the gift gets passed on in one way or another. DNA is part of the story, but it's not the whole story. Upbringing is part of the story, but it's certainly not the whole story, in fact it's much less than we like to think.

So a lot of these healers are ordinary people who've got a spirit gift that's passed down through the family. They may well look at it as a Spirit that is passed on: maybe one of them dies, and it moves into another family member. And why not? They will do real healing, they will do good work for people, then they'll go back to being ordinary people. That is fair enough. They live within the mythology and the belief system and the stories of their people. Some healers, I'd suggest the more powerful ones, are able to step outside of that.

I once asked a native person whether his people get fundamentalist about their creation myth, and he replied no, that they had more than one and they contradict each other! I thought that was a great answer. But he had that ability to step outside the mythologies, and see the stories as just stories, albeit useful and necessary.

At a time like our own where we have no unifying mythology anymore, it becomes the calling of some shamans or teachers to help recreate that mythological foundation, without which people cannot have psychological stability. That, in a sense, is where your healing work starts. (The Medicine Wheel, in my opinion, could be such a mythology.)

Now most healers don't have that kind of power, they're happy to remain within the story that they're given. You see this in our culture, where people learn Core Shamanism, which gives a set of stories about different worlds, and it works, up to a point, but it's also a bit limited in certain ways. And they're happy with that. They may then go and set themselves up as teachers, but they still teach basically the same stuff, they're happy within that story, and being a teacher tells them who they are. That's fair enough, that's where they are, but their power is limited, because they are not able to dance around the stories and pick them up and drop them and play with them.

This is where the artist comes in. The Shaman-as-artist helps people see the world differently, to re-imagine life and our place in the universe. It's not what most Shamans are about. They function within the received wisdom and stories, and they do good work within that. But it is from within their collectively accepted world. It's a higher level of functioning when you're able to stand outside that. I don't mean that in a purely intellectual sense — that is easy. I mean it emotionally and imaginatively: you are able to stand in the Void, in the Chaos, and feel strengthened rather than threatened by that. That is a very difficult thing for most humans.

This level of functioning, the mythopoeic, is called upon nowadays, because we don't have a unifying mythology anymore. The most unifying story we have is the scientific mythology. I'm going to go into this in some detail now, not as a digression, but as illustrative of this other level on which the Shaman can function.

We generally kind of buy the scientific story: it all started with the Big Bang, but we don't know what came before that. And then we were created through Evolution, though we also don't know how life first started. This story is something that most of us believe, and we treat is as fact, as what 'actually' happened. It is our unifying story, though we ignore the bits we don't know, with the comforting superstition that science will eventually explain them. I think I'll make a distinction and say this story is not a true mythology, because it does not have magic and the miraculous, which is something our psyches need to feel fully satisfied.

One of the jobs of the artist-as-shaman in our culture is to persuasively bring magic to that story. Now there is magic there if you think about it. Before the Big Bang, you have the Great Mystery, the Chaos — the vast abyss that the ancient Greeks talked about, that was there before the universe came into being. I say 'before' and 'was', but that is using the language of time, whereas we are now outside of time. There is no 'before' the Big Bang. We are in territory that is unknowable, and that plugs us into the great mystery of existence.

Our scientific culture is focussed on knowing and providing answers. We imagine that eventually science will get there and have an answer to everything. This is one of Elon Musk's hopes for AI: that it will eventually explain everything. But if you watch the progress of science on these big questions, you'll see that the more we know, the greater the unknown becomes. We start getting to know the universe at large through our advanced telescopes, and whoosh, we suddenly discover that 96% of the universe is missing and undetectable, so we give it names – Dark Matter and Dark Energy – as if that tells us something. The same with the origin of life. We imagine it arose of its own accord from the primeval soup. But the more we understand life, the more complex we see its processes to be, the more the likelihood of it arising by chance from the soup recedes. We ignore that, however, because it 'must' have arisen in this way. But if you let it, it will bring you closer to the Great Mystery, just as a contemplation of Dark Matter will. It's exactly the same with quantum reality, which has been around for over a century now. Matter at bottom is seen to be arising out of Chaos. It becomes a probability wave in which effects can come before causes. So we need to surround these scientific stories, which are as good as far as they go, with the unknowability about the big questions, that grows in size the more we know about the small questions. There's also the idea that consciousness plays a part, which quantum mechanics shows. Consciousness at least helps dream reality into existence. This seems to be too subtle for most people to realise, even though it's obvious if you do Shamanic work. You realise that we are dreaming reality into existence. You do your Shamanic journeying, your healing work, and you realise this stuff that happens in the other reality also manifests in this reality. That person in whom you put a bit of soul back has now got a sparkle in their eye and a desire to live that they didn't have before. You may also have noticed it on yourself when you do your own work with the Spirits. The Spirit level is primary.

We have experience of the intellectual insight of quantum physics, but we have, through our Spirit work, an emotional and intuitive understanding that there's a reality which is primary, that affects, even creates, this reality. The Dreaming.

We can bring that Shamanic insight to the modern mythology of science, which isn't going away.

It doesn't mean other mythologies can't live alongside it. You do that whenever you allow yourself to be imaginatively gripped by a mythology. It's good to be able to hold two stories, and take them as equally real. They're not 'just stories'. When God created the world in seven days, we can read that as Spirit creating the universe, and that is true, that is more real than the scientific myth, because the scientific myth stops at the Big Bang, and it doesn't know where to go then. But the answer is there, in quantum physics: the Big Bang came out of the dreaming of consciousness. And that is what we say as Shamanic people.

Spirit dreamed life into being too; in fact, life was always there, because matter is inspirited. What we call Evolution is an ongoing dreaming of new forms of life. Just as the arising of life by chance is a mathematical impossibility, so too is Evolution as driven purely by chance and selection: it would take far, far longer than the timescales we have. It is also an insult to consciousness, it is an aesthetic crime, to suggest that this phenomenal beauty that we call life is a product of cold, blind chance, and of the brute struggle for survival! I would rather argue that Evolution is driven by the play of Soul, as it continually throws forth new forms of beauty. Life forms survive and thrive, not because they are 'adapted', but because the natural world is benign, and takes care of her offspring.

What we have been doing here is re-dreaming the world, while incorporating the modern mythology called Science. That is a level of functioning which an ordinary Shaman may not have, maybe because he or she is not a storyteller by temperament, but also because they may not be particularly metaphysically inclined, they might just be a normal person who has been chosen by the Spirits to be a healer, because someone has to be. And the Spirits may do powerful healing work through them. But outside of that, they may be happily immersed in the collective beliefs and values, and not be very reflective around that, which is a normal way to be.

That said, indigenous people generally seem to live closer to the insight of life as the dreaming than we do. And the Shaman particularly will be being pulled into that deeper reality on a regular basis.

My overall point here is that we have the goods, we have as much power as indigenous people. We need to really claim that. It is a central plank of Chaos Shamanism, which emphasises the individual's closeness to the Great Mystery. If you can live close to that, which means putting your ego on ice, so to speak – we need an ego, but not to be too determined by it, not using it too much as a prop to tell us who we are – then all the power you will ever need will flow through you.

If you want power in that bigger sense – no, aspire is a better word than want. Actually, both those words are wrong, having more personal 'power' is something we shouldn't even think about! What matters is the desire to live congruently with that power, which is about being truthful and honest and having humility. Doing that at every turn, that will give you all the power there is. Again, my words are wrong. It won't be given to 'you'. It will flow through you as needed, but it can never be yours. It is the power of the whole universe; we can be vessels for something infinite.

There is a book, *Fools Crow,* by Thomas E. Mails. Frank Fools Crow was a famous Lakota Medicine Man from the 20th century. He could do remarkable healings on people. It was mainly physical healings that he did. He could do this because he prayed. He would pray for that person's recovery, and he would often be shown some herbs to give them, and they would get well. They were what we might call miracle healings, but they're not miracles from a native point of view, they are the Great Spirit at work.

One reason Fools Crow's healings were so powerful was because he spent so much time in prayer. In the mornings he would go out with his pipe and pray, and in the evenings too. A lifetime of this, done in a heartfelt and genuine way, brings you very close to the Great Spirit, to 'the Holiest of Everything'. It made him a great 'hollow bone' for Spirit, because when you pray, you're putting your ego to one side, it is not about what you want in a narrow sense.

It is worth bearing this well in mind for when we do healing work. I was never taught in Core Shamanism that prayer is part of it. It's your Spirit helpers that do the work, it's not an ego thing. But those helpers are intermediaries for the Great Spirit. If you want to help people through healing work, then spend your life like Fools Crow did, with an attitude of prayer and humility and the closeness to Spirit that comes with that.

We have the ability to live in that way just as much as any human in history, and why wouldn't we? Sure, we can learn from indigenous peoples, especially the ones who haven't been pulled too far away from the original, inspirited way of being in the world that we have largely lost. We can be grateful that there are such people around. But really, it's about living close to that which gives meaning to your life, and making the choice to live honestly with yourself at all times, and with humility. That is what matters, and there is no reason to suppose that any indigenous person you meet has greater integrity than yourself in this regard. Not that we go around comparing.

Part of the reason I am writing about this issue is that I struggle with it to some extent myself, because it is in the culture: that indigenous people have this mysterious thing that we don't have, they are 'Other'. (Tibetan Buddhism also carries this projection.) I think the solution is to keep coming back to your own connection, your own centre, your own integrity, which we value on its own account. If you have a teacher or a

Pope or an indigenous person up there above you, that is not humility, that is disempowerment, it is a giving away of that centre in you. Step one is to admit to yourself what you are doing, and step two is to simply value how you are now, in the moment, without feeling there is any lack in that.

We need to feel we are the real thing. We need on the one hand that firm grip on ourselves, not in a control freak way, but more around being honest at all points, having the courage to do that. And on the other hand, being open to what we can learn from others. They go together, because humility runs through this.

How can Shamanism, the indigenous soul, be reclaimed in our culture so long as we feel the real thing lies elsewhere?

Spirit power is something given to us. We cannot cause it to happen. It belongs to the East of the Medicine Wheel. It comes in of its own accord. Our part is to make ourselves an adequate vehicle for when it does show up. This is the North-South of the Medicine Wheel, Mind and Emotion, where we have choice about who we are. We become an adequate vehicle through honesty and humility and prayerfulness. And through cultivating the sense of belonging to the natural world. The natural world IS the Great Spirit, it is not something separate. Being in nature, enjoying its beauty in a simple way, getting a sense of it as conscious and aware of us as much as we are aware of it, all helps make us an adequate vehicle.

The power doesn't lie in particular cultures and in particular trainings. You sometimes hear about 'powerful' teachings, or 'powerful' teachers. Just ignore all that if you can, though it can be quite difficult to when everyone else is buying into it. Just hold your head up high and look in a level, equal kind of way at these indigenous people, even at the medicine person. We have our own power, our own insight and wisdom. Maybe particularly if you are English you need to do this, because we have a habit of not thinking well of ourselves, we would think it unseemly to do so. Americans don't seem like that so much, they're more likely to give a teacher a run for his money!

I think I've made my point. Own it, we have the power, we can do this thing, we can reinvent ourselves, we can remake that connection to indigeneity, to that sense that we belong to the natural world, which is where our power comes from.

And then we remember who we are and always were. We remember that this notion we have of a separate self is just a brittle illusion. (The modern emphasis on the autonomous self with its raft of 'rights' is not helpful in this respect.) We were asleep, we'd forgotten who we were, and we've come back home. Everything we could ever need, all the wisdom, all the compassion, all the healing power can just flow through us.

It is not a crime to idealise people we have put in a position of being 'spiritual'. It's a stage along the path for most of us, that we find difficult to admit to. Fundamentally, it's about trusting our own guidance, and not looking outside for it. We usually need to start by looking outside, and because it's unconscious, we often do it in a fantastical way, attributing divine qualities to people who do not merit it. But hopefully we eventually sort it out.

There is another reason we do it, which is particular to us: it is the countercultural tendency to be opposed to the modern world you live in, to look down on it as though you could do a better job. This is endemic in much of the modern Shamanic world. In that scenario, indigenous people become everything your culture is not, the ideal original humans, and we need to keep them there as a way of looking down on our own culture. The solution to this is gratitude: gratitude to your own culture for providing you with all those basics such as food, shelter, safety, education, health ... the list goes on. This kind of gratitude is fundamental to indigenous peoples and the way they live. This can be difficult to do if we are politically left leaning, because we (rightly) see what is wrong with the world, we want to alleviate its suffering, but we can find it hard to accept what is right with the world, as though to do so would be to ignore the suffering.

Indigenous people can also play their own part in the ways we disempower ourselves. What they sometimes do is dismiss our own attempts at Shamanism, and Western people then join the bandwagon. We identify with these teachers, we stand in solidarity with these guys who seem to have all the answers, and it affirms the pre-existing attitude of looking down on our own culture. It's a power game of looking down on others, both on the part of the indigenous teachers and their followers. I was guilty of it myself many years ago, when I was around an indigenous person who was dismissive of our attempts at Shamanism. Even the word Shamanism was something you did not say. In a way, it left me with nothing: I could never be part of the ways of a foreign culture, but nor could I take my own one seriously. I eventually had to return from that.

The native person I was around genuinely had a lot of depth to his indigenous perspective. He was deeply versed in the tradition, in the stories, in the practices. He knew a lot, and could give nuanced answers about everything. I learned a lot from that. But would also make fun of what it is we were attempting to do here. Now it's easy to make fun of things, we're human and we're full of holes. The important thing is to affirm that which is genuine in what we're trying to do.

I heard from a friend about some indigenous Mongolian Shamans she visited, who were completely dismissive of Core Shamanism. I suspect this is typical. Don't get me wrong, there is plenty to criticise in Core Shamanism, it has lots of limitations, and I made this clear in an earlier chapter. But I was also careful to affirm where it is helpful. It was what got me going in Shamanism, it changed me.

I think one of the reasons some indigenous people can be so dismissive of our efforts is defensiveness. You look at it from their point of view. They've been overwhelmed by modern culture throughout the world, which is often what happens when one culture is dominant. In many cases it began with invasion, but it is also now just the influence of a rapidly changing modern world that is hard to resist. Their cultures face obliteration, and modern culture is the enemy. It is a culture that accords them very low status, and could destroy what little they have left.

So of course they are on the defensive, who wouldn't be? But that doesn't make it right when our culture gets put down unjustifiably, as a way of them feeling OK about themselves. And that then ties in, in an unholy alliance, with the counterculture bashing of the modern West: the self-flagellation we indulge in, and the guilt we are made to feel about our past. I expect this blind defensiveness from ordinary indigenous people, but I expect better of medicine people.

Another way this defensiveness can come out is in not wanting us to come anywhere near their traditions. 'Cultural appropriation', it gets called. Many Western people take this idea very seriously. It is based on the notion that we have taken nearly everything away from indigenous people, and now we want to steal their traditions as well.

We sometimes behave as though there is some single authority amongst indigenous people telling us what we can and can't do. But maybe all we are hearing is the loudest, most dogmatic voices. Some will say don't you come anywhere near our Sweatlodges, it would be entirely disrespectful for you to imitate them. Other will say go for it, it doesn't matter if you don't know all the details of how to do it, you will still be doing good work, you will still be helping people. It is complicated. There are things to be listened to on both sides.

And it is also where we can claim our power. It's easy to feel disempowered in this sort of situation, and just feel well we won't go near it, because of what they say. But remember there are different viewpoints: they are people, and people are always a bunch of different viewpoints. If it seems like there is just one viewpoint, then you know it's got political, and to be wary.

So in general, be wary of indigenous dismissiveness of what it is we're trying to do, whether it is implicit through silence, or explicit through what is said. They might well see genuine faults or limitations in what we do, and listen to that. But not to the dismissiveness, which may be woven in, and is just so incredibly disempowering for us. It's a protection mechanism for them, and just don't have any of it. This is where they're wrong, and when you can see that they're wrong. That in turn re-empowers us, because it takes them off that pedestal that we put them on. Some of them don't mind being put on a pedestal, because they're human and enjoy being looked up to. You see this a lot around Tibetan Buddhism, which actively cultivates this kind of veneration of its teachers.

There's a story about an ordinary guy on the Indian reservation who goes to the nearby big city, and there he calls himself a local leader. Getting a taste for this, he goes to Washington, where he calls himself a tribal chief. And then he visits Europe, where he is now a Medicine Man. A lot of the Indian stories are based around the trickster figure, who puffs himself up and then comes unstuck. This story is in that spirit, except he doesn't come unstuck. But he does get laughed at on the reservation, where they know who he is. The Indians are just like us. A lot of them will puff themselves up if they can. So keep your eyes open. Watch how they present themselves, the claims they make or imply about how spiritual they are, or allow others to make on their behalf. A native guy I knew had a lot of integrity around this: on any promotional material for his events, we could only state his CV in factual terms: where he came from, and the formal trainings he had had. But nothing to suggest he was on some high level.

You see it in our own Shamanic world all the time. You see teachers preening themselves on their CVs, you see them enjoying the attention and wanting to be loved, you can see their inflation about who they are. You learn so much once you can learn to see these things. It takes quite a lot to see, because we can feel it's wrong and disrespectful to do so. The other pupils will certainly not take kindly to it if you speak it!

But what you are doing when you do that, is to see the teacher or the indigenous person as ordinary. And that gives you your power back. That also means you can dance around the teacher's faults, let them fly past you, while letting in the genuine teachings he has. This can be a bit of a journey. We often start by not seeing the teacher's limitations, and eventually getting burned by them. That gives the chance to claim our power back – which we could never have lost if it had been truly our own in the first place. But when you've been burnt – when you've betrayed yourself, for that is what it ultimately amounts to – you can find yourself never giving away that power, that inner voice, again.

Someone once told me about a visiting Native American teacher who came regularly to their house, where he ran events. The teacher asked to borrow £4000 off them, this was in the 1990s. He said that was the last they saw of that money. When you get burnt like that, you have a chance to learn something. If it takes £4k to learn, so be it. You could argue it is cheap at the price. You take them off the pedestal, and you start trusting your own, instead of the other person's, guidance.

That's such an important step to go through. Not everyone manages it, or maybe they do just to some degree over the course of their lifetime. It's a big ask. You sometimes see people who have maybe been around a teacher for 30 or 40 years, and they start questioning, because something in them is waking up. They start to feel constricted, or maybe betrayed. They feel the teacher has got something wrong in a way they had never allowed themselves to feel previously. They may be quite angry. They may then spend the next ten years wriggling on that hook, all the while loosening up, and gradually trusting their own guidance more. You have to leave people to it, they take their own time with these things, and it may take a whole lifetime to move forward just a few inches.

Another example is that of a Western Shamanic teacher who wrote a spiritual autobiography that was fantastical in places. Anyone outside the cult he had created could see it was a tall story, and he was a guy not to be trusted. And you see his long-term students gradually waking up to it, maybe 15 years later. It's their real learning. Spirit, I would speculate, put them with that teacher so that they could spend 20 years learning that one lesson, which is ultimately a wake-up call to their own power.

This is one of the things we can learn through indigenous people being put on pedestals. We can't help it if everyone else around us is doing it, but then we get drawn into the group dynamic almost despite ourselves, because we are relational beings. We suddenly start changing our behaviour a bit and being a bit more polite and quiet and self-conscious, as though the Pope just walked in. I still have to watch myself in that sort of situation, even after all these years. Most people can't admit to this. They think they are just being respectful to an advanced being.

But just be open and upfront about it, at least to yourself. It's so nourishing and bracing: you pull back, you refuse. It's like, no I'm not having it, I'm a Chaos Shaman and I'm gonna talk to this person just like an ordinary guy, not like someone special. And you might have a welcome surprise, that the teacher is relieved to have a real conversation with someone, where you are levelling with them. I have had plenty of experience of teachers who will not level, they have to top everything I say with some kind of better insight. Or they reply, "Absolutely," to what I say, to show they knew it already. This is all to keep themselves in the teacher position.

So be wary of indigenous teachers who are dismissive of what we do, and their treacherous Western pupils who join them in that! Appreciate the ones who are supportively critical, because there's much we can learn from them.

There is another issue, which is that I've yet to meet an indigenous teacher who can offer practices that are truly suitable and relevant for us. And why would they be able to? Sure, we can enter into their traditions and be deeply helped and nourished by that. But they remain their traditions, not ours. There is a work of translation to be done, in taking the spirit of what they have to offer, and re-imagining it in the context of our own culture. And we will not be able to do that so long as we feel it is they who have the goods and not ourselves. This book on Chaos Shamanism is an attempt to do just that. It began with my 2022 book *The Medicine Wheel*, where I took a traditional teaching, stripped it back to something simple and then unfolded it according to my understanding from within our own culture. In this book, I am trying to do that with the whole of Shamanism, so to speak.

Another example of this comes from a Western teacher who began running Sweatlodges in England in the 1980s. He had been to a couple in America, but no one was running them here. And he thought, well people could benefit from these, but if I don't run them, who will? So he worked it out from scratch, and reinvented them for our culture. I have been to a number of his lodges, and I love them. Some people would claim this to be outrageous cultural appropriation, but I say no, no, no! Compassion, the desire to help people, is what matters.

It is the same with Jim Tree, who I mentioned in Chapter 11. He is Native himself, but in his book *The Way of the Sacred Pipe*, he presents the Pipe Ceremony in such a way that you feel free to do it yourself and develop it as necessary. Some might argue that it is a ceremony foreign to our culture, but I say, who cares?

People have always borrowed in this way. And besides, we are now a global culture, we have that kind of breadth and freedom. We belong to the whole earth in a more tangible way than was ever possible before.

I don't think that trying to return to Celtic Shamanism, or whatever one imagines was originally in this land, is a valid means of reinventing indigeneity for our culture. I think that is another sidetrack. There is no such thing anymore as Celtic Shamanism. The Celts were around thousands of years ago, they spoke a different language, and genetically we have since become mixed with many other invading races. Moreover, we've only got bits and pieces of text about their practices and beliefs and stories. In a way we're much closer to North American Indians. We speak the same language, and they have been living alongside our white American relatives for the last 400 years. There is much in their traditions that is available for us to draw on, and in a more real kind of way, because it's still living. There are people who can speak from the original traditions who want to share with us. Finding something that is our own is not the same as reaching back to the distant past, as though that is somehow deeper and more authentic. It's like no, it's us as we are now that is authentic, this huge melting pot of races with access to the whole world's culture. We are attempting a new synthesis, of modern consciousness with indigeneity. It is THE great project in consciousness for our times. Christianity has gone into decline, and that leaves us free to reclaim what was lost. Modern consciousness and culture has a lot going for it; it is not just some kind of mistake that needs discarding. That is failing to see what is good, and it is disempowering, because it is ourselves we are discarding.

In the next chapters I will say a bit about the Pipe Ceremony and the Sweatlodge as practices we can import and reinvent for ourselves.

One final point on disempowerment. You sometimes see people who are basically copying indigenous people. They take the Native American songs, they take the Pipe like I do, they take whatever, and they start trying to replicate them as though through that they're keying into something deeper. They may be very particular about the exact details of whatever ceremony it is they are running. It is a delusion on their part, and often there is a power game going on: that they have the goods and you don't, because they have been around such and such a native teacher, and they have had the initiation. What matters is how someone strikes you here and now, not the lineages they claim to have hanging off them.

If you're copying something from a Siberian or Native American or Amazonian culture, there's a good chance it's being done quite superficially, that it hasn't got the imagined extra depth and authenticity. The real depth comes from consulting your own experience, being true to that, while maybe incorporating some of these elements that you've learned from the Amazon or Siberia or even from a book. Why not from a book? Be like a magpie, borrow from everywhere. The main thing is that closeness to yourself that you have built up over the decades. That is what gives you the right to be what some might call a cultural appropriator, which is something humans have been doing forever.

26

Ceremony: Giving Thanks

Ceremony, in a way, gets to the heart of Chaos Shamanism. With ceremony we have forms, mainly from foreign cultures, because we don't have that unbroken indigenous connection in our modern Western culture. So how do we relate to those foreign ceremonies? That is the kind of question that Chaos Shamanism asks. And that brings us to a consideration of what the essence of Shamanism is, so that you can reach out from there and have some idea of what to do with these ceremonies. It's as if with these foreign ceremonies we are given the branch of a tree, but we don't have a trunk to hang it on. So it can be hard to make full sense of them. With Chaos Shamanism, I'm trying to say here's the trunk, here's the heart of it, and here's how to hang it, here's how to graft it on. And in such a way that it becomes our tree, and not just something that we bow down respectfully in front of, saying here's the real thing, and we're just beginners.

No, we're the real thing too, about which I've been banging on relentlessly throughout this book. What is this essence of Shamanism, this trunk of the tree? It is the Chaos, the Great Mystery within and around us, this thing that is outside all forms. Chaos is the vast abyss that was there before the world. It brings us right back to creation and its source, which is what we ourselves are. We have this source within us, which is always there, the endless bubbling up of life, of images, of ideas, of feelings, of the sheer desire to be alive. The Chaos is the endless creative fountain of life within us, creative because it was Chaos that gave rise to the whole universe in the first place. The vast abyss is the negative way of putting the Chaos, and it highlights the mystery, the unknowability of Chaos. The positive way is

Chaos as endless creative source, or Cosmos. They are two sides of the same coin. It is like sunyata, or emptiness, in Buddhism, which has been translated as the plenum-void. It is only empty, it is only the vast abyss, from the point of view of ordinary human cognition. Stressing the emptiness can seem like a bleak thing to do, a way of making us depressed about the ultimate nature of existence. But really it is about nudging us to drop all our preconceptions in order to bask in the Great Mystery.

Any spiritual tradition is essentially an aid to bring us close to that source, and for us it's a bit like grandmother's footsteps played backwards. We back slowly towards the brilliant light of the Chaos — which is also the great impenetrable darkness. We don't look directly at the light, for it is too bright. Grandmother is too much for us! *"Humankind cannot bear very much reality"* — and that's even at a low level, where we find home truths difficult.

But even if we are Chaos Shamans and we feel that drive to be deeply true to who we are, to prioritise that in our lives, we still edge slowly and sideways: like Cancer the Crab moving towards the divine light of the next zodiac sign, Leo, while trying to hang on to that which is familiar. We face outward to the known, while Spirit pulls us downwards and inwards to who we really are. It's a demanding place to live from, at least to start with. Being creative means you're always on that edge, you're always asking a lot of yourself, but you wouldn't want to live any other way, once you're used to living on that level. But it takes a lot and it takes time, and we'd rather live with what is familiar.

The purpose of collectives is to provide us with what is familiar. The purpose of religion and its ceremonies, which is the collective at prayer, is to give us that familiarity, while sneaking in something that asks a bit more. This is how you do a Sweatlodge, this is how you do a Pipe Ceremony. We need those specific forms, but there are profound meanings contained within them. They're bringing us closer to the Chaos, or maybe just reminding us of it, and that's the real purpose of ceremony.

I've got a book called *Fools Crow: Wisdom and Power*. It's the second of two books by Thomas E. Mails about the great 20th century Lakota Medicine Man Frank Fools Crow. The first is simply called *Fools Crow*. They are well worth reading, as are other books about some of these guys like Lame Deer and Rolling Thunder and Black Elk, and just imbibing what they were like. (See **Recommended Reading and Watching** at the end of the book.) It's the transmission I was writing about in Chapter 7, but it's from a book!

These two books on Fools Crow are particularly good for imbibing what it is to be a holy person, what it is you need to ask of yourself to become a hollow bone for the Great Spirit. Fools Crow did what we would call miracle healings all the time, and it was because he remained close to the Great Spirit, he created a foundation of that in himself. Of course, he also had a particular gift as a healer, which most of us won't have. But that's how it works, as Fools Crow himself says: you begin by letting the Spirit reshape you, being honest with yourself, being close to yourself, being prayerful and ethical over decades, and gradually you become an adequate vehicle for this much bigger power to flow through you. And then you can teach, then you can heal, then you can run ceremonies, all these things, according to your nature and temperament.

He also says that it's very important to do the ceremonies as they are prescribed, to remain true to the form of them. I thought that was an interesting point, because Chaos Shamanism might seem to be subverting that, by saying the forms don't matter so much, because we need to get to the essence behind the forms. But that's not what I'm saying. Those forms are necessary for the collective, which needs them as a reminder of the Sacred, because ordinary everyday life can be all-consuming in its responsibilities and relentless practical demands. Spirit can seem like something woo-woo or unreal, even though it's more real. The purpose of ceremony is to remind us that the Spirit is what matters, and if you are already close to that, then it brings you even closer. That's why Fools Crow did his Pipe Ceremony every morning and every evening. He said he can do this work without the forms, he can tune into the Great Spirit, but he still used those forms because they were sacred for him, and their power built over time.

We need on the one hand to take the ceremonial forms very seriously, and yet remember that they are also, in the last analysis, provisional and temporary and culture specific. They're both of these things at the same time, it's not one or the other. Ideally, you need to engage with a particular form over a period of time, and engage with yourself over a period of time, before you have the right to start being fluid around it and even reinventing it. If you're in a traditional culture, you probably wouldn't want to reinvent it, you'd just be going deeper into those particular forms, because if you approach them with a fluid and open mind, then they don't become rigid, they remain a lens, a gateway. But they so easily also become barriers, rigid dogmas.

But for us, we don't have the forms, we do have to reinvent, that's where we find ourselves. So we need simple ceremonies that we can then build on, and we probably do need to build particular forms that we always do in the same way, while reminding ourselves they're not the thing itself, they are a gateway, a lens.

I was in a Welsh church recently, where they had a priest's vestments on display. They were striking and beautiful. It reminded me of just how elaborate church ceremonies can be, particularly Roman Catholic. And that in turn reminded me of just how elaborate something like the Sweatlodge ceremony can also be. These tapestries of ritual feed our imaginations, they nourish us deeply, they create a world of the Spirit for a whole community to live by. You hear of people who do not subscribe to Christian doctrine, but go to church nonetheless, for the ceremony. And maybe that's enough. Maybe it is enough to invoke the Sacred, without having to have any particular belief behind it.

I want to describe and discuss two ceremonies, just because they're the ones I know: the Sweatlodge and the Pipe Ceremony. I want to talk mainly not about their forms, but about what is essential to them, namely giving thanks and prayer.

Both ceremonies, like all ceremonies, begin with gratitude, with giving thanks. This is something humans forget to do. That's why it needs to be in a ceremony. We forget because we're busy and we easily take things for granted – we are not very thoughtful in that way. I think this is a big deal in our modern culture, because our attitude to what is conventional, what is established, to authority can be very 'anti' if we're in the Shamanic world or the counterculture. When we're anti like that, it can be hard to experience gratitude, because what we could be grateful for is provided to us by what we're against.

We are provided with food and shelter and health and education and safety and so on: there is a lot that is very basic to be grateful for. But people can feel that being appreciative of and grateful for those things means that they're being complacent and uncompassionate, because they've got to keep an eye on the underprivileged, those who are suffering, because people don't care about them. How can you sit there enjoying your cappuccino when people in Africa are starving? But it's not an either/or. We can be grateful for what works, without that meaning we don't care about the sufferings of the world. Even then, the news will give you any number of desperate situations around the world to feel compassionate about. It can overwhelm you.

Two points arise from this. Firstly, charity begins at home. I always say yes to anyone who comes my way in need of the kind of help I can offer, and I deliberately do not get involved in suffering that is remote from me. How would I know what helps and what doesn't help? The other point is that people often NEED the establishment to be the bad guys, because that makes them feel good about themselves, it makes them spiritual and even Shamanic. Pointing out the people that they think government should be taking more care of affirms this position, and makes them the compassionate ones, because they care, unlike the greedy capitalists who really run the show. As if they could do any better at making the very complex decisions that the government has to make.

I am pressing what amounts to a political point, which I have already made more than once, because it is an attitude that gets in the way of basic gratitude towards life, for what works in a fundamental way. If you can't experience gratitude for this because your politics won't allow you to, then you are not going to get very far Shamanically. Even if you didn't vote for this particular government, they are still keeping the whole show shambling along, the show that feeds us and protects us in its imperfect way. Appreciate that. Our gratitude extends back ultimately to the earth herself, because everything comes from her.

Moreover, that which we are grateful for is usually not perfect. The food we have may be produced in ways we are not happy with; the metals in our phone may be the product of mining methods that do not respect the earth; the medical care we get may involve drugs that do harm as well as good; and so on. But even with these limitations, we still have all those things to be grateful for. Again, we need a supportive attitude to the society that produces these things. Outright opposition takes us away from gratitude. Mining, for example, brings us riches from the earth. It needs to be done with respect, and made beautiful afterwards. Oil brings us further riches from the earth that are at the root of our prosperity and well-being. Appreciate her bounty, and use it wisely. This does not mean you don't care about the environment. There is no point opposing the direction of the modern world. It is much better to work with what is happening, tweak it, and call for an appreciation of the earth as a living being.

I recommend once a day, just stop for a minute and remember all these good things, and feel your appreciation. It is a feeling thing, not an 'ought to' thing. It is for your own well-being and balance. It is not about making you a good Shamanic person: that is religion. You can make it ceremonial. You can lie on the earth if you like, feel her and thank her, and sense her care for you. Gratitude connects you to everything, it is profound. It is a connection to who we really are, which is infinite, everything.

It's worth remembering too that your gifts are not yours, that is why they are called gifts. If you have a high IQ, if you are smart, that isn't something you earned. You were born with it, it was given to you. We don't usually like to remember this. It's hard not to identify with our gifts, it's just what humans do. You can spend your whole life priding yourself on being smarter than the people round you. Or better looking, or wealthier. Or taller, if you are a man. And so on. It's good to be thankful for these things too. No false modesty here, acknowledge the gifts and be thankful for them. And that will haul you off the over-identification with them, and into a foundation in yourself that is more real, that has more humility.

There are all these things that we can be grateful for. We can spend our life being grateful, walking around with the feeling of gratitude, hardly being able to believe that we're alive, for life itself is a gift — and a complete mystery. Just to be alive is a joy, it's rich. Of course there are difficult things that we have to engage with, and sometimes it's really bloody miserable and we don't know if we want to be here or not, but at the end of the day it's meaningful and it's joyful. There's something rich here, we know that we have to stay for this journey, we have to be here for this innings, however difficult it is at times.

It's not about being happy. That's the mistake people can make these days. When you look back on your life at the periods that you remember most, that really mattered, that were the most fulfilling, they were probably the bits where you really grappled with something; there were difficulties that you faced and overcame, and that changed who you were. You probably weren't happy for much of those times, but they are the times you remember, they are what you're proud of.

We're not mainly here to be happy, we're here to find meaning, and that's often a difficult process. Through the meaning we grow and unfold; it's where the life is bubbling up through, and we meet the new life that is wanting to emerge. That's often a difficult process. But we are grateful for that opportunity. I often say to people in the context of astrology readings, and whatever difficult event has happened to them, that one day they are going to look back and be grateful through gritted teeth for that awful person, the 'worthy opponent' it is sometimes called, or the health crisis, or their spouse leaving, whatever it was. Here we are, grateful for the suffering that came our way, that was brought to us, maybe by the Spirit, for we learnt so much from it.

I think Christianity can turn this kind of suffering into a bit of a cult, where it becomes the main thing, and we're meant to be grateful to Jesus for being tortured to death on our behalf. The Christians are onto something, but I think it gets all twisted up and made too central. I'd rather think of the Native American Sundance, where your flesh is ceremonially pierced and torn. There is a closeness to the Great Spirit to be found here, within the privation and suffering. And therefore the sense of gratitude.

Be grateful to people who are successful, because they often create prosperity. I'm grateful for the fact that I can just find something on Amazon and buy it. I may not be entirely happy about everything Jeff Bezos, the founder, does, but I am grateful for the opportunity to encounter all those books I would otherwise never have done. That's difficult for a lot of people because Jeff Bezos is hugely wealthy, and as humans it serves us to envy and judge people like that. It is our comfort zone.

Envy goes deep. It is the first sin in the Bible after Eden, when Cain kills his brother Abel out of envy at God favouring him. So here is a big challenge: be grateful to Jeff Bezos for what he has given us. But as I say, that doesn't mean being uncritical of him. It is a complex picture, like everything in life. In this way gratitude makes us big-hearted, it goes against the very human tendency to live from the small, narrow mean-spirited place that can colour our whole view of the world. This kind of gratitude is a revolutionary act for many people, for it can challenge who we are at a deep level.

Be grateful for all these wonderful technologies that we have. There are only going to be more of them, they are a natural thing for humans to keep creating, so embrace them. Our task is not to judge and oppose them — that is too easy, it is complacent, it is even a kind of spiritual bypass. It is what religions have always done: put themselves above the world. Our task is to find new ways of bringing these technologies into balance with the natural world. We need to be a kind of anchor on the earth while humanity, Icarus-like, heads for the Sun, attempts to become godlike.

In conclusion, we're grateful just to be here, and everything and everyone that comes with that. We begin any ceremony by remembering and expressing our gratitude for all those things, because they so easily get forgotten. Express it once a day at least, have it in mind. Just feel appreciativeness for the house you've got, however inadequate it may be, and for the clothes you wear, for the people who made them. All those people and things that are near you. Giving thanks opens us up to the Spirit. We remember that we are given everything.

27

Ceremony: Prayer

Giving thanks is essential to Ceremony, and how it begins. Then comes prayer.

I was shown many years ago how to do the Pipe Ceremony in a Navajo style. The person running it talked about prayer, and about how the Navajo would gather together – it's a community event – for a Pipe Ceremony. You hold the Pipe and you pray to it, and through that to the Great Spirit. It would be relatively informal, it's not holy and solemn in the way that a church is. Of course there is the respect there, the sense of the Sacred, and people are homing in on that. But normal stuff happens, kids run in and out. You don't have kids running in and out of church. The reason being that for indigenous people, the Sacred and the everyday are much more connected, they're the same thing. They don't have a separate thing called the Sacred. In a way they do, because they have ceremonies. But it's not separate in the way that it is for us. It's an integrated aspect of life. I wrote previously about this provisional distinction in the chapter on Soil.

Having first given thanks, people would pray for what they want. Again, the prayers could be quite informal. Some people would go on for three-quarters of an hour, they might crack jokes, there is humour. They just go around the houses and talk about everything in their lives. Maybe what they want is their car fixed, because they haven't got the money to do it, and they really need it, because they need to get to work or something. This is on the reservation – the 'rez' – where very few people have any money. And so they pray for that, and why not? Prayer is something that's dead practical, again because the Sacred and the ordinary are not separate. So why shouldn't you get your car fixed?

The fact that they feel they can just talk on when they pray reveals another point. For them, prayer is not about asking an almighty being to grant you favours, rather it is a conversation with the natural world. This is an important point. You're not asking God. If you like, you're letting your heart merge with the heart of the world, the heart of the Mother. Because you are nothing but her, and she provides, she takes care of us.

The Earth is also the Great Spirit, in other ways she's not, it depends how you want to look at it. You can make these distinctions, but that's how I'm looking at it here. And we are her. We have this idea that we're a separate human being. It's just how people are, we suffer from this delusion, and prayer takes us away from that delusion. Like giving thanks, it reminds us that we're connected, and that's why prayer works.

It's a conversation in which you're asking the Great Mother, please help me with this. You have the space in the prayers just to talk and to take the time you need, you're not under pressure to come out with something important. You can talk around it and let what's in your heart and what is important there emerge. We don't always know what's in our heart, so we don't necessarily know what's important. We might think we know, that we'd like a new car or a pay rise. But you might find in your talking, that there's something underlying, that is what really matters to you, there is strong feeling there, coming straight from the heart. It can surprise you.

Often what is important is below the surface, because we tend not to live in that deeper place. When you circle around your life in the course of your conversation with the natural world, what is truly important can emerge naturally, maybe even when you are being humorous. Humour is play, and when we are playing, the whole of us is present, it is sacred in that way.

And then out something comes with a force that surprises you, and how could that not be answered? This is how prayer works. We say something that matters to us, that's in our heart, and that connects us to everything, to the whole universe, we are pulsing with her. The earth feels the power of what we have said, and in her compassion, in her care, she cannot but respond. That's how it works.

The prayer will be answered, but probably not in the way that we think. How could it? We are these individual humans with just a tiny sliver of consciousness – this perspective is traditional – in the context of the vast, infinite consciousness of the universe. The universe, the Great Spirit, sees things in a way that we never could, and it is her that we are asking for help, so how could we ever know the way in which she will respond? This attitude gives us humility and the wisdom that comes with that, the ability to see clearly without the ego getting in the way.

The answer to the prayer might even bring a difficulty with it. The Great Spirit is always wanting us to learn, because that is what we are here to do. Maybe we get the opposite of what we think we want, and we realise that if we had got that job or that woman or whatever, it wouldn't have worked, it wouldn't have been good. And in that we learn something. So we never know the outcome. All we do know is that strong feeling around the matter we have prayed on, and what we think it's about. That's as far as we can go.

The person I learnt the Pipe Ceremony from always led it beautifully, but I don't think she properly understood prayer, even though she had been around a Navajo teacher for years. She said that you need to pray for exactly what you want, and it will inevitably happen. If it doesn't happen, it's because you didn't pray for exactly what you wanted. It seemed to me that she was treating the Great Spirit like Santa Claus: you gave him your list of things you wanted for Christmas, and if it was precise and neat and properly spelt, you would get all of them. Her upbringing had been Roman Catholic, and maybe that influenced how she saw prayer. I agree with her that you need to be exact about what you are praying for, but it is an exactitude that is true to the feeling behind the prayer. It is the feeling that gives power to the prayer. You cannot be exact about the outcome, unlike how she saw it. She was driven by blind faith, and I don't think she ever stopped to consider if and how her prayers were ever answered.

Praying gets us close to ourselves. If you pray regularly, even quite informally – just tune into your heart and talk to the Great Spirit – you will end up living closely to yourself. And what else are we here to do, but that? It will make you very sure-footed. You will be less likely to make wrong steps, because you know who you are and you know intuitively, in your body, what is the right thing to do and what is the wrong thing. Animals live closely to themselves in that way, they are deliberate in their actions, and we can learn from that, us newborns, newborn because we are the only animal that does not know who it is.

You will also be more attuned to the needs of others, for you will be paying attention to them with your heart. They can be prayed for too. It is usually best to pray in a general way for others. If they are ill, pray for a recovery, but not for a specific treatment. If they are in a difficult family situation, pray for its improvement, but be cautious about praying around the person you think is the cause of the trouble. Pray for the specific help that they have themselves asked for, or that is obvious. But otherwise be circumspect, for we do not know what is going on, and its wider picture. They may have just the difficulty they need in their life, and they are railing against it! Or it may be that their time has come to die. Death isn't necessarily a bad outcome. But we can pray for their suffering to be alleviated, and for the best possible outcome for them.

I think prayers for others are particularly effective because they're compassionate. The Spirit takes particular note of those. A bit like when you do Shamanic Journeying work for others: it can be very easy, you have a following wind. When you do things for others, there is a very clear path to Spirit, a lot of power can flow through that.

Prayer is something that you can be living all the time. I've cited twice the Achuar people, for some of whom everything they do is a prayer, which is remarkable. It means that all the time you're living close to your heart and to the Sacred. You're feeling what you're doing, it's imbued with meaning, it's connected to your reason for being alive. If they're living in the jungle, maybe they're out collecting some kind of vegetable, they're doing it so that they can feed their family, and that's a prayer, and it is done with gratitude for the plant that gives up its life, so that your family can live.

A traditionally trained friend – I think she was from the Blackfoot people – told me that all some elders do is pray. This was in the context of talking about activism and its limitations. I learned from that, because they are elders. If you want to help the world, prayer is perhaps the best thing you can do.

When you're doing something for others, look on it as an ongoing prayer. Whatever you're doing, even if it's for yourself, it is a kind of prayer. There's an intention there, and if it is in your heart, then it is naturally prayerful. I am writing this book in a way for myself, for I love doing it, but also with the people who might read it in mind, and how it might be of benefit to them. It is that feeling which keeps me going. There is an edge of Spirit to it, a feeling of inspiration. In this way it connects me to the Great Spirit, makes me a vehicle for her.

When you're living in that prayerful mode, you do the things you really need to do, and it hauls you away from any kind of self-destructive behaviour, too much alcohol or sugar, or whatever it is you do. If you're close to yourself, you know it's not doing you any good, and you're not going to pray for that, are you? You end up praying for what's really in your heart.

Here's something. Sometimes in the evening I'll have a really hot bath, a bit like being in a Sweatlodge, and it melts me out of my head and into my heart. That can be quite good, for sometimes in the evening I can feel a little bit uncomfortable in myself, and that maybe it would be nice to have some alcohol to alleviate that. I don't feel that so much these days because I've been off the drink entirely for a good while, and it has come to feel more like a poison. But you know that little hole can open up, and you want to fill it with something, and therein lies addiction. But what you're really needing is to feel that connection with your heart. That's what a really hot bath will do for me, and the little hole goes. And that's what prayer also does. It is worth any number of hours of psychotherapy and self-analysis! It keeps you living in a sacred way, and that puts you in balance, makes you whole, for your being has a sacred centre around which to organise itself. As Jung said, all psychological ailments are in the last analysis about the need for meaning. Prayer, broadly interpreted, is one of the best ways to address that.

Prayer is at the heart of both the Pipe Ceremony and the Sweatlodge. You could argue that whatever the ceremonial form, it is there to help us come to the point where we can pray in a good way, an authentic way, a way that is close to who we are and what we really need.

I read a description of a Pipe Ceremony by someone on Facebook a few years ago. He's someone who does know a lot about indigenous ceremonies, and it's great to have that kind of resource around. He described it in a traditional and detailed way. First you do this, then you do that, then you call in the directions in this particular way and in this particular order, and this is what you do with the Pipe and so on. Then he said that now you do the prayers, almost as an aside, and then continued with his description of the technicalities, as though getting them right was what was essential. It sounds ridiculous when described in this way, but that is what he did. He likes to be seen as the authority in these things, and he gets it by knowing all the details and citing his connections to indigenous teachers. Many people fall for this, and he has no shortage of followers. It is exactly what Chaos Shamanism has arisen as an ongoing protest against. People often do not know how to look deeply, and they mistake forms for essence. That is one definition of religion, and it will always attract a following. But it leaves you open to people who want power over you, and maybe you secretly want someone powerful and authoritative in your life? Does your power come from your heart, which prayer will bring you closer to? Or does it come from your sense of alignment with someone who claims to know the right and wrong ways of doing something?

28
The Pipe Ceremony

Having discussed at length something of the essence of ceremony — giving thanks and prayer — it is time to move on to a description of the Pipe Ceremony and Sweatlodge.

I would add two more features to the essence of ceremony. Firstly, the building and strengthening of community. That will be described further as we dive into the Pipe Ceremony. Secondly, the immersion in a collective mythology, a particular way of seeing and feeling the universe, that strengthens our metaphysical roots. The Medicine Wheel acts as a mythology for both of the ceremonies I will be describing.

The Pipe is made up of a stem and a bowl. They stand respectively for the male and female principles in the universe. When you join them together, you have wholeness, you have the entire universe, you have the Great Spirit. You normally keep the stem and the bowl apart. You only bring them together for the ceremony, and they are separated at its conclusion.

The Pipe is a sacred object. You keep it in a special place, wrapped in a special cloth. You occasionally visit it and talk to it and clean it. You only bring it out for the purposes of praying. Over time it acquires power, the power of the Great Spirit. The Pipe isn't 'just' a symbol, it doesn't just STAND FOR the union of male and female in the universe, it IS that wholeness, it IS the Great Spirit. That is why it is a sacred object. The Sacred is that which we value most highly. It is not just something we bow down in front of because that is what you do.

We go into a quieter, more reverent kind of attitude when we're in the presence of the Sacred. But that's not the same as the kind of solemnity that you have if you're a church mouse. There's still room for humour and joking. I read once that the difference between being serious and being earnest is that serious also has a sense of humour. Any ceremony is serious, but it's not earnest, unless it's religion and everyone is being terribly hushed and respectful. When there's humour, then there's play. What we're often laughing at is irony and contradiction, the daftness of life, and then you have wholeness. And the purpose of ceremony is to make us whole. The lightness and humour are an important part of it, at least if you are a Chaos Shaman.

The Ceremony begins by putting the bowl and stem together. You don't put tobacco in at this point. Now you are in Ceremony, that special place where we are attuned to that which has the highest value. Whoever is holding the Ceremony will at this point talk to the Pipe and give thanks to it, and call in the Spirits and the Powers of the Directions one by one, each with its particular qualities, and give thanks to them too for presiding and helping. His or her speech is often beautiful and elegant. They talk to the Spirits and Powers like they are talking to a person.

Then the Pipe is passed round clockwise from person to person. You hold the bowl in your left hand and the stem in your right. You give thanks and make your prayers, and when you have finished, you pass it on to the next person who does their giving thanks and their prayers. You don't have to get it right. Halfway through my prayers, I might well remember something I haven't given thanks for, so whoops there's something I didn't give thanks for, so I chuck that in and then carry on with my prayers. We can be informal about this, but in a serious way. Something I do when we've been around everyone and they've all done their prayers, is that I say now we'll have a second round for any prayers you might have forgotten. That is completely untraditional, and I haven't heard of anyone else doing that, but it serves a useful purpose, because often there are things we've forgotten about. Also, if you know you've got a second round, you know you don't need to get it completely right the first time, and that takes the pressure off. And that means you're more likely to remember them all first time. It's always good to spot these kinds of pressures and take them off.

When someone has finished one of their prayers, you may hear some people exclaiming "Aho!" What they are doing is saying it is one of their prayers too, and they are affirming it. That is a great community thing. You can also pray silently for some or all of your prayers, because you might not want everyone to know what it is that you're praying about or giving thanks for. That is fine. However, the more you can pray out loud, in some ways the better, because it connects us all as a community. It's great to be able to open yourself to other people about what matters to you. It creates community, even amongst people you may not know. That can be a beautiful thing, that is equally true for the Sweatlodge. It creates a particular type of consciousness that in the Russian Orthodox church is called 'Sobornost'. I have heard it described as a collective consciousness in which the sense of individuality is heightened rather than subsumed.

Often we are, in this sense, one or the other. It can be that you have to get away from other people to come back to yourself. When you're with others you can kind of lose yourself. You get full of your impressions of them, or maybe drawn into their more superficial, less considered and heartfelt place. And there is always the subtle collective pressure to conform, to think and act and believe like they do. There is always that kind of pressure if you think independently. If you don't think independently, then it's probably just fine, you feel at home, that is what community is for you.

We can lose ourselves in the same way in religious collectives. A cult is this kind of religious collective, but which doesn't have official recognition, it is not yet respectable. That is the only essential difference between, say, Scientology and the Catholic Church. (You might go no, Scientology has bizarre beliefs. And you think Christianity doesn't?) They are mixed things, they perform a function and are not all bad. Society itself is in many ways like one big cult. But we do it to ourselves, out of our need to have shared beliefs and rules for living. There is no dark force doing it to us, no brainwasher in the sky. There is always a choice to step out of it, the red pill.

Ceremony can give a taste of a very different kind of collective consciousness. Maybe it was different amongst a people numbering a few thousand. They were not subject to the vast collective thoughtforms that we live in nowadays. Maybe that made it easier to step into the Sacred. Or maybe it could be the opposite: our large societies have multiple norms and belief systems, and that leaves us freer to step outside of them. But then the mythologies are less unified and less compelling. It is complex, and one of the things I ponder.

Our individuality, our sovereignty, is founded in the personal connection to the Sacred, to that which carries most meaning and value for us. In the best kind of ceremony, that personal connection is supported and heightened. And/or, as usual, it may be a mixed thing. People may have the leader or the tradition on a pedestal, and accordingly be giving something of themselves away. But there can also be a degree of sobornost.

It is one of the beauties of Ceremony that it brings people together at a deep level. You may not know the other people. It is what we might nowadays call a transpersonal experience.

Hinduism and Buddhism have an image for this in the form of Indra's Net. Imagine the universe as an infinite net, with an infinite number of intersections, at each of which there is a jewel that reflects all the other jewels in the net. That is sobornost on a universal scale, and that is what the experience of sobornost on a local scale, whether in the Pipe Ceremony or in the Sweatlodge, can plug us into.

In Ceremony, we are surrounded by beauty: in its forms, in the way people are, in the presence of the Spirits (who love to be there) and in the type of community that is created.

Back to the Pipe Ceremony itself. After everyone has made their prayers, whoever is holding the Ceremony puts the tobacco in the bowl, lights it, draws on it, and passes it to the person on her left. You don't generally inhale, and you don't have to take any, you can just touch the Pipe to your lips if you want. The tobacco itself is a sacred herb, it is a medicine, even though we have turned it into a poison through our addiction to it. There are usually other herbs mixed in, each with specific meanings.

The smoke carries your prayers out to the universe in order that they can be answered, so it is good to blow it upwards. The smoking of the tobacco is contemplative, reflective and enjoyable. You're sitting there quietly remembering your prayers, remembering everyone else's prayers, and also just enjoying the taste of the tobacco: it does have a full rich taste to it, and even without inhaling, the nicotine alters your consciousness. It is, as I said, a medicine.

The tobacco has a Spirit that needs to be treated with respect, and part of this is that all the tobacco in the bowl needs to be smoked. The Pipe is passed around the circle until it is all used up. At this point the ceremony is over. The leader separates the bowl and stem, while giving thanks to the Pipe and to the Spirits and to the Directions for the ceremony, and for listening to everyone's prayers. People give thanks to the leader of the ceremony and bring them gifts such as chocolate or tobacco. It is good to give thanks in this kind of way. It is part of the etiquette.

It's quite a responsibility to be holding the Ceremony. It demands of you. It might be simple, but you're having to be a kind of hollow bone, you're carrying the Great Spirit, and that draws everyone else in around it. It makes a big difference who's leading it. They need to be qualified, but that isn't fundamentally about knowing all the forms. The real qualification for leading anything is that you've spent many years with yourself, you've become close to yourself, you know about gratitude, you know about prayer, you know about your demons, and you know how to be in good relationship with them. You can tolerate yourself!

The Pipe Ceremony is essentially very simple, but the qualification for leading it traditionally takes many years of training. We may not have someone to train under in our culture, in fact we probably don't. But we can do these things ourselves, we just need honesty at all points: why we're doing what we're doing, and truthfulness with ourselves and with others. None of the kidding of yourself that you are doing it just for the benefit of others, when you are also building your own ego as a teacher and healer and leader, which is very common. It usually takes years to purify ourselves of all that. Of course, it's usually better to have a Ceremony than not at all. But keep that high bar in mind.

A further point on what I call the real qualification for leading Ceremonies or any kind of teaching or healing work, which is those years spent at our own coalface, is that it means we treat other people better. If we are a teacher of any kind, we will have people's trust, and we do not want to betray that by acting in our own interest, at the expense of the student. We need self-mastery, the Strength card in the Tarot. I don't mean dominating ourselves. I mean the ability to hold oneself, to remain in balance, remain at the Centre of the Wheel, whatever may be going on. A therapist once said to me that the cardinal sin in her profession is retaliation. That maybe sums up what I mean here. Don't take anything personally. If someone comes along and attempts some kind of power struggle with you, don't retaliate. Catch yourself, or it will downgrade your relationship with everyone present. Some people will pay good money to come to a workshop so that they can prove they know more than the teacher. You need to be a bit fierce if necessary, you have to be able to protect yourself and the group. But make sure it's not personal: only those years at the coalface can ensure that. Even then, an edge might slip out, so apologise if you do that. Otherwise it creates an authoritarian atmosphere, which students will either conform to out of fear, or they will quietly leave.

Just because a Ceremony is simple doesn't mean it is less profound than a more elaborate traditional one. It all depends on the intentions of the people there. For now, I think it is best that we have simple ceremonies that we can fully claim as our own, rather than elaborate ones whose complex symbolism comes from another culture. There is no hurry to elaborate them. These things are slow, they need time to take root.

29

The Sweatlodge

There's a lot to say about what it takes to be able to hold a Ceremony well. It wasn't something I was ever taught. My two main experiences have been firstly of teachers who encouraged people to go out and teach and lead almost as soon as possible, regardless. I have seen the egotistical messes that has created over the years, and the harm done. My other experience has been of a traditional teacher who made one feel the opposite, that one needed a special invite to come anywhere near doing what he taught: he was a good teacher, but the special invites only went to young, pretty women!

I have had to work it out for myself. It is a theme I have returned to throughout this book. My main cue is that in a traditional society, it takes many years of training before one is considered ready to teach or to hold a ceremony. That is why I say spend years with yourself first.

Then we can come into good relationship with ourselves. We have, if you like, followed the injunction above the ancient Oracle at Delphi: "Know Thyself." We are no longer determined by our tribulations, the dark stuff in us. We can live with them, and not slip into avoidance through alcohol or other addictions, or through taking it out on other people. It means we can treat others well, and we can be objective about them, see what it is they need, because we are no longer in the way with our own needs and desires. It can still be a struggle if you are a male teacher, for example, and you have a female student you find attractive. You can end up thinking highly of them in ways they do not merit – as happened in the example above – and the unconscious flattery does not serve them at all.

This self-mastery, this knowing of ourselves, extends into the metaphysical, the Sacred. We live connected to that deep thing in us that is always wanting to unfold, to move forward. That is what is really fuelling us — that, and the compassion, the desire to be of service, that arises naturally with it. It is that deep desire for the metaphysical, to be true to that within ourselves, that motivates us to come into good relationship with our shadow: otherwise, why go to all that trouble, why not just become an addict or a wife-beater, it is much easier?

In terms of the Medicine Wheel, we are attempting to live at its Centre. It is a lifelong undertaking.

With the Pipe Ceremony or a Sweatlodge, if you're in a traditional situation, you would have a proper training in the forms of that as well as the work with yourself for years. We haven't got that here, so what we do is we take a simplified form and we run with it. We know it helps people, and that is the justification for doing it. If somebody suggests no, you shouldn't, because you haven't had the proper initiation, your answer is well it helps people, that's what matters. It's compassion that matters, not being right about the details of how things are done or whether you've had a teacher.

The Pipe Ceremony can be done very simply, and the Sweatlodge too can be quite simple in its forms, albeit profound in its effects.

Someone I know who started running Sweatlodges in the UK in the 80s had been to something like two in the USA. There were no Sweats here, and there was no way he'd had any kind of training. But he'd seen enough of the form to be able to do something that would work. So he and someone else worked it out and they started running them. In a traditional situation, that would be outrageous, and correctly so, because there's no training at all. But over here, there were no Sweatlodges, and people would not have had the benefit of Sweatlodges.

This same guy had the same chutzpah with his Pipe. It is said that you are meant to be given one from a traditional source, and only then are you empowered to lead them. The Pipe has to come to you. There is a lot in that, but probably not over here. This guy was indeed given one, by someone who bought it at Camden Market. I was also given one, by someone who'd ordered it online. I also later went and bought one, but there was some magic around the process that felt to me like a thumbs up from the Spiritworld.

We humans can work things out, and we can be guided by Spirit. Shamanic people say often enough that they were guided by Spirit, or that they get taught by Spirits. Well, there you go, the Spirits will teach you! What does that mean? You might have guides turning up and you hear them saying things. Or you might be nonverbal, like I am in that realm, and you just get a strong feeling that comes from somewhere deep about the right and wrong way to do things. If you follow that feeling about what's right, if you train yourself in learning what feelings to follow and what not to, it will work, it will go well. If you're too headstrong about it, if you're too set on your own pre-planned ideas about it, then you'll tend to override those feelings that are Spirit-driven, and it won't go so well.

As back-up for what I'm saying, I went to a Sweatlodge run by a woman from a Lakota reservation. She didn't really know how to run one. She said she'd got a spirit in her handbag that she'd brought over from America for the Sweat. She was playful and humorous. She knew very little of the forms, and she was telling us in the Lodge just to go out and run Sweatlodges ourselves. She really didn't feel it mattered how it was run, and you got the feeling that she felt that the thing about you've got to do it this way, and you can't come near our traditions, was a male Elder attitude that she was in full protest against. So that relativised the charge of cultural appropriation: "That's just rigid old men who are doing that, they would. I'm a woman, I say it differently, you go and do this, you share this, it's about compassion. That's what matters, it will help people." You could see she had a compassionate heart and that she knew very little in a formal sense about how to run a Sweatlodge. That was great, it was so refreshing, it almost felt she had been sent my way as a counterbalance to all the disempowering dogmatism I had encountered.

My description of the Sweatlodge in this chapter won't be anywhere near enough to go on. You will need to go to a few before you think of running them. And then work out your own way of doing it. Alternatively, you may prefer a long apprenticeship with someone, and then run them in the way you have been taught. It is horses for courses.

For the Sweatlodge, you first need to build a structure, and you need to look that up. It's basically a dome made out of sticks planted firmly in the ground, then bent over and tied to each other. After that, you throw blankets and a canvas over it to keep the heat in. In the centre of the Lodge is a pit for the stones. You have a fire some distance away, in which the stones are heated up before being brought in.

There is a Spirit Road that connects the fire to the Sweatlodge, you put down flour or corn grain or something like that. The stones in the fire are male, the Lodge is female, the womb. The stones impregnate the Lodge, and something new is born, the newborn being ourselves. The Ceremony is infused at all points with this kind of beautiful symbolism.

Once the stones are red hot in the fire, people gather inside the Lodge, and the first set of stones is brought in by the firekeeper, who ideally stays with the fire rather than coming in the Lodge, so as to keep the connection between the Lodge and the fire.

The door is shut, the stones are welcomed in, and thanked for giving their lives in order that we may heal. The stones are living beings, they may have been in this form for millions of years, and now they will crumble. The trees ('the standing people') out of which the wood for the fire came are also thanked. Herbs are sprinkled on the stones, and the Spirits and the Directions are called in one by one.

Then the first round of prayers begins. Like the Pipe Ceremony, everybody prays in turn, and after each person has prayed — or maybe just given thanks in this first round — water is poured on the stones by the leader. The steam carries their gratitude or their prayers out into the universe, much as the smoke does in the Pipe Ceremony. People may also pray/give thanks silently.

The steam also begins to seriously heat up the Lodge, and people may find themselves struggling with it. Bear it, it is good to bear difficulty, it is part of life. Particularly for men, because women learn to bear suffering through childbirth. We men get into warrior mode, and it gets things done, but we can lose the heart connection through that, and the Sweat is good in this way too. The purpose of the steam is to melt us out of our rational minds, and into our hearts. It needs to be turned from an enemy into an ally. Yield to it, allow it to penetrate and heal you. The steam is a beautiful thing.

A sauna can have this melting effect too, but it doesn't have the sacred and ceremonial dimension that a Sweatlodge has.

There may be songs too, usually at the start and the end of the rounds. When the round is over, the door is opened by the firekeeper, and after a short break and water to drink, more stones are brought in, and the process repeats. If we have given thanks in the first round, we may then pray for ourselves, what we want to let go of, what troubles us, in the second round. In the third, we may pray for what we want to bring in to our lives, and in the fourth round we may pray for others. This is a schematic, an example of how it may go. There are all sorts of ways and permutations.

Each round is usually also associated with a Direction, whose Powers are called in for that round, and thanked at the end of that round. The door of the Lodge will also be facing a particular Direction, and that can give an overall emphasis to the Ceremony.

As in the Pipe Ceremony, there is a deep sense of community, of sobornost, as people pray sincerely and openly about things that really matter to them. It is intensified in the Lodge, because of its bare physicality. You go in naked, spiritually if not literally; you are huddled in the dark with a community of people; you yield to the Ceremony and to the steam, and in this sense the old you dies; and you are reborn as you emerge crawling at the end of the Ceremony. You are surrounded by the four Elements in a basic way – the earth that you sit on, the water that is poured on the stones, the water that you may drink ceremonially between rounds, the air and steam that you breathe, and the fire that heats the stones and heats you. It is raw and primal, and beautiful.

Twenty years ago, it was quite common for people to go naked into the Lodge. Nowadays, people usually wear something. There are good reasons both ways. Nakedness emphasises the primal nature of the ceremony, and the death and rebirth we are undergoing. It brings us back to essentials, and it is my preference. If I was a woman, however, I wouldn't want to go in naked amongst men for obvious reasons, and maybe that cultural shift has been in that sense a good thing.

We crawl into and out of the Lodge, partly for practical reasons, because it is a low structure. But also for reasons of humility. We touch our head to the ground as we enter and leave and say, "For all my relations," our relations being everything that lives.

I will say a bit more about the Directions in the Lodge. In the chapters on Sun, Rain, Soil, and Wind, I talked about the

Directions primarily in terms of their elemental associations, because they are good for describing the intricacies of the human psyche. But primarily they are Directions which we can stand and face and talk to. They each have their own Powers, and they are invoked by eloquently listing some of the associations of that Direction.

There's a Direction for each round. You can go East then South then West then North, that is what I am used to, but there are bound to be those who do it differently. If you begin with the Powers of the East, that is inspiration, the power of Fire. You are calling that in at the start, because the East is beginnings, and that's maybe the round in which you give thanks. Next is the South, the Watery place of the child, where we can feel tender and vulnerable and in pain. That is often the place we're praying from in the second round, when we're asking for help with our difficulties in life.

The third round is the West, the adult, where we are praying for those extra things that can help our life unfold. That new job, the creative project, a better house, maybe a partner and children, those things in this practical Earthy reality that we live in. But also, as the looks-within place, where the Sun sets at the end of the day, there may be inner qualities that we want to develop.

Finally, the North, the place of the Elder, who has lived his own personal life, and is now at the service of the community with his experience and compassion. And so we pray for others in this Direction. Others matter more to us than we matter to ourselves, something we began to learn as an adult in the West, when we had children.

The Sweatlodges, like most ceremonies, were traditionally carried out for a particular purpose, you didn't just do it because it was Sunday. You did it because someone needed help or healing. It's a community thing, because if one person is ill, the whole community is out of balance. Maybe that's why they're ill, maybe there's something out of balance in the community, or in their family, who knows? It can really help people heal when you've got a collective praying for them; they don't even need to be in the Lodge, if they are too ill. It's the power of sobornost.

When the fourth round is over, thanks are given to the leader, to the people who've kept the fire, to whoever's provided the land to let you have the Ceremony, and to the Spirits for being present. You may want to thank the weather Spirits for holding out and allowing you to have a fire, there may be all sorts of thanks you want to give. It truly comes from the heart at this point, after the melting and community and prayers of the ceremony.

Sweatlodges are one of my favourite Ceremonies. They're a lot of work. I really recommend them, do go in one or two, even if you don't want to run them. There are different ways of doing them. You don't have to stick to the traditional way of building them. I used to have a mini collapsible Sweatlodge. I got four boards that I strapped to five posts. Each of them was a wall of the Lodge, painted in one of the four colours of the Directions. The fifth wall was the door. I'd sling a wood lattice on the roof, and then a tarpaulin over that. It was very quick to put up and take down, and it was only about five feet square. You could probably get five people in at a squeeze, but it was dead easy to heat up, just two or three stones for a round, so you didn't need a big fire. This style is definitely not traditional, but it works. You do get very small Lodges traditionally, and I was told that you put the stonepit next to the door instead of in the middle, so that people can stretch their legs a bit in the Lodge. So that was what I did. It was dead handy for when I just wanted a few friends round to sweat.

In any Lodge, you have a bucket of water for the stones, and you are meant to use up all the water and all the stones. At the end of the formal Lodge, everyone leaves who wants to, and you just keep going till all the stones and water are used up. Maybe you bring in all the remaining stones at once, and pour all the remaining water on at once. That is called a Thunder Round, and you get extreme heat. In the mini Lodge, it would be even more extreme in such a tiny space. The only way you can bear it is by lying face down on the earth. Personally, I love being pushed in that sort of way.

But that doesn't necessarily make it the most powerful or transformational type of Lodge, not at all. It is the Spirits who decide that! A Lodge with gentle heat, Deer energy, may bring people into deep places, may be very healing. People in the Lodge may well experience the heat differently. Some may experience it as very hot, some as fairly mild, and that isn't necessarily to do with whether they are nearer the back or the door, the back being naturally hotter. It may just be the Spirits giving different people what they need.

Magic can happen in there. You might find that the Sweatlodge covering has disappeared, and you can see the sky and the stars. Some people have visionary experiences. I know a couple of people who saw one of the stones floating in the air above the stone pit — that was in a special type of Lodge, and had been intended.

Along with my flatpack lodge, I used to have a permanent earth Sweatlodge in my back garden. It was quite complex to build, and I was given advice on its construction by my native Canadian friend. It was nine feet across on the inside, with walls of adobe. The outside was covered in turf. It looked very natural. But its bones were made of the steel reinforcing rods that you get in concrete, bent over to make a dome shape. Inside this was placed chicken wire, to provide a lattice for the adobe. Outside the steel frame was a layer of plastic, to stop the inside getting damp in our climate, and having the adobe gradually rot. Outside the plastic was more chicken wire, for the turf which was placed on top and down the sloping sides.

There were a few more details I haven't mentioned, but the Lodge was a powerful presence. Some great Lodges happened in there. One thing I hadn't foreseen was that the thick earth walls, while providing the good heat insulation I had hoped for, also absorbed most of the heat from the first round of stones. So I used to put an electric fire inside for two hours before the Lodge began. Another time I would make it smaller inside, because it was a lot of work – a lot of wood and stones were needed to get a moderately hot lodge.

When you're leading a ceremony, something is working through you. I haven't led a Lodge now for some years, but in the last one I led, which was in turn the first I had led for some years, something new came in. A feminine presence was around me, I would speak from that, and I would pour water from that. It was just very easy, very smooth.

I had someone next to me in the Lodge, a big guy who had been worried about coming in, because he gets claustrophobic in these small spaces. The last Lodge he'd been in had been run traditionally, and he was seated near the back, which tends to be the hottest part. He'd been told that if he needed to leave the Lodge during a round he could, but that he couldn't come back in for the rest of the Ceremony. He was put under this pressure, that if he left he wouldn't be able to come back, and he'd sat in the Lodge struggling with claustrophobia. So he was reluctant to join my Lodge. His experience had been one traditional way, and maybe that is fair enough – though I have my doubts about that. 'Traditional' doesn't always mean right, it can just mean it's the way they've always done it, so it's the way they have to keep doing it. Or it may be that the tradition does have room for flexibility and sensitivity, but the leader was being macho, getting too much into his warrior thing. I was told you get a kind of competitiveness amongst some native Sweatlodge leaders, as to who can run the most Lodges one after the other without collapsing from exhaustion.

But I don't work in any of these ways. I said to the guy, OK, you sit right next to the door, so if you do need to leave you can leave straight away without having to clamber over everyone and make a scene, and you can come back in in the next round. I took all the pressure off him, and that's what he did. He ended up staying throughout the whole Lodge without a problem, because he knew he could leave. He was actually having visionary experiences.

Here's a rule: if common sense and tradition are in conflict, go with common sense.

In many traditions, women on their Moon time aren't allowed in the Lodge. I don't know the reasons for it. Someone I know who runs Lodges in a traditional way in Canada and the US started running them for non-Indians, and on one of his early Lodges he told a woman on her Moon time that she would have to sit outside. This would be fine for the woman in a traditional context, there would be nothing personal in it. But he noticed this woman was feeling left out, and he decided accordingly that he would not have this rule among non-Indians. This might seem straightforward to us, but it is not necessarily straightforward, if you are trained and immersed in a tradition, to start changing it. A priest in a church couldn't just change the service because he disagreed with it. If he could, before you knew it there would be no tradition left. So this was a big deal for this guy, and to his credit that he did it, even though he remained a rigid old so-and-so in other ways, probably just the sort of male Elder that the woman from the Lakota reservation was protesting about.

We need tradition, we hunger for it without knowing it. Yet you also need flexibility and even a bit of heretical ferment around the edges to keep it alive. You see that hunger in the way people will hang on to bits and scraps of tradition from faraway cultures, or from faraway times and call it Celtic, as though that aligns them with the power they imagine their ancestors to have had.

It can be tempting, because of the lack we feel. But we need to place ourselves firmly in our actual situation. We do not have traditions, but we do have simple Ceremonies that we can build on, that we can truly claim for ourselves, without looking over our shoulders to those who have the 'real' power. We also have it. I have been thrown out of Facebook groups for saying this kind of thing, because people NEED their indigenous people on a pedestal, and they feel I am being disrespectful. If people are giving their power away, there is a reason for it, and they won't thank you for pointing it out: you are liable to be excommunicated!

We have everything we need. We have the natural world just as much as anywhere else, from which we can draw inspiration directly. And we have the freedom to reinvent, which means we have free rein to be true to our own Spirits in a deep way, that may not always be possible if people find themselves within a tradition that has become dogmatic, maybe due to defensiveness around the overwhelming modern culture.

Take the simple forms very seriously. Treat your Pipe and your Sweatlodge as sacred objects. Chaos Shamanism is NOT about treating forms as dispensable in a superficial kind of way. No, we take our simple Ceremonies very seriously, so seriously that we experience the deep essence, the taste of Spirit, that they are designed to promote. But we also dance around them, we are free to be creative with them in a way that indigenous people are not.

There was never any sense from the native Canadian who ran the Lodges that we could learn to run them like he did, though he did introduce us to what they call a 'family lodge', that we were free to run, that is dead informal. You take it in turns to pour the water, and people might miss a whole round while they go and have breakfast or something.

This is something I've thought about over the many years since I've seen him. If you're a teacher, you need to be able to give your pupils something they can seriously run with, something to do themselves. They need to be able to find their own way into it, otherwise they get disempowered, they just remain in awe of tradition, and that's no good at all. So it's interesting for me why he didn't do that. What was it that he was doing as a traditional teacher? You come all the way over to Europe, and you run Ceremonies from your tradition, which has its own place, has its own use, but you don't give people something to run with, that they can develop themselves. What then is the point in it all? Why did the Spirits send him over here with that kind of fundamental limitation, that leaves the pupils high and dry once he goes?

If you are an indigenous teacher, adapting your tradition for our culture takes a lot, it's a whole journey for you. Very few have done it. There have been one or two Native Americans who have done it, like Harley Swiftdeer and Hyemeyohsts Storm. You can see plenty of criticism of them on the Internet from traditional Indians, some of it justified, though by no means all. But they gave teachings that helped people, and that is what matters, even though you are probably well-advised to steer clear of the groups that formed around them, which I have experienced as religions just like any other. Sun Bear was another guy who went to the trouble of adapting and sharing the teachings, and inevitably got a lot of stick from the traditionalists for doing so. But you don't hear the same stories of bad personal behaviour with Sun Bear, as you do with Swiftdeer and Storm. So good on him I say, and good on them all, whatever their limitations. Rolling Thunder is another guy who got stick for teaching traditional ways. They get called charlatans, but what is a charlatan? You may not be perfect, and your Indian lineage may be open to question, but the product works, so where's the problem?

It's politics, and you get the same with Tibetan Buddhism. There is a deity called Dorje Shugden who people meditate on, but which was controversial in Tibet. Some schools claimed the deity to be demonic. That political divide translated to the West, with the Dalai Lama taking the side of those who claimed it to be demonic, and another school, now with many Western adherents, reverencing Dorje Shugden. It became a public battle, with Western disciples taking sides in this medieval Tibetan conflict.

So just ignore all this stuff. Just do what works. With teachers, I recommend that you benefit from the teachings, but be wary of getting involved with the groups that form around them.

With the Ceremonies, you don't have to get them 'right'. I sometimes forget things, I might forget to call in the Directions or something. But then I'll make up for it later. You do your best to get it right, but really it's Spirit that is running these Ceremonies.

30

Teacher Plants

I feel qualified to say something about what are called Teacher Plants, even though it's not something I really do. This is because they were foundational for me way back in 1978, at the tender age of 20. A group of us found thousands of what used to be called magic mushrooms in the Mendip Hills in Somerset in the UK. We were all students at the University of Bristol. Over the next few months, I was taking them regularly. They became large doses, 100 at a time, something like that. We had dried them to preserve them, and made a tea, which we drank. It had a profound effect on me. I didn't have any kind of guidance or anything like that. I was on my own, which is how it's felt most of my life.

I've never ended up with a teacher that I've been able to stick with. It's not like there are people close to my heart that I'll always look up to. It's more like I got taught stuff, but somehow the Spirits put me on this path where I have to work it out on my own, and that's not a bad thing. The teachers I ended up around all had holes that were too big for me to stay around very long. A good thing about teachers with big holes is that you can develop a critical faculty, it helps you claim your power back. So thank you, teachers, for those big holes!

Anyway, I could probably have used a bit of guidance with the mushrooms. Over a period of just a few months, the autumn of 1978, these teacher plants – to use the modern parlance – helped me make my metaphysical quest central. They deepened me, and friends noticed that I became more serious. They opened me up. Whenever I took them, I ended up in a deep place, though probably the predominant experience was not pleasurable. There were times when I was in the heavenly realms, it was beautiful. But quite a lot of the time, it was dark, there'd be a crashing depression descending on me, and my father's face would appear to me in this sort of demonic form, like Adolf Hitler.

I was always struggling to get away from these difficult experiences, always hoping the next trip would get back to being one of the nice ones. It was decades before I looked back and realised that these so-called 'bad trips' are maybe best seen as initiations into the shadow. It was arguably a premature initiation into the shadow for me, because I wasn't able to do anything with it, I was just sort of thrown by it. But even then, it deepened me. The shadow may not be a pleasant experience, but it is a deep experience.

It is a deep experience because we are taken to meet our demons, which tend to live below the surface of conscious experience. We would rather not experience them, because they are painful and because it can feel humiliating to have to own that we have this darkness within us. It can demolish our 'positive' self-image in a way that many people cannot perhaps handle. So they remain below the surface, unacknowledged and sincerely projected onto others, who become the bad guys: politicians, parents, exes, neighbours. Maybe they merit being the bad guys in some ways, but it carries an extra charge, we make them worse than they are, we 'awfulize' them, it is very personal.

So I was initiated into a consciousness of this darker side of life. Of course my father wasn't really a demon, he was just an ordinary guy with a marked authoritarian streak about who I was meant to be. He wasn't even aware he was doing it. But I had spent my childhood subject to that, and here I was aged 20 being shown what it had done to me. It had made me authoritarian too — or probably I had that in me anyway — which I transferred into the spiritual realm. I became quite dogmatic.

It was the Spirits who showed me the psilocybin mushrooms, it was the Spirits (or you could say, the Unconscious) who then revealed to me my heavenly and shadow sides, and who then prevented me from finding mushrooms in any numbers ever again. People say to me it's easy to find them, you live on Dartmoor, here is where to look. But there are never any there, and to be honest I'm not particularly bothered. These days I will very occasionally take mushrooms or LSD if they come my way, as a sort of inspirational reset. I took Ayahuasca a couple of times in the Amazon in 1999. It is never world-shaking for me. I like it, I always have a good time these days, I think because I have a better relationship with my shadow. Something useful usually comes out of it, but I had the deep initiations all those decades ago. It was foundational, and it is still with me.

These experiences gave me a new metaphysical centre. Eighteen months later I found myself being swept into a Buddhist group, and wanting to make their practices a full-time thing. The strength of my response, its consuming nature, took me by surprise. I had thought of my metaphysical quest as just a side of me, a serious side, but not as central as it turned out to be.

These deep changes were arguably something that was going to happen anyway, but the teacher plants certainly sped it along.

They were an initiation for me into what gave deep meaning to life. They opened me up, so that immediately following the initial experiences I fell in love with a young woman in an entirely consuming way. That was another initiation, coming hot on the heels of the first one. Nothing much came of it. I was heartbroken, but it was for the best: what a projection for an ordinary young woman to carry! It was a tough initiation into my own heart: I needed to be hurt, cauterised, and then spend the rest of my life remembering it, allowing the emotional and imaginative depths that it portended to gradually emerge. Oh to have had someone to guide me in all this! But I'm not sure I could have listened. I was far too rebellious against anyone who appeared to be any kind of authority.

I've always felt about these plants that they can indeed be an initiation, but after that comes the real work. They are not an ongoing path in themselves. I was glad when someone I was doing some astrology for, told me that they'd been working with a teacher in the Amazon jungle. They'd been taking Ayahuasca under his guidance, in a proper traditional way. The teacher said that after you've done your Ayahuasca sessions, the real work begins. The Ayahuasca is just a starting point. I thought, good, that's what I've always thought, but nobody seems to say it. It's not a path in itself. It's an initiation, and occasionally we may return to it for a bit of inspiration. Maybe it is an ongoing path for some, you can usually never rule anything out about anything. But I'm going to stick my neck out and say that for the great majority of us, it is not an ongoing path. It becomes a distraction if we treat it in that way, or make a bit of a cult of it.

There seem to be plenty of people at the moment who assume that this is what Shamanism primarily IS: the ingestion of plant medicines. I have had the experience of someone finding out I do Shamanic things, and immediately wanting to know if I had access to plant medicines. Shamanism has its fashions like anything else, and this one will probably pass.

I met an academic researcher into teacher plants, and my impression of him was that he had taken too many drugs in his life! He would talk at length about the profound experiences he had had, as if that was the main thing, and which substances could take you furthest, to what was most ultimate: to where this reality shockingly broke down completely, and you saw things as they really are, outside the constructed reality that the brain provides. He had certainly had these experiences, but his emphasis was wrong. They are to be talked about circumspectly, if at all, and as a guide and inspiration for living on this planet, in this material reality. These experiences partake of the Sacred. In this reality, he was middle-aged, yet dressing and behaving, in some ways, like a teenage rebel. It is a bit like people who identify with the profound experiences that can occur in Shamanic journeying or in meditation. You can end up with arrested development in this reality, however profound your experiences may be in other realities.

There is a regular psychedelic conference in the UK called 'Breaking Convention'. I'm sure it is a useful event, but the title to me is wrong. It is a countercultural cliché to be anti-establishment, to think you know better, and ultimately it goes nowhere. Something like 'Making Peace with Convention' would be a genuinely radical title for the counterculture, and make the point that we need to move towards society, bringing our wisdom with us. It is we who need to change in order to be more part of society, rather than it being society that needs challenging to be more like us, something that will never happen to any great degree.

The emphasis needs to be incarnation, the West of the Medicine Wheel, because that is what we are here to do. Teacher plants give us an experience of the Fire of the East. That then needs to be integrated; it needs to be used to help us incarnate further, more deeply, instead of using them as an escape, a spiritual bypass. It is a dance.

Several years after my experiences with psilocybin mushrooms, I felt myself arrive fully back in this reality. I had been subtly away all that time because of the depth and intensity of what I had been through. I was not aware that I was subtly not here, until I found myself back. You see this in some people who ingest a lot of these substances. Yes, they are privy in an ongoing way to some esoteric experiences, which gives them a sense of validation, and there is often a gentleness about them. But you can see they are not quite here, and there are probably psychological reasons why they do not want to be fully here.

You maybe need to be especially aware if you have an addictive temperament. It may be that you need a regular input of non-ordinary reality to stay balanced – the sign of Pisces can be like this – and if you're not getting it by non-chemical means such as music and meditation and the natural world, you may feel drawn to having that experience by chemical means.

You're not supposed to say things like drugs and magic mushrooms and psychedelics and tripping any more, you're supposed to say Teacher Plants and Plant Medicine and Psilocybin. People can get quite serious and religious about it, and in a way that is fair enough, but it can also close things down a bit. There's a big no-no around doing these substances 'recreationally', people look down on that. But I think why not do it recreationally sometimes, just have some fun, don't be so serious? When we play, things can happen that couldn't otherwise. When we play, we are whole. The best creativity comes out of play. I try to keep this book as play as I go along, but I don't always succeed when I have a load of video transcripts to edit. The videos themselves, however, remain a lot of fun.

The psychedelic world, like the Chaos, is feminine. We yield to it, just like we yield in the Sweatlodge. It tempers and broadens and deepens the ego in this world.

My main point about these plant medicines is that they are a deep initiation. They can open you up in all sorts of ways. Some people have visionary experiences that they will never forget, as can happen with 'big' dreams. You need to keep them with you for the rest of your life, and let them inform it. You've been shown something outside of this constructed reality that we live in. We get these glimpses sometimes, don't we? That this reality is just a construction, it is a shocking realisation, but it goes incredibly deep. The world and ourselves seem so ultimately real to us. It's the Matrix, and these plant medicines can take us outside of that. Maybe it's like what happens when we die, because similarly this brain-constructed reality breaks down. It opens us up to the love and connectedness that is the real nature of the universe.

I recommend Oliver Sacks' *The Man Who Mistook His Wife for a Hat*. It is an account of what reality can be like for people with neurological damage. Basic categories like left and right, or the ability to categorise itself, disappear, and the people who are impaired in these ways do not realise that anything is awry. The book is an ongoing meditation on the constructed nature of this reality, which can be shocking if you allow it in.

Like all forms of Shamanism, the Teacher Plant way becomes religion to some degree; it is inevitable. The Chaos perspective is the dance around that. Someone came to me who had a traditional teacher in the Amazon. They had been taking Ayahuasca and everything that comes with it for some years. There was a lot of practice and discipline around it. It was a whole path, and it was the central thing in their life. At a certain point, this person got the feeling that they wanted to stop doing it, and go back to Europe and do art work and have children. They were in conflict about this issue, which is why they had come to see me for some astrology. Their main doubt was that if they left the Amazon, they would be backsliding spiritually, because they would have left that particular discipline behind, which the teacher emphasised had to be kept up. And leave it to do what? To have children. How, they thought, could a mere personal desire possibly be as spiritually significant as this profound way they were learning in the jungle?

What do you do when the teacher says one thing, and your instincts are telling you something else? It can be a good crisis to have. My answer was that you always need to follow the voice in you, you're here to learn to follow your own guidance, that has grown out of all the work you have done so far with this traditional teacher. A good teacher will always guide you to do that. To that extent, I think I'm a good teacher. (I'm probably crap in some other ways!) I just say identify what's in your heart – and sometimes that can take a while – and then follow it. It is what we are here to do.

Unlike the Amazon teacher, I don't need disciples, I don't try to hang on to them, because I put my trust in Spirit. If there are people wanting to be around me and perhaps learn something, I will trust that and say yes to them. If there is no one coming my way, I will trust that too, I won't think there is something wrong, or that I am inadequate. It is a liberating way to be, and the way to be of most help to others, because Spirit can get on with its own designs, without me and my anxieties about who I am getting too much in the way.

I don't have a particular tradition that I am trying to draw people into. Maybe one day I will start some kind of loose community around Chaos Shamanism, who knows? I will let Spirit decide that one.

Spirit tends to show itself through what we want to do, often moment by moment. It certainly doesn't show itself through what we 'ought' to do – that is religion. This person's life in the jungle had turned into an 'ought', and the 'want' was back in Europe.

So this indigenous Amazonian teacher was limited. He hadn't created an ethos where his pupil felt free, rather the opposite, and that speaks of his own needs. A lot of teachers are like that, maybe most are to some degree. But they perform a useful function. They provide the initial framework that we often need, to get our house in order, cut down on the drinking and all that, and take our first steps. And then they get attached to having us in that pupil position, they feel validated by it. They will all, of course, say you are free to come and go and do other things, but that may not be the underlying vibe. I banged on earlier about taking indigenous people off the pedestals we often put them on, and this is a good example.

My advice to this person was, "Follow what's in your heart. I'm not going to tell you what to do, that's definitely not my job. My job is to bring you closer to what's in your heart."

This is a crucial point that many people reach, whatever path you are on. The teacher has brought you so far. You have sailed alongside their ship. But now it is time to take a deep breath and head out on your own into the wide ocean. It is something you know you have to do. It takes courage, it will give you the adventure of your life, and you will not be at rest until you do it.

The Amazonian teacher reminds me a bit of the Buddhist teacher I once had. He had founded a Buddhist Order, and I read a seminar extract once in which he was asked if there could be positive reasons for leaving his Order. He was a logical, cerebral kind of guy, and he laid out at length, with remorseless logic, why to leave was inevitably 'spiritual catastrophe'. That says it all. It was why I eventually felt I had to leave. It was a huge thing for me, because it had become my whole life. So I could sympathise with this person and the conflict they were in.

Like everything, we need a perspective that has room for Spirit to have had a part in leading us into the problematic situations we find ourselves in. The whole journey can prove to be exactly what we needed, from the initial supportive framework, to the conflict at the end, in which we learn to seriously trust our inner guidance, as we begin to dare put that new voice before the guidance and judgement of the person who had been our teacher.

The Plant is a teacher too, and needs to be treated in the same way. The Teacher Plant gets us going, helps us find that initial vision of life, outside the bounds of conventional ways of seeing the world. But eventually we trust our own guidance, we do not need to get it from a substance anymore, however sacred. It brings me back to the earlier point, where I said that Teacher Plants are not an ongoing path. That is a good point to end on.

31

Chaos Coda

As I made the videos out of which this book has come, I created a list of points that hadn't been mentioned. Some of them have been inserted in earlier chapters. But I also thought, in the interests of the Chaos, that I would gather some together randomly at the end.

Faith

Faith has always underpinned my life. I had a deep experience of it when I was 22, listening to a Buddhist talk about faith. I had a deep, joyful experience of homecoming. I felt I'd found something I'd been looking for all my life without knowing it. Buddhism was the nearest vehicle to hand. But there was always a wholeness, a soulfulness that was lacking for me in Buddhism.

Shamanism gives me that fuller experience of faith. Faith in what? Not in anything objective. That is why it is a nonsense to talk about the existence of God as if he can be objectively defined and apprehended. It is faith in the subjective pole of existence, which begins with the personal experience of Spirit, and expands to the realisation that the one Spirit underlies and underpins everything.

Spirit is vast, compassionate, all-powerful, and all-knowing. It is not an aspect of life, it IS life. You look at what went into building the old churches, and it is apparent that our ancestors experienced a level of faith of which we have no conception. We truly live in the Dark Ages.

This is why I object to the teaching of Shamanic healing ways as a mere add-on to other modalities, which may themselves have the need for rational respectability lurking behind them. That is all wrong, it is the cart before the horse.

Shamanism begins with the experience of faith in the Spirit, and in the natural world, to which we belong, as the expression of Spirit. You may or may not end up doing healing work, coming out of that foundation of faith, that takes years to build, and which is the stuff of life. Fools Crow's remarkable healings were always based in prayer to the Great Spirit, to 'the holiest of everything', as he more literally translated Wakan Tanka.

How to Know What You're Talking About

I've called this chapter Chaos Coda, like the last movement of a symphony. I'm picking up all these bits that have sort of got scattered along the way, and bringing them in to the musical journey. It's teaching in a Chaos kind of way. Traditionally, teaching is something that is spontaneous. You don't get traditional teachers with a course and a plan, which is normal for us nowadays; indeed, it seems the responsible way to be. They do it orally, spontaneously, according to who they're with, or according to what has appeared in their mind. You trust what it is that you have an urge to speak about. This is a point I made earlier, and I am repeating myself. There's plenty of repetition throughout this book, because I am not trying to communicate a list of ideas to be noted down and remembered. That is the kind of teaching that is the passing on of information. That is one level, and it has its own validity. The kind of teaching I am doing here is more like a meditation on certain ideas, a contemplation from different angles, that we keep returning to, and allowing these ideas to percolate into our being and change us. It is not a book to be speed-read, like Bill Gates would do: 140 pages an hour, and he remembers nearly everything. It is not about cerebral understanding. You need to feel in your being what you are reading, and that is slow, it takes time.

That's why it's best done orally in many ways, because then the teacher's being is better able to communicate itself. If you haven't done so already, watch a few of my videos on YouTube at Chaos_Shamanism, and then you may be able to hear me speak as you read this.

Teaching is as much about the way a teacher is, as it is about what it is he or she has to say. You pick up on how they are. If they are close to who they are, in balance with themselves in a deeper kind of way, then you will be drawn into being closer to yourself in the same way, almost as a process of osmosis. That is why in Hinduism they have a ceremony, or a practice, called Upanishad, where you just sit silently with the teacher, who is also silent, and your beings commune.

This is obviously harder to do with a written page, but consciousness works in mysterious ways, and particularly if you have made the connection by watching a few of my videos, you may find yourself tuning into something as you read. I'm not making any great claims about myself in this respect, but there does seem to be something about the way I am that people sometimes benefit from. That can be an online thing; through Zoom I have had that kind of feedback. I do get to know people through Zoom. When I eventually meet them physically there is something extra there, quite a lot extra, but I still get a lot just from the Zoom.

What is it that you might pick up on around me? I've been around these kinds of ideas for many years, thinking them through, learning by watching how other people work. And when I talk nowadays, I feel what I am saying in my body, there is a wholeness to it. I feel I know what I'm talking about.

In the mid-80s, when I began teaching at the tender age of 28, I was essentially just passing on things that I had been told, with a little bit of experience round the edges of it, but not much. That is a valid thing to do. It was initially some meditation techniques that I was passing on, and then a few Buddhist ideas.

I'd been promoted beyond my station, really, as a Buddhist teacher. Of course I wasn't really a teacher, not at that age. I didn't know much in my being. In fact, I'd probably argue now that I was in some ways the opposite of a teacher at that time, a teacher in a real sense being someone who teaches by how they are, as much as by what they say. I was the opposite of a teacher because I was at odds with myself, I was wilful, I was taking these perfectly good Buddhist ideas and imposing them on myself, trying to force myself to become something. I wasn't entirely like that, but sufficiently so as to be not a very good exemplar of the teaching.

By my mid-40s I was teaching Shamanism, and it was in a less conflicted way, but still something came to feel not right about it, there was a big part of me missing from it, and so I took a 15-year break from teaching. That missing bit, looking back on it, was knowing with my being, in my viscera, if you like, what I was talking about.

In Buddhism there's a list of three levels of comprehension. Buddhism is very good at coming up with lists. They're called Sutta-maya-prajna, Cinta-maya-prajna and Bhavana-maya-prajna. That's a bit technical, but what it basically means is listening, understanding, and insight, or making it your own. You begin by just listening to what is being said, and the way it is being said. Then when you chew it over, you understand it to some extent, you make sense of it in your own experience. It's not like this list is made up of entirely separate categories, they flow into each other. And then finally, bhavana means becoming, it really gets into you, you become the teaching. I realised, as I thought about this list for the purposes of this book, that that's what's happened to me, I have to a degree become what I am teaching. (I was also learning in the act of teaching, which is so often the case if what you are doing is alive.)

When I returned to teaching in 2020, during the pandemic lockdowns, and started running a Medicine Wheel course online, I started getting comments that I was authentic. I thought well I should hope so, I mean what I say. But it was more than that, because what had become natural for me, was actually quite a strong experience for some other people. Like this guy's in what he's talking about, he means it, he's living it, it IS him. And I thought, yes that's true, and then I realised, in the act of writing this, that this is bhavana-maya-prajna, the third and deepest level of understanding from my Buddhist days, which are decades behind me now.

The way I am just seems quite normal and natural to me, it's not some sort of whopping transcendental insight, which is what I'd always imagined. It's quite ordinary, quite normal. In fact, that's what we're doing with any spiritual path: at the end of the day, it's just about coming back to yourself. This is well known in e.g. Zen and Tibetan Buddhism. You spend all those years faithfully doing your practice, trying to become good, trying to become holy, trying to discipline your mind, all these things. All the time you're trying, and then after 20 or 30 years you realise, oh, there was never anywhere to go, it's just about being close to yourself. It doesn't have to be good, it doesn't have to be right, it can be messy, in fact it will be messy because we're humans on this planet and we have a body. But within that messiness we're with ourselves, we're close to ourselves and where else is there to go? There's nowhere to go, so stop judging yourself for not being this idea of who you think you should be.

Suddenly you own yourself, you own your life, you own who you are, because you're not sitting there in judgement over it, going, it's not good enough, and I've got to be this or that, because I'm a spiritual person. And secretly I'm better than other people, because I'm trying to be good and they're not, they're just worldly, all of that sort of stuff. Just drop all of that, you can just be who you are.

Many of us can't easily get away from that first stage, where you make all that effort for all those years, or cane yourself for not making that effort. What making all that effort did to me was to split me apart like a hammer hitting a walnut. Crash! By my mid-30s, I couldn't do anything anymore, apart from just about keep life going. That was when I started to listen to myself, instead of imposing ideas from without as to who I 'should' be, however meritorious those ideas might be in themselves. I began to listen to what I was, and then it all slowly began to change. It took many years of listening before I was ready to start teaching in the way that I do now.

You end up as a teacher not because you have listened to teachings, but because you have listened to yourself. That is where the real teaching lies. Traditional Shamans are taught by their Spirits, and probably a lot of that has to do with doing their healing work. It's the same thing, framed differently. Listen, without standing in judgement over yourself, and the Spirit will speak. If you are angry or jealous, just be with it. We all get like that. Don't feed it, but let it be there. Only stand in judgement over it if you act on it, even in thought, for that is also an action. Just be comfortable with being the human that you are, warts and all. Then you will have arrived. Then you will be like the animals, who know who they are.

The Flatpack Helpline

I was once on an online course with Lewis Mehl-Madrona. He's an American, part Cherokee-Lakota, and a conventional doctor who was also brought up with the traditional healing ways and outlook. (I recommend his book *Coyote Medicine*, his own story of how he became a healer.) He said he'd been at a powwow, hanging out with his people. Some of the elders, including him, had gathered together. They were sitting around talking about what they should call themselves in doing their healing work. They thought well if we call ourselves Healers, that's a bit pretentious, that is making a claim about who we are. And Medicine Man, that sounds a bit like a Spaghetti Western. In the end they settled on Fix-it Men. It's a bit like a plumber: your pipes aren't working, so you get the plumber around to fix them. Similarly, you've maybe got personal or health problems, so you get the Fix-it man round and he'll fix that for you. So it's all on a kind of level, it's not putting you up on a kind of plinth of being holy and all the rest of it. I thought, yeah, I'll go with that. But only up to a point. It's not entirely right. I don't think you can actually fix people. Well maybe you can with their physical health, or rather the Spirit does it, working through you. But the soul stuff, you can't fix that for people. 'Fix-it man' gives the wrong impression there. All you can really do is show them how to fix themselves, guide them to that, give them the confidence to do that, let who you are, Spirits included, rub off on who they are. And so I thought, no we're not really the Fix-it men either. But how about the Flatpack Helpline, like you get with IKEA? If you can't assemble your bookshelves from the instructions, you ring them up, and they will clarify the instructions for you so that you can do it yourself.

The instructions we give aren't just verbal, as I was saying in the section above on teaching. The instructions are also in how to be, just from the way we are, hopefully. But they still have to do it themselves. It keeps the responsibility firmly where it needs to be.

I think that Shamanic healing work, as it comes down through Core Shamanism, can sometimes give the wrong impression. Like we can retrieve your soul for you, or all will be well if you have this entity that is sucking your energy removed. And I'm sure some healers don't mind being seen as powerful in this kind of way. I have met some. But really, I think that kind of work needs to come last. Don't even think about entities. It is easy to start thinking you are possessed by them, and it creates a paranoid, disempowered world. Do a bit of energy clearing, sure, like giving someone a bath. As for soul retrieval, it is primarily something people need to do for themselves. It happens in its own time, in a natural way. Our job is to help the person move closer to that lost bit of themselves, whose very absence may have been a necessary source of learning for them, a part of the larger destiny of their lives. In guiding them to pay attention to it, and to be welcoming to it, and to perhaps change their lives to allow room for it to be born, we are helping them read the code of their life, we are being the Flatpack Helpline.

Wild Shamans

The great psychologist Carl Jung once said that if you observe wild animals, you will see that they are deliberate in all that they do. It is a startlingly original observation, yet very simple. Original, because it is contrary to how we normally think of wildness. We tend to think of something that is out of control and has no rhyme or reason to it. We think of Chaos, in its conventional sense! But Jung is saying the opposite of this. He goes on to say that a person who is wild will be a respectable citizen, because they will be self-possessed and considered in all they do, mindful of the rules of society. It doesn't sound very exciting, put that way.

Another way of putting it is that if you are wild, you know who you are, just like the wild animals know who they are. It is our bodies that tell us who we are. Our bodies are a continual flow of feeling and instinct and intuition (I've never achieved complete clarity on the different meanings of those words), that tell us who we are and how to live. I watch my cat, and everything he does is purposeful. Sitting in front of the fire, I can see his presence and intent in doing that.

Shamanism is about becoming wild again. I say 'again'. It is something we have as very young children, before we begin the necessary process of adapting to the rules of the society we live in. It is something we need to find again as adults, but in a different, more self-aware way. It is about being true to who we are in the context of a society with whose customs and rules we may have to reach an accommodation. Being wild does not mean rebelling, though that might be a necessary early stage.

It requires courage to be wild, for it is no different to the voice of the Daimon, or the Spirit, coming through our body. But it's not just about you. In our individualistic society, we think of the lone hero, courageously breaking free of the chains of an authoritarian, brainwashing society. But it's not really like that. Wild humans are also deeply relational. It is better to think of yourself as primarily relational, connected, rather than individual, for the self is an ephemeral, protean thing, that dissolves upon examination.

The wild person is like the Wolf that showed up in 2021 and suggested I write a fantasy trilogy about Shapeshifting. He remained around me for the entire time I was writing. He is there now as I write. He is on hind legs, and is unmistakably wolf, even though dressed like a Victorian gentleman in a tailcoat and side-whiskers. He is eminently respectable, he knows how to conduct himself. He is self-possessed, and the fierceness is not far below the surface. There is no compromise of his natural self. But he understands the need for an ordered society.

Society and its rules easily go too far, and we become afraid and condemning of the natural self, that is outside of that control. That is why Elvis Presley was banned in some states of the USA. The raw, liberated physical and sexual energy that he conveyed, which had been inspired by the black people he grew up around, was threatening to the safe, over-controlled ethic of the wider society. He attracted moral condemnation for being wild.

The wild energy is very real, and it is beautiful and dynamic when it is unleashed. Most of the time, there will just be a sense of contained power, of someone who is very present in a physical kind of way, and who you're not going to mess with. Self-possession is maybe the keyword when considering wildness, but it is not a controlled thing, it is free and natural. You're in your body, you're listening to your body, you're listening to who you are at all points and acting from that. When you act from that inner guidance, you never make a false step, you always do the right thing, things work out as they need to; not necessarily as we want to, but there's a sense of rightness, and we don't lurch from one disaster to another. You have probably noticed that some people do that in their lives, they're always lurching from one mess to another.

If you have that kind of self-possession, then before you act you stop and you think and you consult yourself. It's all those sorts of qualities. I'm making wildness even sound a bit boring! But actually it's not. You put some dance music on, and that animal will take over, not in a random sort of way, but in a very vigorous, yet self-aware way. The physical, animal energy will rise up and move through your body, and you will have joy and ecstasy, which means out of your body — something else comes in and takes over, and this is natural. It happens too during sex. We yield to the body, something else takes over, our ordinary self recedes, and the aware animal does what is natural to it. The room can be full of Spirit presences. They like us to have sex in this way.

If you're wild, you're this contained power that can rise up forcefully, like a horse bursting into gallop. We can see the whole Shamanic way as becoming wild in this sense. Knowing who we are, finding the balance at the Centre of the Wheel. The balance is always to be found by listening deeply to ourselves, to what our body is telling us. Everything we need in any situation is there in us.

I'll say something further about Trance Dance, because I see the dance as a way to wildness. That's when you let your body take over. Some people might see the Devil if you do that, that is how far Christianity got in suppressing the wildness. The dance, this movement of the Spirit, is a joyful thing. It's what humans love to do, but for us it's also a practice for wildness. I described this at length in the chapter on **Meeting the Spirits**. It is essentially about embodying the Spirits, which live according to their rules, that are not human rules. This is what is terrifying for some, for they sense it.

Part of our Shamanism needs to involve a reclaiming of embodiment. You won't become wild through classic Core Shamanism, because it doesn't involve the body. It's safe in that respect, it is a modern expression and even affirmation of our historic religious repression of the body, that is 1000 years and more old.

When you dance, have live drumming if you can, but otherwise a fast and loud base beat. The more you can yield to the body in the dance, the more you can then just carry that in a contained way into your day-to-day life. You will always have that poise, that self-possession, that thing in your body that knows. The wildness is your true self, and your mind is its servant. It becomes so that it is always with you, always guiding you. You feel alive, you feel vital, you feel in your body, even when you're shopping or unloading the dishwasher. And don't forget your animal helpers, and your sense of them being around, even if you can't see them. They are also your guide to the wildness. It is they who you dance, or rather they who dance you. You haven't understood what these animal helpers are truly about if they're just guys you go and meet in journeys. They can't show up fully, they can't love you and guide you as they might, if you don't feel them in your body. They are the wildness. They are also the Chaos, for what is the Chaos but the spontaneous life of the animal that pours through us at every moment, coming from we know not where?

Recommended Reading and Watching

Books

Ariés, Philippe *Western Attitudes toward Death*

Audlin, James David *The Circle of Life*

Baring, Anne *The Dream of the Cosmos*

Borrows, John *Drawing Out Law*

Boyd, Doug *Rolling Thunder*

Bregman, Rutger *Humankind*

Browning, Christopher *Ordinary Men*

Campbell, Ffyona *The Hunter-Gatherer Way*

Clerc, Olivier *The Gift of Forgiveness*

Davis, Wade *The Wayfinders*

de Waal, Frans *Mama's Last Hug: Animal Emotions and What They Teach Us about Ourselves; Are We Smart Enough to Know How Smart Animals Are?*

Descola, Philippe *The Spears of Twilight*

Duran, Eduardo *Healing the Soul Wound*

Ehrenreich, Barbara *Dancing in the Streets: A History of Collective Joy*

Fox, Kate *Watching the English*

Goddard, Barry *The Medicine Wheel*

Goddard, Barry *The Stolen Queen*

Goddard, Barry *Surfing the Galactic Highways: Adventures in Divinatory Astrology*

Greene, Liz *The Astrology of Fate*

Haidt, Jonathan *The Righteous Mind*

Harpur, Patrick *Daimonic Reality; The Philosophers' Secret Fire*

Harris, Judith Rich *The Nurture Assumption*

Healy, Nan Savage *Toni Wolff & C.G. Jung: A Collaboration*

Hillman, James *The Soul's Code*

Hollis, James *The Middle Passage* (Inner City Books, 1993)

Johnson, Robert *Owning Your Own Shadow; Lying with the Heavenly Woman*
Jung, CG *Memories, Dreams, Reflections*
Lenihan, Eddie *Meeting the Other Crowd: The Fairy Stories of Hidden Ireland*
Lomborg, Bjorn *False Alarm*
Mails, Thomas E. *Fools Crow; Fools Crow: Wisdom and Power*
Mehl-Madrona, Lewis *Coyote Medicine; Coyote Healing; Coyote Wisdom*
Milton, Richard *Shattering the Myths of Darwinism; Alternative Science*
Morris, Jan *Conundrum*
The Native American novels of Leslie Marmon Silko, Louise Erdrich, Sherman Alexie, and D'Arcy McNickle
Plomin, Robert *Blueprint: How DNA Makes Us Who We Are*
Rosenberg, Marshall *Nonviolent Communication*
Ruiz, Don Miguel *The Four Agreements*
Rutherford, Leo *The View Through the Medicine Wheel*
Sacks, Oliver *The Man Who Mistook His Wife for a Hat*
Sanchez, Victor *The Teachings of Don Carlos*
Sarangerel *Chosen by the Spirits*
Tree, Jim *The Way of the Sacred Pipe*
Tupy, Marian, and Ronald Bailey *Ten Global Trends Every Smart Person Should Know*
Van Ysseltyne, Jan *Spirits from the Edge of the World*
Vitebsky, Piers *Reindeer People*
Vuillard, Eric *The Order of the Day*
WaiHong, Choo *The Kingdom of Women*
Wolff, Toni *Structural Forms of the Feminine Psyche*
Yalom, Irvin *Momma and the Meaning of Life*
Znamenski, Andrei *The Beauty of the Primitive*
The Anthology of Scottish Folk Tales (The History Press UK, 2019)

Films and Documentaries

American Beauty Dir. Sam Mendes, 1999
DreamKeeper Dir. Steve Barron, 2003
Elvis 2022
Face To Face | Carl Gustav Jung BBC, 1959
Kiss the Ground Netflix, 2020
Matter of Heart (Documentary on Jung) Dir. Mark Whitney, 1986
Smoke Signals Dir. Chris Eyre, 1998
Surviving Death Netflix, 2021
Wild Wild Country Netflix, 2018
2 Spirit Documentary: *vimeo.com/ondemand/twospirits*
YouTube: *Chaos_Shamanism* and *Astrotabletalk* (Barry Goddard)
YouTube: Jordan Peterson interviewed by Cathy Newman
YouTube: *Nonduality and the Consciousness of 'Things'* (Thich Nhat Hanh)
YouTube: Snow Raven, *Indigenous Wisdom From Arctic Siberia.* Also Francis Whiskeyjack, Kaaren Dannenmann, and Edna Manitowabi.
YouTube: *The Moral Roots of Liberals and Conservatives* Jonathan Haidt, TED Talk, 2008
YouTube: *The Science Delusion* Rupert Sheldrake, TED Talk

About the Author

Barry Goddard was destined as a young man to run the family veterinary business. He was, however, seized by a desire to become a psychonaut: an intrepid explorer of inner worlds. Buddhism being the nearest vehicle to hand, he followed that tradition for much of his 20s and 30s. Eventually, it left him feeling thoroughly out of sorts, while Shamanism, about which he knew nothing, seemed to beckon irresistibly. As did astrology, which had always fascinated him, while again knowing little about it. Shamanism, which treats the Earth herself as sacred, eventually renewed and restored him. At the same time, he set out to be an astrologer which, from a Shamanic point of view, means your spirits are in the sky. Barry has been doing astrology readings since 2002, a craft he views as divination rather than science, in which the gods speak through the astrologer. Since 2006 he has been well-known for his blogs and social media posts on astrology and shamanism. During the first Covid lockdown he began running an online group on the Medicine Wheel, after a 15-year break from teaching. He realised he had quite a lot to say, having been deeply drawn to the Wheel for over 20 years. Out of this arose his first book, *The Medicine Wheel*. Hot on its heels came *Surfing the Galactic Highways*, an astrology book. And then, at the suggestion of a Spirit Wolf, came *The Shapeshifters Trilogy*, a shamanic fantasy novel. In 2024, he wrote *Chaos Shamanism: Reclaiming Your Indigenous Soul*, which emerged from a series of YouTube videos, in which he attempted to grasp and expound what is essential to Shamanism, outside the multiplicity of forms by which modern practitioners are surrounded. Barry lives on Dartmoor, a wilderness area in the UK. He likes to take visitors on walks to the local fairy glens, of which there are many.

Also by Barry Goddard

The Medicine Wheel (Moon Books 2022)
978-1785359675

Surfing the Galactic Highways: Adventures in Divinatory Astrology (Moon Books 2022)
978-1803410104

The Stolen Queen (Pine Winds Press 2025)
978-1805141952

EASTERN RELIGION & PHILOSOPHY

We publish books on Eastern religions and philosophies. Books that aim to inform and explore the various traditions that began in the East and have migrated West. If you have enjoyed this book, why not tell other readers by posting a review on your preferred book site.

Recent Bestsellers from MANTRA BOOKS Are:

The Way Things Are

A Living Approach to Buddhism

Lama Ole Nydahl

An introduction to the teachings of the Buddha, and how to make use of these teachings in everyday life.

Paperback: 978-1-84694-042-2 ebook: 978-1-78099-845-9

Back to the Truth

5000 Years of Advaita

Dennis Waite

A demystifying guide to Advaita for both those new to, and those familiar with this ancient, non-dualist philosophy from India.

Paperback: 978-1-90504-761-1 ebook: 978-184694-624-0

Shinto: A celebration of Life

Aidan Rankin

Introducing a gentle but powerful spiritual pathway reconnecting humanity with Great Nature and arming all aspects of life.

Paperback: 978-1-84694-438-3 ebook: 978-1-84694-738-4

In the Light of Meditation

Mike George

A comprehensive introduction to the practice of meditation and the spiritual principles behind it. A 10 lesson meditation programme with CD and internet support.

Paperback: 978-1-90381-661-5

The 7 Levels of Wisdom

Mónica Esgueva

A straightforward and compelling approach on how to reach the highest levels of consciousness, wisdom, and inner peace.

Paperback: 978-1-80341-470-6 ebook: 978-1-80341-471-3

Compassion Based Living Course
Heather Regan-Addis and Choden
A practical guide to living a compassionate life.
Paperback: 978-1-80341-676-2 ebook: 978-1-80341-709-7

The Sacred Gathas of Zarathushtra & the Old Avestan Canon
Pablo Vazquez
The ancient and mystical poetry of Zarathushtra and the first Zoroastrians: Now accessible to the public in a modern translation.
Paperback: 978-1-78535-961-3 ebook: 978-1-78535-962-0

Radiant Bliss
Sue Bushell
Embrace Your Journey: Unfolding Peace, Power, and Purpose Through Yoga
Paperback: 978-1-80341-818-6 ebook: 978-1-80341-822-3

Ordinary Women, Extraordinary Wisdom
Rita Marie Robinson
The Feminine Face of Awakening
A collection of intimate conversations with female spiritual teachers who live like ordinary women, but are engaged with their true natures.
Paperback: 978-1-84694-068-2 ebook: 978-1-78099-908-1

The Riddle of Alchemy
Paul Kiritsis
What is alchemy, exactly? Is there any empirical truth to ancient speculative pursuits toward metallic transmutation? How does alchemy intersect with Western mind sciences and science in general?
Paperback: 978-1-80341-637-3 ebook: 978-1-80341-688-5

Readers of ebooks can buy or view any of these bestsellers by clicking on the live link in the title. Most titles are published in paperback and as an ebook. Paperbacks are available in traditional bookshops. Both print and ebook formats are available online.

Find more titles and sign up to our readers' newsletter at www.collectiveinkbooks.com/mind-body-spirit. Follow us on Facebook at facebook.com/OBooks and Twitter at twitter.com/obooks